AF749930

RELIGION AND CRIMINAL LAW

RELIGION ET DROIT PÉNAL

EUROPEAN CONSORTIUM FOR CHURCH AND STATE RESEARCH

RELIGION AND CRIMINAL LAW

RELIGION ET DROIT PÉNAL

Edited by

MATTI KOTIRANTA
NORMAN DOE

PEETERS
LEUVEN – PARIS – WALPOLE, MA
2013

A catalogue record for this book is available from the Library of Congress.

D/2013/0602/21
ISBN 978-90-429-2501-4

En hommage à Alexis Pauly
Pour sa fidélité aux travaux du consortium

CONTENTS

Preface 1

Matti Kotiranta – The relation between religion and criminal law as a topic of discussion throughout Europe: an introduction to the national reports 3

Richard Potz and Brigitte Schinkele – Religion and Criminal Law in Austria 13

Eva Brems – Religion in Belgian Criminal Law 21

Hristo P. Berov – Religion and Criminal Law in Bulgaria 27

Achilles C. Emilianides – Religion in the Criminal Law in Cyprus 35

Záboj Horák and Jiří Rajmund Tretera – Religion and Criminal Law: The Czech Republic 41

Lisbet Christoffersen – Religion in Criminal Law: Denmark 49

Merilin Kiviorg – Religion and Criminal Law in Estonia 55

Kimmo Nuotio – Religion in the Criminal Law of Finland 63

Isabelle Riassetto – Religion et Droit Pénal en France 75

Richard Puza – Religion in Criminal Law: Germany 97

Constantinos G. Papageorgiou – The Special Treatment of Religions in the Context of Greek Penal Law 115

Balázs Schanda – Religion in Criminal Law: Hungary 121

Paul Colton – Religion in Criminal Law in Ireland 129

Enrico Vitali – Religion et Droit Pénal en Italie 155

Ringolds Balodis – Legal Protection of Religion in the Republic of Latvia 163

Andrius Sprindziunas – Religion and Criminal Law in Lithuania 177

Alexis Pauly (†) et François Moyse – Religion et Droit Pénal – Luxembourg 189

Sophie van Bijsterveld – Religion and Criminal Law in the Netherlands 199

Michał Rynkowski – Religion and Criminal Law: Poland 205

José de Sousa e Brito – Religion and Criminal Law in Portugal .. 215

Andi Bogdan – Religion and Criminal Law in Romania 225

Matúš Nemec – Religion and Criminal Law in the Slovak Republic 233

Agustín Motilla – Religion in Spanish Criminal Law 241

Lars Friedner – Religion in Criminal Law: Sweden 255

Norman Doe, Russell Sandberg and Frank Cranmer – Religion and Criminal Law in the United Kingdom 261

PREFACE

The 20th annual conference of the European Consortium for Church and State Research took place at the Church Training College in the famous cultural landscape of Lake Tuusulanjärvi at Järvenpää, Finland, on 2-5 October 2008. The theme for the meeting was 'Religion and Criminal Law'.

The conference was organized and prepared on behalf of the Consortium by Professor Matti Kotiranta, University of Joensuu. The conference papers, reproduced in this volume of proceedings, were prepared and circulated in advance, and the delegates consisted of both Consortium members and the national reporters. The conference was attended by forty-two people representing the countries of the European Union.

The opening ceremony included speeches by Rt. Rev. Matti Repo, Bishop of Tampere, representing the Evangelical-Lutheran Church of Finland, Mr. Joni Hiitola, representing the Finnish Ministry of Education, and Professor Sophie van Bijsterveld, President of the European Consortium for Church and State Research in 2008. Professor van Bijsterveld addressed the topic of religion in criminal law from the perspective of international human rights documents and the principle of freedom of expression. As she put it: "It seems that there is a new element in the international dimension. Fundamental choices on the balance between freedom of expression and religion, made on the basis of a national understanding, can trigger consequences on a worldwide scale, as the 'Danish cartoons' showed in spring 2006. What does this mean for the way we deal with religion and freedom of expression at the national level? Has an implicit hierarchy of rights emerged that is now being challenged? What concept of pluralism do we embrace? And what sort of society do we envisage as a consequence? What role is there for criminal law? Is criminal law meant to be effective, symbolic, or does it fulfil other functions? What does all this mean for the way the state, the law, or criminal law in particular, deals with or protects religion as a whole?"

The first session, chaired by Professor Mark Hill, dealt with the penal protection of religion. On the basis of the wealth of information contained in the extensive national reports, the discussion considered the legal framework (e.g. the degree to which religion is governed by the criminal laws of the countries of Europe), the social reality (e.g. whether religion at the present time has a function in criminal law, or to what extent criminal law coverage is favourable or hostile to religion), and the dynamics (e.g. current or likely future developments) at work in the countries of Europe. The second session, chaired by Professor Silvio Ferrari, considered criminal offences committed in the name of religion, an area which has experienced very different approaches across Europe. The final session, chaired by Church Counsellor Lars Friedner, dealt with criminal law and sects. Here one can mention that criminal law may configure special offences out of behaviour considered typical of some sectarian religious movements (e. g. malicious abuse of ignorance or weakness). In addition to this, questions might be asked about what offences are linked to the sectarian milieu. What are the material and psychological elements of each offence and its punishment?

I wish to thank all those who have made contributions to this volume and to the meeting of the Consortium: members, reporters and invited guests. I would also thank most cordially all those who helped organise this conference: the sponsor for the event, the Evangelical-Lutheran Church of Finland, without which the conference would not have been possible, and most especially Mr. Risto Junttila, secretary-general to the Church Council, and his secretary, Mrs. Tuija Korva, who both helped in organising the meeting in Järvenpää. Special thanks also go to Ms. Sirpa Koski of the Finland Travel Bureau for making the flight arrangements, to Ms. Kati Väliaho, marketing secretary of the Church Training College at Järvenpää, for the accommodation and other arrangements, and to the vigorous stewards of the conference, Ms. Siiri Toiviainen and Mr. Heikki Repo, both students of theology.

Finally, I am indebted to Professor Norman Doe for preparing this volume of proceedings. It has been a great pleasure and privilege to work with him. I also thank Peeters, in Leuven, Belgium, for the publishing work.

Joensuu, November 11, 2009
Matti Kotiranta

Matti Kotiranta

THE RELATION BETWEEN RELIGION AND CRIMINAL LAW AS A TOPIC OF DISCUSSION THROUGHOUT EUROPE: AN INTRODUCTION TO THE NATIONAL REPORTS

Although there has been a desire in modern Europe to keep legislation on freedom of religion outside the domain of the criminal law, the multicultural character of the society in which we live has raised once again, and in a new form, the issue of whether particular protection should be granted for religious feelings.

The stimulus for this discussion has arisen from the conflict in priorities between the principles of freedom of expression and freedom of religious conviction brought about by the multiculturalism, and most especially the presence of Islam. The discussion flared up in 2006 in response to the extensive debate within Europe over the cartoons of the Prophet Mohammed, which concerned freedom of expression and freedom of religion as specifically European values, and which even elicited a statement from the chairman of the European Commission, José Manuel Barroso.[1]

[1] "The publication of cartoons in Danish and other European newspapers and the reactions to this have revealed sensitive and fundamental issues. The cartoons have aggrieved many Muslims all over the world. ...The Commission's concern is not with the peaceful response of the majority to the cartoons. It is with the violent reactions of a minority. Reactions which have been disowned by many Muslims... Our European society is based on respect for the individual person's life and freedom, equality of rights between men and women, freedom of speech, and a clear distinction between politics and religion. Our point of departure is that as human beings we are free, independent, equal and responsible. We must safeguard these principles.

Freedom of speech is part of Europe's values and tradition. Let me be clear. Freedom of speech is not negotiable. Like all freedoms, its preservation depends on responsible use by individuals. Governments or other public authorities do not prescribe or authorize the opinions expressed by individuals. ... Freedom of speech is the basis not only of the possibility to publish an opinion, but also to criticize it..... Freedom of religion is not negotiable either. Just as Europe respects freedom of speech so it must, and does, respect freedom of religion. Religious freedom is a fundamental right of individuals and communities, it entails respect for the integrity of all religious convictions and all ways in which they are exercised. Muslims must be able to practise their faith in the same way as the adherents of other religions and convictions practise theirs." Excerpts from José Manuel Barroso, the official statement. "The EU and the cartoons of the prophet Mohammed". See closer http://www.europa-eu-un.org/articles/fr/article_5696_fr.htm. 15 February 2006: Brussels.

The president of the *European Consortium for Church and State Research,* Sophie van Bijsterveld, also drew attention to the challenges for freedom of expression raised by multiculturalism in her speech at the opening ceremony of the Järvenpää conference:

> "Not very long ago in the Western world we could read with a smile about heated parliamentary and public debates on freedom of expression and whether this new right included the liberty to express views and doctrines that endangered public order and tranquillity. Today, again, questions on the nature and the scope of freedom of expression are highly topical. Even within the context of the countries of the EU, freedom of expression has changed from something secure and certain into a contested concept. Moreover, it is not merely a subject that attracts academic interest. In many countries it is discussed in daily newspapers and at the workplace. At a time when freedom of expression, at least in theory, has spread all over the world and is solidly entrenched in international treaties, it has become less easy to deal with. Why?
> It is not because we have come to believe that it is an absolute right: it is subject to limitation, and indeed restricted. It cannot be used to justify discrimination on the grounds of race, ethnicity, homosexuality or physical or mental handicap, for instance. And it is not only civil law that offers protection against such discrimination; criminal law does so as well.
> It is not limitations on these grounds that trigger the new debates. At the core of the current debate is the relationship – the somewhat uneasy relationship – between freedom of expression and religion. Questions arise in the context both of attacks on religion and of statements made from a religious point of view which excite political controversy. These questions are often dormant in socially, culturally and politically relatively stable times, but they are ready to surface at times of change.
> The issue of the relationship between freedom of expression and religion has an international dimension as well, and not merely the international dimension we have become familiar with over the last decades. As we all know, international human rights treaties guarantee liberties of expression and of religion, and ban discrimination. These liberties are meant to function within the national context."

Although the overriding principle in the European context has been that legislation on freedom of religion should not form part of the criminal law and that the two should be kept separate, it is precisely this emergence of a multicultural society, as mentioned above, that raises serious questions about the protection of religious feelings. These issues were approached under three headings in the course of the conference: protection for religion in criminal law, crimes committed in the name of religion, and religious sects in criminal law.

From blasphemy to minority rights

As becomes evident from the national reports, the relation between religion and criminal law is a very broad and complex one. Historically, the recognition of crimes against the freedom of religion has largely served to protect the majority churches from heresies and atheism. Blasphemy has been punished severely throughout history. The current direction of opinion in Europe, however, has clearly been towards acceptance that the need for such protection in criminal law has either substantially diminished or ceased to exist altogether. Thus the legislation against blasphemy has been repealed in most parts of Europe, i.e. in Eastern Europe and many parts of Western Europe, including countries with a State religion, such as Sweden in 1970 and the United Kingdom in 2008. The guiding principle in Western Europe has been that of freedom of expression and the need to "exclude" religion from the sphere of criminal law. At the same time new legislation has been adopted to afford protection to certain minorities, such as sexually deviant groups, the handicapped and linguistic or racial minorities, and this has also been interpreted as extending to religious minorities, the protection of which in law has thus been restored, but in a different way.

Religion is coming to be recognised as a new category at the level of the EU and an important change has come about, although its precise terms are not yet entirely clear. Historically, protection was afforded to the major churches and their confessions, whereas now the EU seems to be more interested in minorities. Up to the late 20th century it was the principle of protecting the subjective religious convictions of individuals that was regarded as being of greatest importance, but the focus of attention appears now to have shifted to the more general area of the cultural dimensions of religious sensibilities of minority groups.

Does religion have a place in criminal law?

The first major issue as far as criminal law is concerned, and a problematic one in many respects, is the place that churches and religious communities in general should occupy in criminal law. At what point do religion and criminal law coincide, or do they coincide at all? Secondly, how does one define a crime, and what is the general nature of criminal law? Criminal law is a universal practice which defines how deeds that are damaging or threatening to society should be punished; it has nothing to do with religion. One is therefore quite justified in asking whether any protection for religion is required in criminal law at all. Thirdly, does the state wish to protect churches and religious communities, and does it even have any need to do so?

The fourth problem as far as criminal law is concerned is how to combine the criminal law of the State with the religious laws and other regulatory instruments of religious groups. What is blasphemy from the point of view of criminal law, for instance? Who is to be accused and who defended? Is it in general even possible to formulate a single definition of religion?

It is true that a certain priority obtains between the protection of religious convictions and freedom of expression, so that one may then ask, fifthly, whether separate protection should be afforded to religious sensibilities and whether in this case sensibility should be interpreted as collective, or is it sufficient for an individual to feel subjectively that a certain deed is an affront to his or her religious feelings?

Religion is the right of an individual

The source and measure of morality in criminal law is in the last resort society itself and the values prevalent in it at a specific point in time. It is precisely here that the greatest change has come about: society no longer possesses a monolithic foundation that is grounded in religion.

It should nevertheless be borne in mind when considering the limitations on criminal law that its purpose is not to maintain morality as such. As Professor Kimmo Nuotio observed in his own contribution: "In the case of a crime against religion it should be possible to point to a specific object of protection. When the majority of members of a community belong to one and the same religious denomination, one can set out from the assumption that the existence of an insult can be determined without any separate investigations." In the case of more esoteric religions and the things that are sacred to them, however, the decisive element should be an estimation of whether the deed took place with the intention of being insulting, and whether an insult occurred at all.

As Nuotio points out, it is far more difficult to prevent infringements of freedom of worship in a multicultural and multireligious society than the legislators in Finland, for instance, have ever appreciated.

Similarly, it is not a straightforward matter to render protection of freedom of worship consistent with considerations of freedom of expression. This is evidently the reason, in fact, why the laws protecting religious observances have been laid aside in so many countries. Experiences in other

EU countries do not appear to support the notion of any pressing social demand for declaring infringements of freedom of worship as punishable offences or the suggestion that the absence of any regulation in criminal law might lead to more extensive insults against the religious feelings of people. It is noticeable, for example, that the churches have not been particularly anxious to retain the blasphemy provisions within criminal law.

Although the notion of crimes against freedom of religion is gradually disappearing from our law books, religion is becoming a relevant topic in legal circles once more in connection with anti-discrimination legislation. It has been observed in a European context that religion and religious observances are very much a matter of the inalienable rights of the individual. Religion in this sense may be regarded as a part of the identity of the individual in civil society, just as much as are the other prohibited grounds for discrimination, such as national or ethnic origin, colour, language, gender, marital status, sexual orientation, opinions on social matters and political or occupational activity, for instance. Thus religion is mentioned in this connection in those elements of criminal law which deal with discrimination in society or at work.

What is the status of religion and the church in modern criminal law?

Professor Nuotio made an interesting suggestion that crimes against freedom of religion should be defined in law once again, but in ecclesiastical law rather than criminal law. This is something of largely historical significance in Finland. In such a case, criminal punishment, such as imprisonment or a fine, implies important restrictions of human rights and can therefore be applied only in accordance with State law in a criminal procedure. Religious law in a modern State can only apply such penal sanctions as excommunication, interdict, dismissal or deprivation of office, suspension, censure, reparation, which are internal to the religious community in question. There are nevertheless certain basic freedoms and human rights that exist in modern constitutional democracies that are *imperative* for all citizens and do not permit deviations even when the members of some religious group might desire this. One may also ask whether churches should have some kind of ready-formulated opinion on what it would like the relation between religion and criminal law to be. Should it be possible to resolve infringements of freedom of worship through a suitable arbitration body, for example, so that representatives of religious organisations can explain how it is that certain ways of acting are found objectionable. Similarly, if damage were done to a church building (for instance) the church in question could settle the matter of compensation out of court as is done in the conciliation process applied to certain crimes. There would be plenty of room in this field for the churches and religious communities to consider their own role as a party to or victim of crimes and shape this role in such a way as to give expression to their own ethical views.

The national reports examine themselves the relation between religion and criminal law in each country separately in accordance with the *grille thématique* constructed by Professor José de Sousa e Brito. It is to this that I now turn.

Religion in criminal law – *Grille thématique*

The *grille thématique* is a set of instructions to national reporters for them to use as a tool for the comparative study of state laws by specifying with respect to each type of offence the same questions and the possible alternative answers to them. It is designed so that the main patterns of historical evolution are made clear and eventually a critical evaluation on the basis of the common constitutional principles becomes possible.

Since in many countries the criminal law includes offences which are less than crimes these were also to be dealt with in the national report.

Offences with religious motivation, whose description in the law makes no reference to religion (in particular crimes linked with terrorism or with Islamic *jihad*) were not to be included, nor were the crimes of genocide or against humanity. The religious motive is one element among others that may be referred to in the legal description, but it might not explain a particular trait of the way the crime is regulated by law.

It was decided that military offences related to conscience objectors were more appropriately studied in relation to conscientious objection. Therefore they were not included.

National reporters were encouraged to include other offences than those mentioned below. The topics and questions in the *grille thématique* were as follows:

Penal protection of religion

This subject has gone through a radical change in the passage from state religion to the separation of state and religion. The secular state raises questions about the difference between the general limits on the exercise of the liberties of expression, manifestation, reunion and action and those related to religion. Judicial decisions are confronted with such difficulties and often only they reveal the true limits of conflicting liberties. The domestic court decisions and the corresponding decisions of the Council of Europe judicature should be reported in such cases.

1. Defamation or outrage reflecting upon the content of religion. What offences correspond to blasphemy or have replaced it as a matter of legal history? Is there equal protection regarding all religions? With respect to each offence: How do the relevant statutory provision read? What is the protected good (God's honour, religious feelings of the believers, public peace)? What are the objective or material and the subjective or psychological elements (intention or also recklessness, knowledge or also reckless knowledge) of the offence and what is the punishment for it? Is incitement to discrimination, to hatred or to violence towards a person or a group of persons because of their religion, specially incriminated? Are the convictions of philosophical associations (*Weltanschaungsvereine* such as Freemasonry or anthroposophist associations) equally protected?

2. Defamation or outrage against a church or religious community. The same questions as n° 1.

3. Desecration of a place of worship or of sacred objects of any religion. The same questions as n° 1.

4. Hindering or disrupting a religious meeting. What are the material and psychological elements of the offence and what is its punishment? Are the ceremonies of philosophic associations (*Weltanschaungsvereine*) equally protected?

5. Menaces, violence or application of force against another's freedom of religion or of conscience. Are they punished through the general offences of assault, coercion, etc. or is there a specific offence? In this case what are the material and the psychological elements of the offence and what is its punishment?

6. Discrimination because of religion. What are the discriminatory conducts that are criminal offences? What are the material and psychological elements of the offence and what is its punishment?

7. Disrupting a funeral. What are the material and psychological elements of the offence and what is its punishment?

8. Abuse of a corpse or desecration of a sepulchre. What are the material and psychological elements and what is its punishment? What is the ruling if the offence is committed because of the religion of the buried person?

9. Proselytizing. On what occasion was such an offence abolished or deemed unconstitutional? Are some forms of proselytizing (e. g. publicity of a sect) offences?

10. Apostasy. On what occasion was such an offence abolished or deemed unconstitutional?

11. Misuse of religious garments or false state of office. Are there any rules concerning the case when a person tries to give the impression that he or she is a clergy but in fact is not?

Offences by the cult ministers

Some offences can only be committed by ministers of religion.

12. Disclosure of a secret obtained in the exercise of ministry. What are the material and psychological elements of the offence and what is its punishment? How are the conflicts between a duty to keep the secret and a duty to denounce solved? Is the secret of confession more fully protected than other professional secrets?

13. Celebration of religious marriage before civil marriage. What are the material and psychological elements of the offence and what is its punishment?

14. Offences against public peace in a place of worship or during a religious practice. What are the kinds of offence (outrage or public defamation of public authority, incitement to civil disobedience or others) and what are the material and psychological elements of each and its punishment?

Offences linked to acts of worship or to rites

Acts of worship or rites may be crimes *sui generis*. Such is the case with female genital mutilation or female circumcision. Ritual homicide is included only as an aggravation of homicide. Bigamy and polygamy (and ritual usage of drugs) are not included because their legal description is not linked to religion.

15. Female genital mutilation/cutting. Is it a special crime or a form of aggravated assault or of common assault? In the first two alternatives what are the material and psychological elements of the offence and what is its punishment?

Religious motivation as a cause of aggravation or instead of attenuation of the offence

The law may provide that religious motivation is an aggravating circumstance of some offence (e.g. religious hostility in homicide or assault).

But the religious motivation (religious duty) may also be an attenuating circumstance.

16. What are the offences aggravated by religious motivation?

17. What are the offences attenuated by religious motivation?

Criminal law and sects

The law may configure special offences for behaviour considered typical of some sectarian religious movements (e. g. malicious abuse of ignorance or weakness).

18. What offences are linked to the sectarian milieu? What are the material and psychological elements of each offence and its punishment?

Richard Potz and Brigitte Schinkele

RELIGION AND CRIMINAL LAW IN AUSTRIA

1. Defamation or outrage against religion, a church or religious community

There is no offence corresponding to blasphemy as such. Blasphemy was abolished with the great Penal Law Amendment 1975. Since then the Penal Code simply provides for "Disparaging Religious Doctrines" (§188). Accordingly, a person who disparages or derides in public a person or a thing which is the object of worship in a church or religious community within Austria, a religious doctrine, a legally admissible observance, or a lawful establishment of such a church or religious community, and does so in circumstances which are calculated to give rise to public nuisance, is to be punished with imprisonment for up to six months or a fine up to 360 daily rates.

This statutory provision aims to protect the practices of religious cults against disturbance as well as the manifestation of personal convictions without interference and compulsion; in other words, it aims, primarily, at the peaceful co-existence of citizens with different religious and philosophical convictions. However, this also implies the protection of the religious feelings of believers. As far as typology is concerned, this offence represents an "abstract strict-liability tort": actual realisation is not required.

Philosophical convictions or philosophical associations are not treated in the same way. However, it may be noted that regarding such associations, the occurrence of analogous facts is rather unusual. Depending on the factual circumstances, the offences under §111 of the Penal Code "Defamatory remark" or §115 "Personal insult" might be relevant here.

A more serious punishment is available for "Incitement to violence". According to §283 a person, who publicly provokes or incites a hostile action towards a church or religious community or towards a certain group belonging to such a church or religious community, to a race (ethnicity), a nation, an ethnic group (tribe), or a country in a manner calculated to endanger public order, is to be punished with imprisonment for up to two years. The same applies to any person who stirs up hatred towards one of these groups, or abuses or humiliates it in such as way as to interfere with human dignity.

2. Desecration of a place of worship or sacred object of any religion and hindering or disrupting a religious meeting

A person, who hinders or disrupts a legally admissible sacred service or an act of worship of any church or religious community (in Austria) with violence or threats of violence is to be punished with imprisonment for up to two years (§189 para. 1). Furthermore a person, who gets up to mischief in circumstances calculated to give rise to public nuisance: (1) at a place dedicated to the lawful practice of a religion of a church or religious community; (2) during a lawful sacred service; or (3) concerning an act of worship of a church or religious community, is to be punished with imprisonment up to six months or a fine up to 360 daily rates (para. 2). Paragraph 1 describes conduct punishable *per se* as a form of unlawful coercion (§105, §106) or a dangerous threat (§107). Therefore, §189 para.1 qualifies these offences. Paragraph 2 refers to behaviour which is not liable for prosecution if there is no religious connotation.

There is no equivalent protection for ceremonies of philosophical associations (*Weltanschauungsgemeinschaften*). However, usually such associations neither have similar places of worship nor practise their belief in a comparable manner. In case of hindering or disrupting a meeting, every assembly enjoys the general protection afforded by the Police Administration Act. A person who disrupts public order by unjustified and inconsiderate conduct may be charged with an administrative offence (Cf. 12 below).

3. Menaces, violence or application of force against freedom of religion or conscience

Menaces, violence or application of force against the freedom of religion or conscience of another are punished through the general offences of assault, coercion, etc. However, there is also the specific offence of §283 (see above in section 1).

4. Discrimination because of religion

There is no specific criminal offence concerning discrimination on grounds of religion.

5. Disrupting a funeral and abuse of a corpse or desecration of a sepulchre

A person who knowingly disrupts a funeral ceremony by noise or other behaviour calculated to give rise to nuisance is to be punished with imprisonment for up to three months or a fine up to 180 daily rates (§191 Penal Code).

A person who takes a corpse or parts of it or the ashes of a deceased person from the custody of the person or authority entitled to dispose of them, removes a corpse or parts of it or the ashes of a deceased person from a burial or other resting place, or abuses or dishonours a corpse, the ashes of a deceased person or a burial, resting or memorial place is to be punished with imprisonment for up to six months or a fine up to 360 daily rates. A person who takes away jewellery from a burial, resting or memorial place is to be punished with imprisonment for up to three months or a fine up to 180 daily rates (§190). The object protected by these offences is the general feeling of piety towards the dead.

6. Proselytizing and apostasy

The Penal Code currently in force does not include any offence concerning proselytizing.

According to the Penal Code from 1803 (§107 lit c), as well as that from 1852 (§122 lit d in connection with §123), a person who induced a Christian to apostasy or intended to disseminate unbelief, or to spread any heresy towards the Christian religion, was to be punished with imprisonment for between six months and one year. If the behaviour gave rise to public nuisance or public danger, or was based on incitement, this offence was punished with a severe prison sentence of between one year and five years, and up to ten years' imprisonment depending on the gravity of the malice or danger involved.

Although these offences were repeated in the re-enactment of the Penal Code in 1945, the prevailing opinion suggests that they expired *per desuetudinem*.

Moreover, according to §304, a person, who organised assemblies, gave or published a lecture, recruited believers, or undertook any other action with the purpose of establishing or promoting a religious community (sect), which had been ruled by the state administration as no longer to be recognised, was guilty of committing an offence and was to be punished with imprisonment for between one month and three months.

Apostasy was neither an offence in the Penal Code 1803 nor in the Penal Code 1852; however, it was grounds for exclusion from intestate succession up until 1868.

7. Misuse of religious garments or false impersonation of office

As far as the protection of religious garments is concerned, the Austrian Concordat 1933 as well as the *Protestantengesetz* 1961, *Orthodoxengesetz* 1967 and *Orientalisch-orthodoxes Kirchengesetz* 2003, refer to the legal provisions on the improper use (and public vilification) of military uniforms. The criminal offence of abusing a uniform was abolished by the Criminal Law Amendment Act 1934 and replaced with an administrative offence by the Act for the Protection of Uniforms 1934. This Act was abrogated on the basis of the Federal Law Repealing Obsolete Statutes 1999 without providing an alternative. Therefore, since then reference can only be made to §35 Military Law, regulating the admissible wearing of uniforms of soldiers and militia, violation of which met with an administrative fine up to 700 Euros (§53). There are no rules on false impersonation of office with regard to clergy.

8. Protection of confessional secrets

Disclosure of a secret obtained in the exercise of ministry does not constitute an offence under the Penal Code. The Criminal Law, however, takes account of confessional secrets with regard to the "Omission of preventing an action liable to prosecution". Under §286 of the Penal Code, a person shall be punished who wilfully and knowingly fails to act concerning the intentional commission of a punishable action which is imminent or which has already begun, or omits to notify the appropriate state authority or the threatened person, when such notification would prevent commission of the offence. Paragraph 2 excuses those who learn of such action through information confided to them in their capacity as spiritual advisers.

Moreover, there are other procedural rules which protect confessional secrets. Clergy and other pastors must not be interrogated as witnesses in criminal, civil, administrative, or taxation proceedings, or in the proceedings of the Constitutional Court or High Administrative Court, with regard to information imparted/confided to them in confession or otherwise in strict confidence in their specific capacity of spiritual adviser (§320 Code of Civil Procedure, §151 lit 1 Code of Criminal Procedure). However, as to knowledge outside these cases, clergy and other pastors are bound to testify as witnesses. A dispensation, given either by the person suspected or from the church authority, is not permitted, even if the clergy were willing to give evidence. What constitutes a "spiritual adviser" is determined on the basis of the self-understanding of the church or religious community concerned. Any examination which interferes with these regulations is either void (§§281, 345 Code of Criminal Procedure) or it represents a ground of appeal (§321 Code of Civil Procedure).

9. Celebration of religious marriage before civil marriage

Celebration of religious marriage before civil marriage is not a criminal offence in Austria. According to §67 of the Law on Personal Status 1937 an administrative punishment (fine or imprisonment) was to be imposed on a person who underwent a religious marriage ceremony before the marriage had been contracted before a registrar. There was to be no punishment if one of the parties suffered from a critical disease and there was no possibility of postponement of the marriage. This provision was struck down as unconstitutional because of its incompatibility with Article 15 of the Constitutional Act on the Fundamental Rights of Citizens and Article 63 sect. 2 of the Agreement of St. Germain. The reasoning of the Constitutional Court was that the religious marriage ceremonies of legally recognized churches and religious societies represent a public manifestation of religion under Article 15 of the Constitutional Act. Following the Law on Unification of the Provisions of Marriage and Divorce in the State of Austria and the Rest of the Territory of the Reich coming into force on 6 July 1938, a marriage before an organ of a religious community had no legal effect in the eyes of the state. Since then, as the procedure for and determination of the timing of marriages fall within the scope of their "internal affairs", legally recognized churches or religious societies are entitled to regulate and administer marriages independently.

10. Offences against public peace in a place of worship or during a religious practice

See above section 2.

11. Female genital mutilation/cutting

According to §90 of the Penal Code, physical injury in not contrary to law if the injured or endangered person agrees to it in advance and the injury or danger as such does not contravene good morals (para. 1). However, it is inadmissible to consent to genital mutilation or any other genital injury which causes a lasting impairment of sexual sensation. Female genital mutilation qualifies as a serious physical injury with serious continuing effects, and is to be punished with imprisonment for between one year and ten years (depending on the concrete circumstances of the case).

12. Offences aggravated by religious motivation

Aggravated damage to property: According to §126 of the Penal Code, a person who commits damage to property being an object dedicated to the sacred services or religious worship of a church or religious community, or to a grave or other burial place, a tomb or a memorial located in a cemetery or in a place used for religious practice, is to be punished with imprisonment for up to two years or to a fine up to 360 daily rates; in the event that the action causes damage exceeding 50.000 Euros, it is to be punished with imprisonment for between six months and five years. This provision – amongst others – also applies to public monuments or objects preserved for their historical or artistic value.

Aggravated theft: According to §128 of the Penal Code, a person who commits theft at a place used for religious worship, or steals an object dedicated to the sacred services or religious worship of a church or religious community, is to be punished with imprisonment of up to three years. When the value of the stolen object exceeds 50.000 Euros, the penalty may be more severe.

Criminal protection of spiritual advisers: If a criminal offence against honour (Penal Code §111 "Defamatory remark", §113 "Reproach for a criminal offence already served or remitted", §115 "Personal insult") is committed towards a spiritual adviser of a church or religious community during the exercise of office or a sacred service, the public prosecutor has to prosecute the perpetrator with authorization from the injured person and the appropriate higher authority of the body in question. The same applies when an offence is committed against such spiritual advisers with regard to their professional actions in a printed form, on the radio, or in any other way which renders it accessible to a broad public (Par. 117 Sect. 2 Criminal Code). What constitutes spiritual advisers is determined on the basis of the self-understanding of the church or religious community in question (cf. Article I §3 *Concordat*, §9 *Protestantengesetz* and §3 *Orthodoxengesetz*).

13. Offences attenuated by the religious motivation

The Penal Code does not specifically provide for offences attenuated by religious motivation.

Neither Austrian doctrine nor the decisions of the Courts deal thoroughly with problems arising from offences committed because of the religious convictions of offenders; the matter is addressed mainly from the perspective of guilty knowledge. According to prevailing opinion, the fundamental assumption is that offenders are conscious of the wrongful nature of their acts. Thus, error as to the prohibited nature of an action is regularly precluded. However, in relation to crimes of omission – referring to the criterion of reasonableness – moral conflicts arising from religious or philosophical convictions are taken into account as appropriate. Finally, religious motivation may be considered with regard to the assessment of punishment or even as a legal reason for exemption from punishment. Such matters are relevant, most especially with regard to religious precepts concerning medical treatment (e.g. prohibitions against blood transfusion), in connection with the offence of failure to discharge the duty to render help to others (§75 Penal Code) or even murder by way of omission (§2 in connection with §75 Penal Code).

14. Offences linked to the sectarian milieu

There are no specific offences linked to the sectarian milieu.

Eva Brems

Ghent University

RELIGION IN BELGIAN CRIMINAL LAW

1. The protection of religion in the criminal law

The content of religion: Defamation concerning the content of religion (blasphemy, sacrilege) is not a crime as such in Belgium. In addition, proselytism and apostasy were never offences under Belgian law. Article 22 of the *Act combating certain types of discrimination* (10 May 2007; B.S. 30 May 2007) criminalizes incitement to discrimination, hatred or violence against a person, group, community or its members, on grounds of certain protected criteria. These include religious belief as well as worldviews, and therefore equal protection is offered to the convictions of philosophical associations. The punishment is a prison sentence (between one month and one year) and/or a fine.

A church or religious community: Defamation against a church or religious community is a crime to the extent that it falls under Article 22 outlined above.

Religious objects: Article 144 of the Criminal Code provides: "He who offends through acts, words, gestures or threats, the objects of a religion, either in places that are designated or usually serve for the practice of religion, or during public ceremonies of that religion, will be punished with a prison sentence of 15 days to 6 months and a fine."

This provision applies only to all serious religions (including non-recognized religions), not to philosophical associations. The specific intent of the perpetrator, as determined by the circumstances of the case, is a crucial element. The determination of the precise objects that are protected depends on the religion. The protection extends to objects used or exposed during a religious ceremony. Even though formal protection relates to objects, it is understood that the underlying value is the protection of the religious feelings of believers.

Religious garments: Article 228 of the Criminal Code penalizes the unauthorized wearing in public of clothing that is the external expression of an officially-recognized function. Both doctrine and case-law are divided as to whether this includes religious garments, in particular the robes of a priest. The punishment is a fine.

Religious services: Article 143 of the Criminal Code forbids disrupting, hindering or interrupting through the creation of disturbances or disorder, the practice of a religion, taking place in a location that is designated or usually serves for the religion or during public ceremonies of that religion. The punishment is a prison sentence of 8 days to 3 months and a fine. This provision protects religious services of all serious religions (not only recognized religions). It does not protect ceremonies of philosophical associations. The intent to disrupt the religious service is an important component of the offence, as well as the realisation of the consequences (actual disturbance).

Religious practice: Article 142 of the Criminal Code makes it a specific offence to either force or hinder anyone to practise a religion. The material element of the offence concerns the use of violence or menaces. These can consist of psychological pressure. The provision mentions the exercise of a religion, the attendance of the exercise of a religion, the celebration of certain religious festivities, respect for certain religious holidays and therefore to open or close one's workplace or shop and to perform or cease from labour. The offence requires a specific intent to interfere with a person's religious freedom. The intended effect has to be realized. The punishment is a prison sentence of 8 days to 2 months and a fine.

Article 145 of the Criminal Code criminalizes insulting a minister of a cult in the exercise of his function by acts, words, gestures or menaces. The punishment is a prison sentence (15 days to 6 months) and a fine. Beating the minister of a cult in the exercise of his function is punished with a higher prison sentence (2 months to 2 years) and fine. If the beating has serious results, the sentence is higher (Article 146 Criminal Code).

Discrimination on grounds of religion: Discriminatory conduct on grounds of religion is criminal only in the case of public officials. For private citizens it is prohibited under civil law. Article 23 of the *Act combating certain types of discrimination* applies to every public official or public servant, every bearer or agent of public authority who discriminates against a person, group, community or its members in the exercise of his or her function. The punishment is a prison sentence of 2 months to 2 years. When an official acts on the orders of a superior who has authority over him or her, only the superior will be prosecuted. While discrimination on grounds of religion by private persons is not a crime, it should be noted that the same Act prescribes fixed amounts of damages in such cases. In the perception of some, the civil law approach to discrimination therefore comes close to a penal law approach.

Disruption of a funeral and desecration of a sepulchre: The disruption of a religious funeral is covered by Article 143 of the Criminal Code (see above). Article 453 of the Criminal Code criminalizes desecration of a sepulchre. The punishment is a prison sentence (one month to one year) and a fine. Article 453bis stipulates that the sentences can be doubled when one of the motives of the offence is hate, contempt or hostility against a person on any one of a list of enumerated grounds, which includes religious belief and a worldview. Desecration requires a material act, directed against a grave or (even temporary) resting place of a dead human body. The act need not necessarily touch the resting place. Cremation and ashes fall within the scope of Article 453. The offence requires only general intent. It exists only when the result hurts or offends the memory of the deceased, yet this is evaluated in an objective manner. No specific intent is required.

Article 526 of the Criminal Code criminalizes the destruction, pulling down, mutilation or damaging of tombs, memorials or gravestones. The punishment is a prison sentence (8 days to one year) and a fine. This provision concerns only the material act of destruction, regardless of whether this affects the memory of the deceased. A general intent only is required.

Article 315 of the Criminal Code, combined with Article 4 of the Act of 20 July 1971 on burial grounds and disposal of the dead, criminalizes the desecration of a burial ground. The offence consists of the violation of the general respect that is required for the place itself and for the dead resting there. It does not require material acts; it may consist of offensive or inappropriate language. The punishment is a prison sentence (8 days to 2 months) or a fine.

2. Criminal offences linked to the exercise of a religion

Breach of professional secrecy by a minister of a cult: Ministers of a cult fall within the scope of the general provision on professional secrets in Article 458 of the Criminal Code, as it mentions 'persons who because of their function or profession have knowledge of secrets that have been confided to them'. This provision prohibits revealing these secrets except in the case of a summons to testify in court or before a parliamentary investigation committee, in which case the law obliges them to disclose those secrets. The punishment is a prison sentence (8 days to 6 months) and a fine.

Article 458bis provides an additional exception concerning certain offences against minors (sexual assault, rape, murder, manslaughter, offences involving bodily harm, female genital mutilation, abandonment, and neglect). When the minor victim has confided in the minister (or someone else who by virtue of his position has access to secrets), and a serious and imminent danger exists for the mental or physical integrity of the victim, from which this victim cannot protect himself (alone or with the help of others), the minister is allowed to report the offence to the public prosecutor.

Religious marriage without prior civil marriage: Article 267 of the Criminal Code stipulates that any minister of a cult who celebrates a marriage before the civil marriage ceremony has been performed, will be punished with a fine. An exception to this rule exists when one of the persons involved in the marriage celebration was in mortal danger, and any postponement could have made the celebration impossible. In the event of recidivism, the minister can be sentenced to prison (8 days to 3 months). This provision has to be read in the light of Article 21 §2 of the Constitution: "A civil wedding should always precede nuptial benediction except in cases established by law, should this be necessary."

Political criticism by the minister of a cult: Article 268 of the Criminal Code concerns an offence that can only be committed by the ministers of cults. During the exercise of their function, they are not allowed to attack directly the government, an act of parliament, a royal decree or any other act of the public authorities, through words spoken in public meetings. The punishment is a prison sentence (8 days to 3 months) and a fine. This provision has always been interpreted in a restrictive manner and does not appear to have been applied by a court in the 20th (let alone 21st) century. Today it is seen by several commentators as incompatible with fundamental rights, in particular freedom of expression (Article 10 ECHR), freedom of religion (Article 9 ECHR), and the prohibition on discrimination.

Female genital mutilation: Article 409 of the Criminal Code, inserted in 2000, establishes a specific offence of female genital mutilation. The offence consists of the execution, facilitation or promotion of any type of mutilation of the genitals of a person of the female sex, regardless of her consent. The punishment is a prison sentence (three to five years). An attempt is punished with a lower prison sentence (8 days to one year). The law establishes higher sentences if the victim is a minor or if the mutilation is performed for profit (five to seven years), if the mutilation results in a seemingly incurable disease or a permanent disablement (five to ten years), if the mutilation leads to the death of the victim (ten to fifteen years), and if the mutilation is performed by a parent, grandparent or other person who has authority or guardianship over a minor or dependent person or by a person who occasionally or habitually lives with the victim (doubling the minimum sentence if no other aggravating circumstance applies; two years are added to the minimum sentence in other cases).

Religious motivation as an aggravating or attenuating circumstance: For several offences, the law determines that it is an aggravating circumstance if one of the motives for which they are committed is hate, contempt or hostility toward a person because of that person's religion or worldview (or any other matter on a list of prohibited grounds of discrimination). These are:

- offences that involve sexual assault and rape: Articles 372-377 of the Criminal Code (aggravating circumstances: Article 377bis Criminal Code)
- manslaughter and other offences involving intentional killing and assault, as well as the intentional administration of very harmful substances: Articles 393-405bis of the Criminal Code (aggravating circumstances: Article 405quater Criminal Code)
- omitting to help a person in grave danger or to deliver help which one is requested to deliver by law, while one is in a position to do so without serious danger to oneself or other persons: Articles 422bis and 422ter of the Criminal Code (aggravating circumstances: Article 422quater Criminal Code)
- arbitrary and illegal arrest or deprivation of liberty: Articles 434-437 of the Criminal Code (aggravating circumstances: Article 438bis Criminal Code)
- beleaguering a person whilst knowing that one's behaviour will seriously disturb that other person's rest: Article 442bis of the Criminal Code (aggravating circumstances: Article 442ter Criminal Code)
- libel and defamation: Articles 443-452 of the Criminal Code (aggravating circumstances: Article 453bis Criminal Code)
- arson: Articles 510-514 of the Criminal Code (aggravating circumstances: Article 514bis Criminal Code)
- destruction of buildings or constructions: Articles 521-525 of the Criminal Code (aggravating circumstances: Article 525bis Criminal Code)

- destruction or damaging of moveable property: Articles 528-532 of the Criminal Code (aggravating circumstances: Article 532bis Criminal Code)
- graffiti and damaging immoveable property: Articles 534bis and 534ter of the Criminal Code (aggravating circumstances: Article 534quater Criminal Code)

There are no offences for which the Criminal Code prescribes a lower sentence when the motivation is religious. Belgian criminal law does not define attenuating circumstances, but leaves them to the discretion of the judge.

Sectarian activities: There are currently no offences in Belgian criminal law that address the specific situation of sectarian organisations. However, a Bill is pending in the federal Parliament that would introduce two new offences in the Criminal Code relating to 'mental destabilisation of persons and abuse of persons' weakness', which are specifically intended to address abuses by sectarian organisations. The first offence (which would be punishable with a prison sentence of 15 days to 2 years and/or a fine) is defined as: violating the fundamental rights of a person by acts of violence, threats or psychological force against an individual, either by inducing the fear that this person, his family, his goods or his job could be harmed, or by exploiting his credulity to convince him of the existence of false enterprises, of an imaginary power or of the existence of non-existing events (proposed Article 442quater Criminal Code). The second offence (that would be punishable with a prison sentence of 1 month to 4 years and/or a fine) is defined as maliciously abusing the ignorance or weakened position of a person who is particularly vulnerable because of age, disease, physical or mental disability or pregnancy, when the abuse aims at forcing that person to commit or omit an act, even though this entails a serious harm for that person, or actively inciting a minor or a vulnerable person to suicide, resulting in actual suicide or an attempt thereto by that person (Chamber of Representatives, 2007-2008, Doc. 0854/001).

Hristo P. Berov

RELIGION AND CRIMINAL LAW IN BULGARIA

I. The penal protection of religion

The Republic of Bulgaria has been[1] and continues to be an undeniably secular state. There is no doubt about this statement in the literature. However, as a matter of fact there are no explicit regulations from the Bulgarian legislature concerning the secular character of the state. Only the Bulgarian Constitutional Court has mentioned it in its interpretative decision no. 2/1998 (State Gazette [SG] 15/1998). Nevertheless, the constitutional provision of Article 13 (3) defines the Eastern-Orthodox religion as the country's traditional faith, and the same is repeated in the stipulation in Article 10 (1) of the Religious Denominations Act from 2002 (SG 120/2002). The obvious dissonance between this stipulation and the separation of state and church,[2] as well as freedom of religious communities under Article 13 (1) and the prohibition on the use of religious convictions and religious communities for political goals, result in a certain practical ambiguity in the Bulgarian position. This can be seen in the "declaration" of the Bulgarian Constitutional Court (decision 2/1998) that the Eastern-Orthodox religion has meaning currently in the political life of the state, which was repeated in the Religious Denominations Act of 2002 (Article 10 (1) s 2). The Bulgarian state is nevertheless a secular post-communist state, and it generally does not resort to any kind of religious considerations in its legal system.[3]

Although the secularization of Bulgarian society began even before 1944, it was precisely the separation between church and state, as a result of the communization of the state and society that led to the situation which is outlined in this study. This situation was substantially influenced

[1] Zankow, St., Die Verfassung der Bulgarischen Orthodoxen Kirche 1918, S. 196; Бобчев, Ст., Черковно право, С., 1927, с. 388.

[2] The current Constitution of the Republic of Bulgaria (from 12.07.1991) stipulates in Art 13 (2) that the religious institutions are separated from the state.

[3] Танчев, Ев. в: Стойчев, Ст., (и съст.) Конституция на Република България. Коментар, С. 1999, с. 69.

by the communist model, in which regulation of religion in the legal system and criminal law became less and less important.

In recent Bulgarian legal history, after the establishment of the Bulgarian state (1878), there were three main legal sources of Bulgarian Criminal Law, also referred to as Acts and Codes of legislation concerning the criminal law. The first is the Bulgarian Penal Act (DV 40/1896), the second one is the Act of 1951, and the third is the Penal Code of 1968. Although the latter has been amended several times, it still remains the central source of Bulgarian criminal law.

Religious issues in Bulgaria underwent intense legal changes during the passage from "state religion" to "separation of state and religion" (Constitution of 1947 and the Religious Denominations Act of 1949). The Soviet influence on the entire Bulgarian legal system left religious issues outside the scope of the interests of both the state and society, so that the liberties of expression, manifestation, assembly and action and those related to religion in the criminal law remained only a paper façade.

Even now, almost two decades after the end of communism, it is barely possible to find any serious and relevant jurisprudence on religious matters in Bulgarian criminal law. Most of the topics addressed below, if regulated at all, are not treated within the framework of the criminal law, but rather other branches of Bulgarian law.

1. *Defamation or insult reflecting upon the content of religion*

In Bulgarian criminal law there was an explicit offence of blasphemy (1896-1951) within Article 204 of the first Bulgarian Penal Act (1896). Blasphemy is not listed as an offence in the current criminal law. There is also no offence corresponding to blasphemy. In the case of discrimination, hatred or violence towards a person or group because of their religion (see below, 4 and 5), the convictions of philosophical associations are equally to be protected (see op. cit.).

2. *Defamation of or insult to a church or religious community*

These could also be prohibited on the basis of hatred or violence towards groups because of their religion (Articles 162 and 164, see below 4, 5, 6).

3. *Desecration of a place of worship or of sacred objects of any religion*

This is not an offence according to Bulgarian criminal law.

4. *Hindering or disrupting a religious meeting*

The regulations of Bulgarian criminal law against hindering or disrupting a religious meeting are to be found within the provisions of Article 165 in connection with Article 174a of the Penal Code. According to these provisions, whosoever, by force or threat, obstructs citizens to profess their faith or carry out rituals and services that do not violate the laws of the country, public peace and good morals, shall be punished by imprisonment for up to one year. The same punishment shall be imposed on those who, in the same way, compel another to participate in religious rituals and services. Also, whosoever, by force, fraud, threat, or in any other illegal manner, disrupts or obstructs a meeting, rally or parade permitted by the Law, shall be punished by imprisonment for up to two years.

It seems that the ceremonies of philosophical associations are equally protected on the basis of Article 174a (2) of the Penal Code.[4] There is no "comparative" jurisprudence to allow a definitive conclusion.

5. *Menace, violence or force against another's freedom of religion or conscience*

This is the general and, at the same time, the special norm for protection of freedom of religion or of conscience: under Article 165 (1) and (2), whosoever by force or threat obstructs citizens to profess their faith or carry out their rituals and services shall be punished by imprisonment for up to one year. The same punishment also applies to those who, in the same way, compel another to participate in religious rituals and services. See 4, 7, and 14.

6. *Discrimination because of religion*

It is stipulated in Bulgarian criminal law through Article 162 (1) that: Whosoever propagates or incites racial or national hostility or hatred or racial discrimination shall be punished by imprisonment for up to three years as well as by public reprimand; and (2): Whosoever commits an act of violence against another or damages his property because of his nationality, race, religion or his political conviction shall be punished by

[4] Art 174a (2): an organizer who, in violation of art. 12, para 3 and art. 13, para 1 of the Law for meetings, rallies and manifestations, holds or continues to hold a disrupted meeting, rally or manifestation shall be punished by imprisonment of up to one year.

imprisonment for up to three years as well as by public reprimand. According to Article 162 (2) and (3) the organizer of groups with the aim of the same conduct is to be imprisoned for one to six years as well as by public reprimand; the member of such a group, up to three years as well as by public reprimand.

7. *Disrupting a funeral*

There is no explicit criminal offence in Bulgarian law applicable to this topic. Nevertheless, the stipulations of Article 165 (1) could also be generally applied (see above 4).

8. *Abuse of a corpse or desecration of a sepulchre*

Only Article 195 (1) could be relevant here: "the punishment for larceny shall be imprisonment for one to ten years: [...] 8. If the larceny has been committed from a grave;"

Nevertheless some municipal authorities have promulgated administrative rulings[5] against the abuse of a corpse which however cannot result in punishment under criminal law.

9. *Proselytizing*

Since the establishment of the Third Bulgarian State (1878), there has been no explicit stipulation making proselytizing a criminal offence. See also 18.

10. *Apostasy*

Since the establishment of the Third Bulgarian State (1878), there has been no regulation on apostasy. The matter of apostasy might have been relevant to the former constitutional obligation (Article 38, 1879-1946) that the monarch should be an Orthodox Christian. But since the referendum on the republic (1946) and the proclamation of the republic this is no longer relevant.

[5] E.g. §1 defines under the term vandalism also abuse, disrupting etc. See: Наредба за гробищни паркове и погребално-обредната дейност на територията на Столична община: Р. N° 368 прот. N° 107/2007 Столичен ОС.

11. *Misuse of religious garments or false impersonation of a religious office*

Bearing in mind that the Penal Code does not contain any special provisions in connection with religion, there are no rules concerning cases when a person tries to give the false impression that he or she is a clergyperson. Legal provisions relevant to such issues could be Article 210 (1) nr. 1 of the Penal Code,[6] as well as the administrative guidelines of Article 36 of the Religious Denominations Act,[7] but the subject is not treated by a special criminal stipulation.

II. Offences by members of the Clergy

Some offences can certainly be committed by members of the clergy, but there are no such explicitly defined offences. So they fall within the general framework of the criminal law.

12. *Disclosure of a secret obtained in the exercise of ministry*

In Bulgarian criminal law there is no special stipulation on revealing a secret obtained in the exercise of religious ministry. Nevertheless, the general rule of Article 145 (1) of the Penal Code reads: whosoever illegally discloses a secret endangering the good name of another which has been entrusted to him or has become known to him in connection with his profession, shall be punished by imprisonment for up to one year or a fine of 300 BGN.[8] Another provision (not criminal, but administrative) concerning this issue, is Article 13 of the Religious Denominations Act.[9] It may eventually be possible to state that a religiously obtained secret should also be protected. It remains questionable whether the secrecy of confession is more protected than other professional secrets because of the lack of jurisprudence on these issues, and also because it remains an open question whether confessional ministry is a profession under the Penal Code.

[6] Art 210 (1): the punishment for fraud shall be imprisonment of one to eight years. 1. if the perpetrator has presented himself as an official or as a person acting on an errand of the authority; etc.

[7] Art 36 (1): anyone who acts on behalf of a religious denomination in the absence of due authorization shall be punished by fine of BGN 100 to 300. (2) In the event of repeated offending under para. 1, the fine shall be of BGN 500 to 1000.

[8] Approx. 150 Euros.

[9] Art. 13 reads: "The confidentiality of confession is inviolable. No clergyman shall be forced to testify or disclose information about facts and circumstances that became known during confession."

13. *Celebration of religious marriage before civil marriage*

Prior to the year 2000, the celebration of religious marriage before civil marriage was regulated in Article 176 (3) of the Penal Code.[10] Currently there is no stipulation in Bulgarian criminal law against celebration of a religious marriage before a civil marriage. It is therefore an issue for the administrative branch of government.

14. *Disruption of public peace in a place of worship or during a religious practice*

Article 165 (1) of the Penal Code states: whosoever, by force or threat obstructs citizens to profess their faith or carry out rituals and services that do not violate the laws of the country, public peace or good morals, shall be punished by imprisonment for up to one year. This provision on crimes against religion is a general regulation and can be used in other cases as well. See 4, 5, and 7.

III. Offences linked to acts of worship or ritual

Acts of worship or ritual are generally not understood as crimes *sui generis* according to the Bulgarian Penal Code.[11] Ritual homicide could only be regarded as homicide and has to be categorized under each particular case.

15. *Female genital mutilation/cutting*

Female genital mutilation/cutting has never been a specific crime in Bulgarian criminal law. As a matter of fact, there are no such cases known publicly. However, as a form of "average bodily harm", it could be placed on the continuum between aggravated and common assault.

The relevant regulation is Article 129 (2) of the Penal Code which states: "Bodily harm shall be considered average if it has caused: a permanent weakening of sight or hearing; permanent speech difficulty,

[10] Repealed – SG 51/2000. The former punishment was imprisonment up to one year and public reprimand.

[11] The principle *nulla poena sine lege* is found in Art 2 (1) in connection with Art 1 (2) of the Bulgarian Penalty Code. As a matter of fact the principle "no penalty without a law" should generally exclude such *sui generis* punishments and prohibitions. See also Art 5 (3) of the Constitution.

difficulty with moving limbs, the body or the neck, the functions of the genitals without causing generative disability; breaking a jaw or knocking out teeth without which chewing or speech is impeded; disfiguring the face or other parts of the body; a permanent non-life-threatening health disorder, or a health disorder temporarily life-threatening; injuries penetrating the skull, the chest and the abdominal cavity".

Its punishment is stipulated in Article 129 (1) of the Penal Code: if someone inflicts on another an average bodily harm he or she shall be punished by imprisonment for up to five years.

IV. Religious conviction as a cause of aggravation or mitigation

16. Bulgarian criminal law does not explicitly stipulate that religious convictions are an aggravating circumstance for any offence (e.g. religious hostility in homicide or assault). The same applies to the fulfilment of a religious duty. Nor does Bulgarian criminal law regard religious motivation as an extenuating circumstance.[12]

There are some cases which have reached the Supreme Administrative Court and have dealt with the right of asylum of foreign citizens, who explained that their reasons for applying were motivated by religion – but this practice is not a part of Bulgarian criminal law. As a result of this it could be stated that in Bulgarian criminal law there are no offences aggravated by religious motivation.

17. In Bulgarian criminal law there are also no offences extenuated by religious motivation.

V. The criminal law and sects

18. Bulgarian criminal law does not contain any special criminal offences for behaviour considered typical of some sectarian religious movements (e.g. malicious abuse of ignorance or weakness). There are also no particular cases relating to these issues in Bulgarian criminal jurisprudence, so that members of the so-called "sectarian" or "new religious movements" could not state that any typical behaviour is being especially stipulated or configured against the so-called "sectarian milieu". The

[12] Art 56 of the Penalty Code reads: "Extenuating and aggravating circumstances shall not be those which are taken into consideration by the law in defining the respective crime". It therefore remains questionable whether such circumstances have been taken into consideration, because there is no jurisprudence on such cases.

current Bulgarian Penal Code was adopted in the communist period and intended to establish an atheistic system rather than setting out offences relating to a special religious issue or so-called "sectarian" behaviour.

Nevertheless, after the political changes of 1989, some Bulgarian local authorities have often misused administrative stipulations and prerogatives in order to designate as "sects" even some historically established religious communities in Bulgaria – mostly because of religious illiteracy or misunderstanding of Christian-orthodox doctrine.

Achilles C. Emilianides

RELIGION IN THE CRIMINAL LAW IN CYPRUS

Introduction

The interaction between criminal law and religion in Cyprus has not been so far an issue of major debate. This is probably due to the system of co-ordination prevailing in Cyprus, which has, in general, promoted religious tolerance as between the various religious communities. There is a lack of case-law with respect to the penal protection of religions; indeed the issue has almost never attracted social attention. Thus, the practical application, or importance of the offences relating to religion which are enumerated in the criminal code, has been limited.

1. Proselytism

Article 18 §5 of the Constitution prohibits illicit proselytism in favour of or against any religion. It prohibits in particular 'the use of physical or moral compulsion for the purpose of making a person change or preventing him from changing his religion'. This constitutional prohibition, though, has never been supplemented by law. Thus, there can be no prosecutions which concern illicit proselytism, since according to Article 12 §1 of the Constitution, which corresponds to Article 7 of the European Convention on Human Rights, there can be no crime, no offence and no punishment without law. Unlike Greece – where the great majority of the population also adheres to the Orthodox faith – in Cyprus there have not been prosecutions of Jehovah's Witnesses with respect to proselytism, since it has always been accepted that Jehovah's Witnesses represent a free religion within the meaning of Article 18 §2 of the Constitution.[1]

If the use of physical or moral compulsion would constitute another criminal offence, irrespective of the fact that religion is concerned, then such compulsion could of course be prosecuted, but only on the basis of

[1] *The Minister of Interior* v. *The Jehovah's Witnesses Congregation (Cyprus) Ltd* [1995] 3 CLR 78. Also see Tornaritis, C., 'Is Chiliasm a Religion? Is it Allowed by the Constitution and what Measures are Provided against it?' [1981] 1-2 *Cyprus Law Tribune*, p. 3-5.

such other criminal offence. This would be the case for instance if the compulsion used, in order to make a person change or prevent him from changing his religion, was the direct result of a threat of injury to the person, reputation or property of the person in question. Such behaviour would amount to a violation of Article 91 of the Criminal Code, Cap. 154 and would constitute the offence of 'threatening violence'. However, it is quite obvious that in the aforementioned circumstances, it is the unlawful compulsion by threats, and not the act of proselytizing, which would constitute the offence. In practice there has been so far no misapplication of Article 91 of the Criminal Code; thus, no cases of religious proselytism have been included within its ambit, when there were no threats of violence.

2. Penal Protection of Religion

Part IV of the Criminal Code, Cap. 154, entitled 'Offences injurious to the public in general: Offences relating to religion', protects certain religious manifestations. The criminal offences that are characterised as religious under the Cypriot penal code are as follows:

2.1. *Defamation of religions*

Article 138 of Cap. 154 provides that any person who destroys, damages or defiles any place of worship or any object which is held sacred by any class of persons with the intention of thereby insulting their religion, or with the knowledge that such class of persons is likely to consider such destruction, damage or defilement as an insult to their religion, is guilty of a misdemeanour.[2] The protected good is public order, as well as the religious feelings of the believers, which may be offended by the act of destroying, damaging or defiling a particular place of worship, or an object which is held to be sacred. In order for the offence to take place, the court must be satisfied that there was an intention to insult the religion of the class of persons who hold the destroyed, damaged, or defiled object as sacred, or who attend the place of worship. The mental element of intent is therefore a prerequisite for the existence of the offence.

The offence of defamation of religions applies to all religions and not simply to Christianity. Although there has been no interpretation of the

[2] A misdemeanour is any offence which is not a felony. Article 35 of Cap. 154 provides that when no punishment is specially provided for any misdemeanour, it shall be punishable with imprisonment for a term not exceeding two years or with a fine not exceeding € 2562.90, or with both punishments.

notion of religion in the Cypriot legal order, it is safe to assume that only those religions whose doctrines or rites are not secret, are included in the scope of protected religions, since only such religions are considered not to be secret and therefore to be 'known' within the meaning of Article 18 §2 of the Constitution.

2.2. *Disturbing religious assemblies*

Article 139 of Cap. 154 provides that any person who voluntarily causes disturbance to any assembly lawfully engaged in the performance of religious worship or religious ceremony, is guilty of a misdemeanour. The protected good is public order, which may be disturbed by the act of causing disturbance to the assembly which has lawfully been engaged in the performance of religious worship or religious ceremony. The court must be satisfied that there was an intention to cause disturbance and thus, the mental element of intent is a prerequisite for the existence of the offence. The offence applies to all religions.

2.3. *Unlawful trespass to places of worship and burial grounds*

Article 140 of Cap. 154 provides that any person, who with the intention of wounding the feelings of any person or of insulting the religion of any person, or with the knowledge that the feelings of any person are likely to be wounded, or that the religion of any person is likely to be insulted thereby, commits any trespass in any place of worship or in any place of sepulchre or in any place set apart for the performance of funeral rites or as a depository for the remains of the dead, or offers any indignity to any human corpse, or causes disturbance to any persons assembled for the purpose of funeral ceremonies, is guilty of a misdemeanour. The protected good is public order, as well as the religious feelings of believers, which are likely to be offended by the act of trespassing in the places of worship, or sepulchre, or depositories, or by the indignity offered to the human corpse, or by the disturbance caused to the assembly of persons. Intention must be proved in order for the offence to take place. The offence applies to all religions.

2.4. *An affront to religious sentiment by word or act*

Article 141 of Cap. 154 provides that any person who with the deliberate intention of wounding the religious feelings of any person utters any word or makes any sound in the hearing of that person, or makes any gesture in the sight of that person, or places any object in the sight of that person, is guilty of a misdemeanour and is liable to imprisonment not exceeding one year. The good protected is public order, as well as the religious feelings of believers, which may be offended by the words, sounds, gestures, or objects placed. Intention of wounding the religious feelings is required for the offence to take place. The offence applies to all religions.

2.5. *Circulation of defamatory publications*

Article 142 of Cap. 154 provides that any person who publishes a book or pamphlet or any article or letter in a newspaper or periodical which any class of persons considers as a public insult to their religion, with intent to vilify such religion or to shock or to insult believers to such religion, is guilty of a misdemeanour. The good protected is public order, as well as the religious feelings of believers, which may be offended by the publication. It could be argued that the *actus reus* of the offence is to be determined on the basis of the criteria prevailing in English law with respect to the common law offence of blasphemy, and thus, the manner in which the views are expressed is more important than the views themselves.[3] The publication should have an element of vilification, ridicule or irreverence that would be likely to infuriate others.[4] The court must be satisfied that the offender intended to vilify such religion, or shock or insult believers to such religion. The offence applies to all religions. A prosecution for the offence of circulation of defamatory publications may not be commenced except by, or with the consent of, the Attorney-General of the Republic of Cyprus.

2.6. *Impersonating clergy*

Article 109 of Cap. 154 provides that anyone who impersonates a person employed in the public service on an occasion when the latter is required to do any act, or attend in any place by virtue of his employment, or who falsely represents himself to be a person employed in the public service,

[3] *R* v. *Ramsay and Foote* (1883) 15 Cox CC 231, which was approved by the House of Lords in *Bowman* v. *Secular Society Ltd* [1917] AC 406, HL.

[4] See a critical perspective in Emilianides, A., 'Can God be Offended? The Common Law Offence of Blasphemy' in Slovak Institute of Church – State Relations, *State – Church Relations in Europe*, 2008 (forthcoming).

and assumes to do any act or to attend in any place for the purpose of doing any act by virtue of such employment, is guilty of a misdemeanour and is liable to imprisonment not exceeding three years. For the purposes of Cap. 154, the notion of a 'person employed in the public service' includes a person acting as a minister of religion of whatsoever denomination in so far as he performs functions in respect of the notification of a prospective marriage, or in respect of the solemnization of marriage, or in respect of the making or keeping of any register or certificate of marriage, birth, baptism, death or burial, but not in any other respect. Thus, impersonating a member of the clergy is not a criminal offence, unless such impersonation is linked to the specific aforementioned functions of a religious minister. The offence applies to ministers of all religions.

3. Offences by Ministers of Religion

3.1. *Confessional secrets*

It is not a criminal offence for a minister of religion to reveal a secret he has obtained in the exercise of his ministry. Further, according to the prevailing view – and although there are no court decisions to support such view – clergymen do not enjoy exemption in criminal or civil procedure, as a result of any kind of confessional secret. Only advocates enjoy privilege with respect to professional secrets by specific legal provisions. If a clergyman reveals a secret, then he may be liable only for canonical offences within his own church, but not for criminal offences.

3.2. *Ecclesiastical courts*

In 1989 the Constitution was amended, so that civil marriages were allowed for members of the Orthodox Church, as well as the Maronite, Armenian and Roman Catholic Churches. However, any citizen of the Republic can enter a religious marriage according to the rites of their religion. The Orthodox, Maronite and Roman Catholic Churches, however, do not recognise civil marriages, or the jurisdiction of the (state) Family Courts. As a result the Orthodox Church will not allow an Orthodox Christian to enter a new religious marriage, unless his previous marriage has been dissolved by a decision of the ecclesiastical courts of the Orthodox Church. Thus, an Orthodox Christian who wishes to have a religious marriage following his divorce, ought to have his marriage dissolved by a decision of both the Family Courts and the Ecclesiastical

Courts. Similarly the Roman Catholic and the Maronite Church will not perform a new religious marriage, unless the previous marriage has been annulled before their respective ecclesiastical courts.[5] There have been suggestions that the State ought to discourage the functioning of the Ecclesiastical Courts, through criminalization of the Church's conduct; however, such suggestions have correctly been rejected.

4. Offences Linked to Acts of Worship and Rites

Article 97 of Cap. 154 provides that any person who holds or is responsible for a Moslem feast (a Moslem festival arranged for, or in connection with, a marriage or for a circumcision) or is the occupier of premises on which such Moslem feast is held and engages, whether with or without pay, or knowingly permits a dancing girl (a prostitute or a woman who dances or sings for pay at Moslem feasts) to dance or sing at such feast, is guilty of a misdemeanour and is liable to a fine not exceeding €128.15, or to imprisonment for one month.

Article 233A of Cap. 154 further provides that female genital mutilation or female circumcision, unless performed by a medical doctor for health reasons, is an offence, irrespective of whether the female had consented to the act. The offender is liable to imprisonment not exceeding five years. Female genital mutilation, though often related to rituals, is not an offence linked exclusively to acts of worship under Cypriot law; indeed there is no mention of acts of worship or rites in the *actus reus* of the offence.

5. Religious motivation as a Cause of Aggravation or Attenuation of the Offence

There are no specific provisions in the Criminal Code, or in other criminal laws, providing that religious motivation is either an aggravating or an attenuating circumstance of a specific offence. Further, ritual homicide is not considered to be an aggravation of homicide. However, a judge may have the discretion, on the basis of all relevant factors, to consider whether he should give weight to religious motivation when considering a specific offence.

[5] Emilianides, *The Cypriot Law of Marriage and Divorce*, *Sakkoulas*, Athens – Thessaloniki, 2006 (in Greek).

Záboj Horák and Jiří Rajmund Tretera

Charles University, Faculty of Law, Prague

RELIGION AND CRIMINAL LAW: THE CZECH REPUBLIC

Special provision under the category "defamation of religion" existed in law in the territory of the Czech lands in 1852–1950, and was defined in the Austrian Criminal Code of 1852 (Act nr. 117/1852, art. 303). This was adopted by the Czechoslovak legal order in 1918. The communist totalitarian regime replaced this Code with a new one in 1950 (Act nr. 86/1950), which did not contain any such special provision. In spite of the wide and real persecution of all religions and the promotion of an atheistic world-view, the new code contained several formal provisions concerning protection of freedom of religious confession or the right not to be confessional, in common provisions for the protection of human rights.

The Criminal Code of 1950 was replaced by the Criminal Code of 1961 (Act nr. 140/1961). The 1961 Code did not differ greatly from the previous one, but specified some offences in more detail. The protection of conscience was until the democratic revolution of 1989 merely an empty proclamation; in reality the communist world view of atheism dominated. The Criminal Code of 1961 is still in use – because of its relatively good formal composition – but was amended many times from December 1989 in order to protect human rights effectively in the territory of the Czech Republic. Many of these amendments concern the protection of religion of the citizens and other inhabitants of the Czech Republic – in association with international agreements which bind the Czech Republic.

The Parliament of the Czech Republic is currently considering the draft of a new Criminal Code. However, the following national report is based on the legal order in July 2008. All quotations are taken from legal provisions in use at the time, i.e. the Criminal Code 1961 (its sections and subsections as amended), and other legislation in force: the Criminal Process Code of 1961 (Act nr. 141/1961, as amended), the Minor Offences Act (Act nr. 200/1990, as amended), and the Act on Churches and Religious Societies (Act nr. 3/2002).

There is no protection for the honour of God in the sense of an offence of "blasphemy", because the Czech Republic is a secular state. According to the constitutional provisions (above all in the Charter of Fundamental Rights and Freedoms, published in January 1991, and again after the split-up of Czechoslovakia in January 1993), the Czech Republic may not bind itself either to any ideology or to any religious conviction (Art. 2).

There is protection for the human dignity of believers and their convictions. This protection is provided not only in favour of members of the denominations registered by the state,[1] but also for believers of other religions. We are convinced that protection of human dignity is more than mere respect for the religious feelings of believers or for the public interest to maintain civil peace, but nevertheless it includes both. The common formulations on the protection of conscience are usually sufficiently wide as to protect also the convictions of philosophical associations.

Among those criminal offences of "grossly infringing civic coexistence" (Special Part of the Criminal Code, Chapter V) there are "Defamation of a Nation, Race or Conviction" (sec. 198), "Violence against a Group of Citizens or an Individual" (sec. 196), and "Incitement of National and Racial Hatred" (sec. 198a).

Section 198 provides:

"Defamation of a Nation, Race or Conviction

(1) A person, who publicly defames:
a) a nation, its language or a race; or
b) a group of inhabitants of the Republic because of their political conviction, religion or because they are non-denominational,
shall be sentenced to a term of imprisonment of up to two years.
(2) An offender who commits an act pursuant to subsection (1) together with at least two other persons shall be sentenced to a term of imprisonment of up to three years."

The phrase "a group of inhabitants of the Republic" may refer to a group who have residence in the Czech Republic, and not only to Czech citizens living there.[2]

[1] Some religious communities were recognized (registered) by the state even in the past under the rules of Acts nr. 68/1874, and nr. 308/1991. Their registration is now regulated by the Act on Churches and Religious Societies nr. 3/2002. At present there are 30 denominations registered in the Czech Republic.

[2] See the Criminal Code, Minor Offences Act, a Translation by Trade Links, Prague, 2003, p. 218.

Section 196 provides:

"Violence against a Group of Citizens or an Individual

(1) A person who threatens a group of citizens with death, a bodily injury or extensive damage shall be sentenced to a term of imprisonment of up to one year.
(2) A person, who uses violence (force) against a group of citizens or an individual, or threatens them with death, a bodily injury or extensive damage, because of their political conviction, nationality, affinity to an ethnic group, race, religion, or because they are non-denominational, shall be sentenced to a term of imprisonment of between six months and three years.
(3) A sentence under subsection (2) shall also apply to those, who conspire or mob to commit such act."

Section 198a provides:

"Incitement of National and Racial Hatred

(1) A person who publicly incites hatred of another nation, ethnic group, race, religion, class or another group of persons or publicly incites the restriction of their rights and freedoms, shall be sentenced to a term of imprisonment of up to two years.
(2) The same sentence shall apply to a person, who conspires or mobs to commit an act pursuant to subsection (1).
(3) An offender shall be sentenced to a term of imprisonment of between six months and three years:

a) if he commits an act pursuant to subsection (1) by using the press, film, radio or TV broadcasting, a publicly accessible computer network or a similarly effective method; or
b) if he actively participates in activities of groups, organizations or associations promoting discrimination, violence or racial, ethnic or religious hatred."

Protection of a church or religious community against defamation or outrage is not specially regulated. It is governed by the provisions outlined above.

Section 202 provides special regulation under the title "**Hooliganism**":

"(1) A person who, in a public or publicly-accessible place, behaves in way which is grossly indecent (immoral) or causes disorder,

particularly by assaulting another person, dishonouring an historical or cultural monument, grave or another abode of the dead, or by disrupting an assembly of citizens or ceremony in a gross manner, shall be sentenced to a term of imprisonment of up to two years or a pecuniary penalty.
(2) An offender shall be sentenced to a term of imprisonment of up to three years if he commits an act pursuant to subsection (1) as a member of an organized group."

"Disrupting an assembly of citizens or ceremony" is to be understood, naturally, as covering both religious meetings or ceremonies and those of a philosophical association.

Menaces, violence or the application of force against another's freedom of religion or conscience are punishable under both a *general offence* of coercion or extortion (literally: blackmail) and a *special offence* of restriction of freedom of religion. Sections 235 and 236 provide as follows:

"Sect. 235 – **Extortion**

(1) A person who forces another by violence, the threat of violence or the threat of other serious detriment, to do something, to desist from doing something or to tolerate something, shall be sentenced to a term of imprisonment of up to three years.
(2) An offender shall be sentenced to a term of imprisonment of between two and eight years if:
 a) – e)..........
 f) he commits such act against another person because of such person's race, ethnic background, nationality, political conviction, religious belief or because of being non-denominational.
(3) An offender shall be sentenced to a term of imprisonment of between five and twelve years if by an act pursuant to subsection (1) he causes extensive damage.
(4) An offender shall be sentenced to a term of imprisonment of between ten and fifteen years or by extraordinary penalty[3] if by an act pursuant to subsection (1) he causes death."

[3] The extraordinary penalty is imprisonment of between 15 and 25 years or life imprisonment. It was introduced after the abolition of the death penalty (1 July 1990).

"Sect. 236 – **Restriction of the Freedom of Religion**

A person who by using violence, the threat of violence or the threat of some other serious detriment

a) forces another to take part in a religious service,

b) unlawfully prevents another from taking part in a religous service, or

c) prevents another from enjoying freedom of religion,

shall be sentenced to a term on imprisonment of up to one year."

Restriction of freedom of religion which is of minor seriousness may be punished under the Minor Offences Act, sect. 49 – minor offences against civic coexistence. In its subsection 1 (e) we read that a minor offence is committed by the person who causes harm to another because of his faith or religion. The penalty is atypical, and it is imposed by municipalities.

There are some serious offences under the Criminal Code, committed against humanity, where religion is mentioned: Sect. 259 – Genocide; Sect. 260 – Support and Propaganda of Movements Aimed at Suppressing Human Rights and Freedoms; Sect. 261 – Publicly Expressed Support for Movements Aimed at Suppressing Human Rights and Freedoms

Discrimination because of religion would violate constitutional provisions (the Charter of Fundamental Rights and Freedoms, Art. 1 and Art. 3 sect. 1). Every act of Parliament or other legal regulation which would allow active or passive discrimination is to be forbidden. The review of legislation is exercised by the Constitutional Court. No enquiry of religious conviction is allowed in personal data questionnaires.[4]

Funerals are protected by the common provision on hooliganism (sect. 202, see above). Sect. 202a provides:

"Improper and Indecent Interference with a Dead Human Body

1. A person who illegally opens a grave or tomb with a dead human body or urn holding the ashes of a cremated body shall be sentenced to a term of imprisonment of up to two years or a pecuniary penalty.
2. A person who wilfully removes a dead human body from a graveyard or who handles remains of the dead human body contrary to statutory

[4] Even teachers and pupils of denominational schools are not obliged to declare their denominational membership. Not only in theory but also in reality, many of them differ from the denominational affiliation of a founder of such a school or are non-denominational.

provisions shall be sentenced to a term of imprisonment of up to two years or a pecuniary penalty.
3. An offender shall be sentenced to a term of imprisonment of up to three years if he commits an act pursuant to subsection (1) or (2) as a member of an organized group."

Proselytizing is not an offence. Everybody has a right to change their religion or to be non-denominational. This right had been introduced by the Acts of the Austrian Empire (Acts nr. 142/1867 and 49/1868). Advertising religious groups is not an offence, but it is not common (it could be seen as against good morals). It is excluded from radio and TV broadcasting under special mass-media provisions. But public speeches by evangelizers are allowed; there is only a duty to notify them to the relevant public authority. The same duty applies to those who organise processions. The public distribution of booklets or reviews is common.

The right to apostasy is part of religious freedom. The Charter of Fundamental Rights and Freedoms, Art. 15, sec.(1) states: "The freedom of thought, conscience and religious confession is secured. Everybody has the right to change his religion or faith or to be undenominational." The right to be non-denominational was introduced in the years 1868-1870 by the Act nr. 49/1868 – see above – and by the municipal register rules from 1870. It established civic registers for the births, marriages and deaths of non-denominational people.

The consequences of the misuse of religious garments are not specifically regulated by state law. However, impersonation of state or ecclesiastical officers can be punished as general offences of fraud (sect. 250) or impairing another person's rights (sect. 209).

The Act on Churches and Religious Societies (Act nr. 3/2002) empowers ministers of denominations registered with "special rights" to safeguard secrets disclosed in the confessional, or analogous secrets,[5] with a limitation period of 50 years. The list of these denominations is published by the Ministry of Culture; there are 21 such denominations at the present time. The ministers are freed from the duty to report a criminal act (sect. 168 of the Criminal Code), and they may not be forced into examination as witnesses (sect. 99 of the Criminal Process Act nr. 141/1961, as amended). But they nevertheless have a duty to prevent a criminal act (according to sect. 167 of the Criminal Code). These matters might be a source of disagreement between church and state in the future. We can say that secrets

[5] The formulation "analogous" rights was incorporated into the Bill according to a wish of several Protestant Churches in the Czech Republic.

from confession are more fully protected than other professional secrets. The state recognizes that the secrecy of confession is absolute.

There are alternative forms of marriage in the Czech Republic. The marriages celebrated before the ministers of denominations which are registered with "special rights" by the Ministry of Culture (see above) have legal consequences in civil law. The minister is obliged to notify every celebrated marriage, three days after celebration, to a registering municipal authority. An omission to do so, prescribed in the Family Law Act, is to be punished by a pecuniary penalty under the Minor Offences Act (sect. 42c, subsect. 1 lit. b). The minister of a religious community which is not registered "with special rights" is not punished for celebrating a marriage ceremony but such a "marriage" is not recognized by the state – the couple is regarded as unmarried under civil law.

There is no special *Kanzelparagraph* in the Czech Republic. Ministers of religion are as responsible as other inhabitants for any breach of the law, even in a verbal form, and they can be punished by public authorities according to the common provisions of the Criminal Code and Minor Offences Act. In cases of systematic agitation against human rights by any denomination, the Ministry of Culture can cancel the "special rights" of such a denomination or even its basic registration (Act nr. 3/2002, sect. 21 and 22), i.e. legal existence.

Female genital mutilation/cutting is not a specific crime. It would be punished under the offence of "bodily injury". We are convinced that the Czech courts would use section 222 subsection 1 of the Criminal Code (on serious bodily injury) in such cases.

There are several religiously aggravated offences under the Criminal Code: Sect. 219 – Murder; Sect. 221 – Bodily injury; Sect. 222 – Serious bodily injury; Sect. 235 – Extortion; Sect. 257 – Damaging the property of another. However, there are no offences attenuated by religious motivation.

Finally, there is no special offence connected expressly with sectarianism. Acts of superiors or members of such a movement (even within the framework of a registered denomination), if they contravene personal freedom and human rights, are punished by common provisions. In addition to the above-mentioned provisions, there are also offences under: sect. 231 – unlawful restraint, sect. 232 – deprivation of personal freedom, sect. 238 – criminal trespass, sect. 215 – battery of a charge, and sect. 215a – battery of a person living in the same flat or house.

Lisbet Christoffersen

RELIGION IN CRIMINAL LAW: DENMARK

Introduction: religious norms, criminal law and the protection of religion

The current Danish Penal Code from 1930 is understood as contributing to the modern breakthrough in Danish legislation (Hurwitz 1969). This accounts for the punishments (length and type) as well as for the systematic ordering of the law. The offences, on the other hand, still draw on a legal tradition which is hundreds of years old. Christianity influenced the law from the 13th century and this was greatly strengthened by post-Reformation legislation. The Reformation meant a break with Canon Law. Roman Law came into focus – except when it came to marriage law, penal law and other types of legislation related to the individual. In these fields the post-Reformation inspiration was the Decalogue. From 1683 the systematization of Danish penal law followed that of the Ten Commandments; offences were taken from Mosaic Law and punishments were also inspired by these sources (Tamm 1983; Tamm 2005). Much of this inspiration was down-scaled during the enlightenment and the first penal law following the constitution of 1849, but offences still show the old Christian influence. The Danish penal code, for example, has what is often called a *Samaritan rule* – everyone who, without any special danger to himself or anyone else, is in a position to help another person in obvious danger of his life, must do his best to save such other person; failure to do so may give rise to 2 years' imprisonment.[1]

Crimes in relation to religion

Also the offence of *blasphemy* comes from post-Reformation 1683 Danish Law. It stands alongside other provisions protecting religious aspects of life in a chapter in the penal law concerning crimes against public

[1] Strl §253: "Med bøde eller fængsel indtil 2 år straffes den, som, uagtet det var ham muligt uden særlig fare eller opofrelse for sig selv eller andre, undlader 1) efter evne at hjælpe nogen, der er i øjensynlig livsfare…"

order and peace.[2] The blasphemy rule provides that "a person, who publicly mocks or insults the dogma/creed or cult/form of worship of any religious community lawfully present in the country, is to be fined with a maximum of 4 months' imprisonment".[3] The rule thus covers *religious feelings* related to all types of creed, not only Christianity. Several suggestions in Parliament over the years (since the Cartoons crisis) have proposed to remove blasphemy from criminal law. A leading professor in criminal law supports the suggestion based on the argument that freedom of speech in relation to powerful institutions (monarchy, religion etc) has brought us to the current enlightened stage in Europe; however, a leading professor in constitutional law suggests that the norm is upheld in the code with reference to the 'public peace'-argument in order to protect religious groups from crimes not covered by the prohibitions on defamatory statements.[4]

The blasphemy rule was used in 1938 in a rather famous judgment with regard to changing the content and meaning of Jewish religious writings in Nazi propaganda. In order to protect the (Jewish) religious minorities further, the Danish parliament in 1938 added a paragraph penalizing defamation. This rule was later changed and widened in order to meet international standards, so that the Danish criminal code, as with all other European legal systems, now contains a rule criminalizing defamatory statements about a group of persons on the grounds of *inter alia* their religion or personal beliefs.[5] The legislative question, currently being investigated, is whether or not the possible crimes are all covered by §266 b; or whether or not this rule should be widened if the relevant protection should be secured in the event that the blasphemy rule is removed.

[2] Strl. Kapitel 15: Forbrydelser mod den offentlige orden og fred.

[3] Strl. §140: Den, der offentligt driver spot med eller forhåner noget her i landet lovligt bestående religionssamfunds troslærdomme eller gudsdyrkelse, straffes med bøde eller fængsel i indtil 4 måneder.

[4] See e.g. L 90 2007-08, 2. Samling: Forslag til lov om ændring af straffeloven (ophævelse af straffelovens blasfemibestemmelse), fremsat 28 februar 2008, med bemærkninger samt særligt udvalgsbehandlingen med svar fra Justitsministeren på spørgsmål fra udvalget; beretning fra udvalget samt referat fra offentlig høring 22. Maj 2008 med deltagelse af professor Vagn Greve og professor Henning Koch. [references are made to the relevant suggestion of new laws in the Danish Parliament and the public hearing involving the participation of Professor Vagn Greve, criminal law, and Professor Henning Koch, constitutional law. The Parliamentary committee decided to request a scientific analysis and ask the government to suggest a proposal for new laws. This proposal has not yet been made]. See also Koch 2006.

[5] Strl. §266 b.

Different groups in Danish society tried to get the 12 infamous cartoons evaluated in relation to the blasphemy rule, but no case was initiated as they were far from being blasphemous in the Danish context. There were also two or three earlier cases in the 1970s and 1980s, where songs and paintings showing the Christian God and Jesus in very humiliating positions did not lead to a blasphemy judgment (Christoffersen 2005 gives an overview).

Moreover, as part of the protection of public peace, the criminal law penalizes the disturbance not only of meetings in parliament and public councils, but also religious services or other public religious functions (such as wedding ceremonies or funerals).[6] All religious ceremonies are protected, no matter what confession, but in order to attract protection the ceremony must be public since the protection is designed for the public life of the country. In the same way *desecration of graves* is forbidden along with the *indecent handling of corpses* – again, no confessional distinctions are made.[7] The same paragraph has a special blasphemy provision which penalizes the indecent handling of objects belonging to a church and used for religious purposes; this provision is also being discussed in relation to the blasphemy rule.

Proselytizing and apostasy are of course not crimes in Denmark and this has been the position since full freedom of religion was introduced with the constitution of 1849.

The misuse of religious garments is only protected in relation to the national church, not through a special law but through a general norm that misuse of garments belonging to Danish public authorities (which in certain matters also covers the ministers of the national church) is criminalized.[8] *Secrets of confession* are protected in relation to all functions of ministers of the national church because they are civil servants.[9] The secrecy of confession is only protected in relation to religious leaders from other confessions in those situations in which such leaders exercise public

[6] Strl §137, stk. 2:.. straffes den, der ved larm eller uorden forstyrrer offentlig samling af Folketinget, Færøernes lagting, kommunale eller andre offentlige råd, gudstjeneste eller anden offentlig kirkelig handling, eller som på usømmelig måde forstyrrer ligfærd.

[7] Strl §139: Den, som krænker gravfreden eller gør sig skyldig i usømmelig behandling af lig, straffes med bøde eller fængsel indtil 6 måneder. På samme måde straffes den, som gør sig skyldig i usømmelig behandling af ting, der hører til en kirke og anvendes til kirkeligt brug.

[8] Strl. §132, stk. 1, nr. 1: Med bøde straffes den, som forsætligt eller ved uagtsomhed på retsstridig måde benytter kendetegn eller dragt, som er forbeholdt dansk eller fremmed offentlig myndighed eller militærperson

[9] Strl. §152: Den, som virker eller har virket i offentlig tjeneste eller hverv, og som uberettiget videregiver eller udnytter fortrolige oplysninger, hvortil den pågældende i den forbindelse har fået kendskab, straffes med bøde eller fængsel indtil 6 måneder.

power.[10] That is the case as to the general permission for religious ministers to perform marriages under the marriage act; Danes may choose between civil marriage or religious marriage according to civil legislation (whereas religious laws are not in use with regard to religious marriages). Ministers from religious minorities such as the Catholic Church also exercise public power when they bury the dead, even though authority to decide the funeral for all citizens is delegated to ministers of the national church. All religious ministers (regardless of confession) are however protected by the *secrecy of confession* when administered in prisons and they are not obliged (or allowed) to function as *witnesses* before the courts.

Female genital mutilation is prohibited in Denmark under criminal law, and the act is punishable with 6 years' imprisonment. The rule is new in the criminal code (from 2003).[11] Moreover, in 2008 a new law was enacted to penalize *forced marriage*, technically by making it compulsory to see this as an aggravated form of common crimes of coercion, with imprisonment for up to 4 years.[12] Male mutilation is not criminalized, but there were serious suggestions to do so in public debate in 2009.

The question of *aggravation* has also been relevant in a couple of cases regarding *honour killings*, where the religious dimension has resulted in a more severe punishment – whereas a killing, based on jealousy would often result in an *attenuation* of the punishment.

The concept of *sects* is not known in Danish legislation. If a religious group as part of its activities breaks the criminal law, the religious dimension and a closed milieu might be seen as some sort of aggravation, but there have been no cases.

Religion in criminal law

As can be seen, religion as a protected function does not play a central role in criminal law, whereas there have been attempts to see religiously-motivated acts as more severe than other breaches of the criminal law.

[10] Strl. §152 b, stk. 1: Med samme straf som efter §152 straffes den, som udøver eller har udøvet en virksomhed eller et erhverv i medfør af offentlig beskikkelse eller anerkendelse, og som uberettiget videregiver eller udnytter oplysninger, som er fortrolige af hensyn til private interesser, og hvortil den pågældende i den forbindelse har fået kendskab.

[11] Strl. §245 a: Den, som ved et legemsangreb med eller uden samtykke bortskærer eller på anden måde fjerner kvindelige ydre kønsorganer helt eller delvis, straffes med fængsel indtil 6 år.

[12] Lov nr 316 af 30/04/2008 om ændring af straffeloven (Skærpelse af straffen for ulovlig tvang i forbindelse med indgåelse af ægteskab): Tvinges nogen til at indgå ægteskab, kan straffen stige til 4 år.

However, where religious motivation does play a most crucial role is as the normative basis of the crimes. As far as I can see, the more central discussion for the future will be about which acts are to be seen as crimes and on what philosophical or normative basis in democratic societies with a plurality of religions.

Bibliography

Christoffersen, Lisbet, 2005: "Blasfemisk Blindhed" [Blasphemic Blindness] in *Biskop for Herrren og så mange andre. Festskrift til Kjeld Holms 60-års dag*, red. Anne Ehlers, Niels Grønkjær & Marianne Levinsen, Forlaget Anis, København, p. 189-214

Koch, Henning 2006: "Ytringsfrihed og tro" [Faith and Freedom of Speech] i Lisbet Christoffersen (red.): *Gudebilleder. Ytringsfrihed og religion i en globaliseret verden* [Images of Gods. Freedom of Speech and Religion in a global Wordl], Tiderne Skifter, København, p 72-88

Greve, Vagn 2005: et al *Kommenteret straffelov. Speciel del* [The Penal Law with Commentaries. The Crimes], 8. Omarbejdede udgave, Jurist- og Økonomforbundets forlag

Hurwitz, Stephan 1969: *Den danske Kriminalret. Almindelig del*, [Danish Criminal Law. General Introduction]; 4. Reviderede udgave v. Knud Waaben; Gad

Tamm 1983: Ditlev Tamm: "Majestætsforbrydelsen I Danske Lov" [Crimes towards the Crown in the Danish Law] i d.s. (red): *Kong Christian den Femtes Danske Lov*, Jurist- og Økonomforbundets forlag 1983, p. 641-676

Tamm 2005: Ditlev Tamm: *Retshistorie. Danmark – Europa – globale perspektiver*, [Legal History. Denmark – Europe – Global Perspectives], Jurist- og Økonomforbundets forlag

Merilin Kiviorg

RELIGION AND CRIMINAL LAW IN ESTONIA

Introduction

The new Penal Code,[1] adopted on 6 June 2001, came into force 1 September 2002. It repealed the earlier Code which had been in force since 1 June 1992.[2] The new Penal Code introduced two principal changes. Firstly, both criminal offences and some misdemeanours are dealt with in the same law. A criminal offence is an offence for which the principal punishment prescribed in the case of natural persons is pecuniary or imprisonment, and in the case of legal persons, pecuniary or compulsory dissolution.[3] A misdemeanour is an offence which is provided for in the Penal Code or another Act, and the principal punishment prescribed for which is a fine or detention.[4] If a person commits an act which comprises the necessary elements of both a misdemeanour and a criminal offence, the person shall be punished only for the criminal offence. If a punishment is not imposed for the criminal offence, the same act may be punished by way of misdemeanour.[5] It should also be stressed that only intentional acts are punishable as criminal offences, unless a punishment for a negligent act is provided by the Penal Code. Moreover, an act is deemed to be intentional if it comprises the necessary elements of an offence in which case intent is presumed with regard to the act, and negligence is deemed to be sufficient in the case of grave consequences. Intentional and negligent acts are both punishable as misdemeanours.[6]

Secondly, the 2002 Penal Code introduced into Estonian law the concept of the criminal liability of legal entities. In the cases provided by law, a legal person can be held responsible for an act which is committed by a body or senior official thereof in the interests of that legal person.[7]

[1] RT I 2001, 61, 364 (in force 1 Sept. 2002); RT I 2008, 19, 132.
[2] RT I 1992, 20, 287 ja 288, RT I 1999, 29, 398.
[3] §3 (3).
[4] §3 (4).
[5] §3 (5).
[6] §15.
[7] §14 (1).

Prosecution of a legal person does not preclude prosecution of the natural person who committed the offence.[8] Thus, in principle, a religious organisation can be held responsible in prescribed circumstances. In certain cases a religious organisation may even be subjected to compulsory dissolution. The basis for this may be found in Article 48(3) of the Estonian Constitution: 'associations whose aims or activities violate criminal law are prohibited'. There are no provisions in the Penal Code specifically dealing with religious organisations.

Only a very few cases related to religion have been decided by courts. There have been no cases dealing with criminal responsibility of religious communities. There has been one case dealing with an offence committed by a religious individual.

I. Penal Protection of Religion

The Penal Code has several provisions protecting the individual and collective freedom of religion. It also contains necessary restrictions on the manifestation of freedom of religion. First of all, the chapter on "Offences Against Political and Civil Rights" has a specific section dealing with offences against equality. In terms of criminal law all religions (and beliefs) are equal. Article 152 of the Penal Code provides the penalty for the violation of the principle of equality: "Unlawful restriction of the rights of a person or granting of unlawful preferences to a person on the basis of his or her nationality, race, colour, sex, language, origin, *religion*[9], sexual orientation, and political opinion, financial or social status is punishable by a fine of up to 300 fine units or by detention." The same act, if committed at least twice, or if significant damage was caused to the rights or interests of another person protected by law or to public interests, is punishable by a pecuniary punishment or up to one year of imprisonment.[10] Thus, depending on the circumstances, the offence against equality can be either a criminal offence or a misdemeanour.

There are no provisions specifically dealing with blasphemy or defamation. The previous Criminal Code had an article on defamation (§129). Drafters of the new law were of the opinion that defamation is sufficiently

[8] §14 (2).

[9] The unofficial translation (www.legaltexts.ee) uses "religion", however, the original text in Estonian uses "belief". In the case of confusion, one should probably rely on the equal protection/prohibition of discrimination of religion or belief in Art. 12 of the Estonain Constitution and on Articles 40 and 41.

[10] Amendment in force 16.07.2006, RT I 2006, 31, 234.

covered by other articles dealing with specific circumstances (for example, activities which publicly incite to hatred, violence or discrimination on the basis of religion).[11]

Article 154 specifically deals with violation of freedom of religion. It lays down the penalty (a pecuniary punishment or up to one year of imprisonment) for interfering with the religious affiliation or religious practices of a person, unless the religious affiliation or practices are detrimental to the morals, rights or health of other people or violate public order.[12] Compelling a person to join or be a member of a religious association is punishable by a fine or by imprisonment for up to one year.[13] Article 159 of the Penal Code provides more general protection against violations of freedom of association. As some of the religious communities have chosen to register as ordinary non-profit organisations, this provision provides adequate protection to them as well: "Interference with the foundation of, joining or membership in a non-profit association, if the foundation or activities of the association do not violate the conditions or restrictions provided by law in the interests of the protection of the security of the state and society, public order, morals or the rights of other people, and if joining or membership in the association does not violate the conditions or restrictions provided by law for persons in public service, is punishable by a fine of up to 300 fine units or by detention." [14] Thus, it is a misdemeanour and not a criminal offence (as compared to Article 154 dealing with interference with religious affiliation). "Interference with or violent dispersion of a lawfully organised public meeting is punishable by a pecuniary punishment or up to one year of imprisonment."[15]

There is no provision specifically dealing with proselytizing. It is not as such an offence. General provisions on offences against persons apply to improper proselytism (this term is not used by the Penal Code).

Disturbing the peace of other persons in a public place, or any other breach of public order is punishable by a fine of up to 100 fine units or by detention.[16] Breach of the peace or of public order, is committed: by using violence, by offering resistance to a person protecting public order, by using threats with a weapon, any other object used as a weapon, an

[11] §151 (1).
[12] §154.
[13] §155.
[14] §159.
[15] §158.
[16] §262 "Breach of Public Order".

explosive device or explosive substance, or by a group; it is punishable by a pecuniary punishment or up to 5 years' imprisonment (§263 "Aggravated breach of public order").

There was a misdemeanour case in the first instance court (Harju Maakohus) in 2006, which concerned restricting freedom of religion and freedom of assembly on grounds of public order.[17] A small group of believers gathered by Tallinn railway station. They were singing religious songs using microphones and loudspeakers. The organisers of the event did not notify local authorities of the event, and did not have permission to carry out this meeting. Although the religious meeting had a peaceful character, it was established the people involved were obstructing traffic coming into the railway station, and they were disturbing people selling flowers at the market nearby. Organisers of the event were asked to stop singing. When they disobeyed, six people were arrested. Their activities were found contrary to §7 (1 and 2) of the Public Meetings Act, as they were violating public order and obstructing traffic. Neither Articles 9 nor 11 of the ECHR or Article 40 or 47 (right to assembly) of the Estonian Constitution were invoked. There was no elaboration on justifications and/or proportionality of the restriction. Article 47 of the Constitution sets forth a right to peaceful assembly and meetings without prior permission. However, this right can be restricted in accordance with the law in order to ensure national security, public order or morals, traffic safety and the safety of the participants in such meetings or to prevent the spread of infectious diseases.

Misuse of religious garments could be an aggravating circumstance: "taking advantage of an official uniform or badge in order to facilitate commission of the offence".[18] Only a person to whom a religious association has granted the corresponding permission has the right to wear the professional attire of a minister of religion as prescribed in the statutes of the religious association concerned. The specified restriction does not apply if the professional attire of the minister of religion is ordinary clothing (2002 Churches and Congregations Act, Article 21).

II. Offences by Cult Ministers

The new Code of Criminal Procedure,[19] which came into force on 1 July 2004, sets forth the right of the clergy to keep confessional secrecy. This

[17] Harju Maakohus, Case No. 4-05-936/1 (25 October, 2006).
[18] §58.
[19] RT I 2003, 27, 166.

Code obviously tries to find a compromise between the right of a defendant to a fair trial and the clergy's freedom of religion. According to the Code, ministers of the religious organisations registered in Estonia have the right to refuse to give testimony as witnesses concerning circumstances which have become known to them in the course of their professional activities (Code of Criminal Procedure, Article 72). The same right, according to the law, applies to the professional support staff of the ministers. This right of ministers and their support staff is qualified by the requirement to give testimony if their testimony is requested by the suspect or the accused. Moreover, when a court is convinced that the refusal to give testimony is not related to ministerial or professional activities of support staff, the court may require a person to give testimony. The latter provisions may conflict not only with ecclesiastical law but also with Article 22 of the 2002 CCA. This article categorically declares that a minister of religion shall not disclose either information which has become known to him or her in the course of a private confession or pastoral conversation, or the identity of the person who makes a private confession or has a pastoral conversation with a minister of religion. Thus, by law, the minister of a religion has an obligation of confessional secrecy.

Celebration of religious marriage before civil marriage is not an offence. In accordance with Family Law a clergyman who has received authorisation from the Minister of Regional Affairs is entitled to perform civil marriages. Thus, the State has not recognised the concept of religious marriage *per se* but, rather, has established the possibility of delegating the obligations of the register office to a clergyman of a church, congregation, or association of congregations.[20] Without this authorisation religious marriage simply does not have civil consequences.

III. Offences Linked to Acts of Worship or to Rites

Ritual homicide is not a specific crime or an aggravation. Female genital mutilation is not a special crime or a form of aggravated assault. These cases would be dealt under articles covering offences against persons.

In accordance with the Law on Narcotic Drugs and Psychotropic Substances, consumption of drugs without prescription of a doctor is strictly

[20] On 16.01.2008 there were 152 persons with the right to conduct religious marriages with civil validity. This information is obtained from the Ministry of Internal Affairs, http:www.siseministeerium.ee (01.04.2008).

prohibited (Art. 15^1).[21] Illegal manufacture, acquisition and possession of narcotic drugs or psychotropic substances in a small quantity is punishable by fine or arrest. According to Article 183 of the Penal Code,[22] illegal trafficking or mediation of small quantities of narcotic drugs or psychotropic substances, or illegal manufacture, acquisition or possession of small quantities of narcotic drugs or psychotropic substances with the intention of trafficking, is punishable by a pecuniary punishment or up to one year of imprisonment. What constitutes a small or large quantity of drugs is regulated by the Government regulation in force since 1997. For example, 10 grams of opium is considered to be a large quantity.[23] Illegal possession, acquisition, trafficking, mediation, transportation, import, export, transit or other illegal handling of large quantities of drugs is punishable by up to five years' imprisonment (Penal Code, Art. 184). The same act, if committed by a group or a criminal organisation, or at least twice, is punishable by up to 10 years' imprisonment. Criminal liability follows also, for example, from the illegal inducement of a person to the use of drugs (up to one year of imprisonment – Art. 186). Up to five years' imprisonment is prescribed for inducing a person under 18 to use drugs (Art. 187).

The new criminal code also introduced into Estonian law the possibility of the criminal liability of legal entities. For the illegal handling of large quantities of drugs, a legal entity (including a religious organisation) can be fined. If the religious organisation commits the afore-mentioned crime twice, it can even be subjected to compulsory dissolution. According to Article 48(3) of the constitution, associations whose aims or activities violate criminal law are prohibited.

There is no case law on the use of drugs in religious ceremonies in Estonia. Thus, it is difficult to say whether any exemptions would be allowed on religious grounds. It is doubtful whether individual or collective religious autonomy extends so far in Estonia as to allow the use of drugs in religious practice. Taking into account growing drug related problems and the current climate of zero tolerance to drugs, an Estonian court would most likely find the prohibition of using drugs in religious practice justified under the general constitutional limitation clause (Article 11) and the limitations in Article 40 of the Constitution (namely, public order, health or morals).

[21] RT I 1997, 52, 834; RT I 2002, 63, 387 (revised text in force from 1.09.2002).
[22] RT I 2001, 61, 364.
[23] RT I 1997, 83, 1416.

IV. Religious Motivation as a Cause of Aggravation, or Attenuation of the Offence

Religious motivations do not figure in the specific list of aggravating (§57) or mitigating circumstances (§58). No article of individual offences has listed religious motivations as a specific aggravating or mitigating factor. Moreover, Article 41 (2) of the Estonian Constitution specifically stipulates that 'beliefs shall not constitute an excuse for a legal offence'. However, no person can be held legally liable just because of his or her beliefs.

V. Criminal Law and Sects

No provisions in the Penal Code are specifically devoted to sects. If a religious person or a minority religious group commits a crime it will be tried under the provisions applicable to all.

Kimmo Nuotio

RELIGION IN THE CRIMINAL LAW OF FINLAND

1. The penal protection of religion in Finland

Until 1809 Finland was part of Sweden. The Law of the realm of 1734 was in force in the whole of Sweden. It was the king's law. In religious issues that law was very strict and conservative even when looked at as a product of its time. The protestant church was the State church and the state's laws reflected the deep religious convictions of this church. The Church Law of 1686, a domain of the privileges of the clergy, regulated in detail everyday life of the community. As well as the general criminal proceedings for corporal and other punishments, the church also had authority to punish on the basis of church law. When looking at penal protection of religion, the most important sources of law are church law (including church orders), penal law and constitutional law.

The Law of the realm of 1734 included a penal code, the first chapter of which was devoted to "Blasphemy against God and abandonment of the pure Evangelical doctrine". Blasphemy and heresy belonged together. Blasphemy was punishable by capital punishment when committed on purpose. Section 1 covered not only blasphemy against God but also blasphemy against his sacred word and the sacraments. In lesser cases fines were to be imposed. Also corporal punishment could be imposed. Section 2 dealt with ridiculing church services. Fines were applied in these cases. Section 3 dealt with abandoning the accepted faith, which was sanctioned by expatriation and loss of inheritance and residence rights. Section 4 provided rules on ordering the exile of foreign preachers who did not adhere to the pure doctrine.

The letter of law was very strict, but court practice was not quite as tough. Capital punishment was generally not much in use and the last known peace-time execution, involving a witch, was in the 1820s. The lower courts were dominated by lay persons. The blasphemy case law of that time has not been fully researched. King Gustav III softened many of the 1734 provisions in 1779, but did not alter the blasphemy rules. During the 18th century the Jewish community and some Christian religious communities were granted limited rights to practise their religion behind closed doors.

In 1809, as a result of the Napoleonic wars, Finland became an autonomous part of Russia, but kept its former legal system. The penal (and other) provisions of the 1734 code continued to be valid and applied. The process of legislative development came to a standstill in the first half of the 19th century, and in the course of that century the citizens could already choose between the protestant and the orthodox churches.

During the second half of the century preparations started for a new penal code. Interestingly, this period marks a change in how religious offences are being understood. In 1869 the Church Law was reformed, which was the first step. It became possible to leave the church, and join another. This development can be understood as an expression of the development of a right to religious freedom. In 1889 a law was enacted which granted Christians other than Protestants the formal right to organize themselves. Non-Christian beliefs were not yet legally permitted.

The proposal for a penal code from 1875 sought very little change from what had been the case for almost 150 years. The God of the dominant religion, the Protestant church, was to be protected and heresy was to be rejected. This proposal did not lead to legislation. The next proposal, in 1884, was more modern and closer to the view that in fact the protected interests in religious crimes were the religious feelings of the people.

The official law proposal from 1885 had a slightly stricter view on blasphemy than had been proposed by the reform committee. During the parliamentary proceedings two estates, the priests and the peasants, proposed higher sentences for blasphemy. This proposal, however, did not lead to legislation.

Finally in 1888, the proposal emerged for a new penal code. The provisions of chapter 10 were close to the wording of the 1885 proposal. The provisions concerning religion were debated during the legislative process, but these were adopted with rather small changes. In 1889 the new penal code was accepted, and came into force in 1894 after some delay.

Chapter 10 had six provisions. Public blasphemy against God carried with it hard labour for at most four years, or imprisonment. For less severe cases there was a fine or imprisonment for up to six months. Blasphemy against God's sacred word, or against the teachings, sacraments or religious customs of any of the religious communities recognized, lawful or tolerated in Finland carried a punishment of up to six months, or a fine.

Violent and intentional obstruction of a religious service or other church service or religious practice was made punishable with a sentence of imprisonment up to two years. Disturbance of a church service was also made punishable.

Despite many efforts, full freedom of religion, including the right to practise any religion, was not established before the independence which Finland gained in 1917. The constitution from 1919 granted a right of religious freedom. The content of the penal provisions regarding protection of religion was the subject of fierce political battles before that. The battles also spilled over to prosecutions for blasphemy offences. According to Marxist views these crimes should have been abolished. Many liberal politicians shared that view in the 1910s, and disliked such prosecutions. Later, during the 1920s, prosecutions for blasphemy were directed against freethinkers' journals which attacked religious views, thus testing the limits of freedom of the press and freedom of expression.

In 1922 the Act on religious freedom was finally enacted, and came into force in 1923. It also granted full rights to leave any religious community. Every religious practice, which was regarded lawful and was not against good manners, was regarded as lawful. Should religious worship which was arranged in private be against good manners, a fine could be imposed. Non-religious communities, such as freethinkers, could organise themselves as ordinary registered associations.

The penal code (PC) of 1889/1894 also contained some links with Church Law, which are relevant in this context. The Church law of 1869 had detailed obligations for Church members, and many breaches of these were punishable as so-called police-offences (*politia*) according to the rules of PC Chapter 41 on breaches concerning Church order. The Church itself could refer cases to court. These were lesser crimes, sanctioned with a fine. This system came to an end through the renewed Church Law in 1964.

In 1971 Chapter 10 PC was slightly revised. The blasphemy provision no longer speaks about the word of God and the sacraments but uses the concept of "what is regarded as sacred". The penal value of the central provisions was clearly reduced, with the most severe punishment now being two years' imprisonment. Blasphemy against God attracted a more severe penalty than blasphemy against other sacred beliefs. The two were regulated in separate provisions.

The current penal provisions no longer protect God's honour, but rather religious convictions and feelings and religious peace. Religious peace means religious order, related to the general category "law and order". The offence of breach of the sanctity of religion was reformed in 1998. One common provision applies to both blasphemy against God and blasphemy against sacred beliefs. The penal value of this offence has clearly decreased, as the most severe punishment now is imprisonment for six months.

The provisions have been placed in Chapter 17 on Offences against public order (563/1998), which means that these provisions have finally lost their position as the opening chapter of the penal code, as well as their separate nature as offences with a religious content. The specific offence of violation of the sanctity of religion requires intent on the part of the perpetrator, meaning that as the requirement of culpability one form of so-called *dolus* must be present.

The provisions (see below) distinguish between public blasphemy against God and publicly defaming or desecrating what is held to be sacred by a church or religious community. This structure arose because parliament at a very late stage amended the government bill by reintroducing God as a figure into the provision. The original proposal, which was prepared as part of a larger law reform project, had not provided for such a distinction – the idea being that protection of the Christian God would fall under a single formula. Both the law committee and the constitutional committee of parliament shared this view. The law committee was explicit in mentioning that the penal legislation also needed to be acceptable from the point of view of those who do not share a belief in God (see, Report of the Law Committee, 3/1998; Report of the Constitutional Committee 23/1997).

With regard to blasphemy against God, no specific form of intent is required. No intent to offend needs to be present, whereas in other instances, such purposive intent is required. This difference indicates that the protection of God against blasphemy covers a wider range of actions than the second act description. The point is that in the case of deliberately offensive action even those not sharing the religious belief itself will regard the action as offensive, namely hurting the religious feelings of the community. For this reason efforts have been made to abolish the special clause on blasphemy against God, but the legislator has not yet been persuaded to do so.

It is not fully clear whether the concept "God" in this provision still refers to the Christian God only as depicted in the Bible. It is worth noting that the term "God" has a capital "G", which indicates that it only refers to a specific god, namely the God in which Christians believe institutionally. It is likely that the many gods of the Hindu religion, for instance, would not fall under this. Should one or more of these gods be wilfully and publicly defamed or desecrated, this would have to be handled as a case of offending the beliefs of a church or a religious community. A link between these two cases is the term "what is otherwise to be held sacred"; "otherwise" signals that the sacredness concerns also the first object of blasphemous acts, namely God.

As concerns these other instances of sacredness, the solution of the provision is of an institutional nature. It would for obvious reasons be difficult to define directly in positive terms and in more detail what sacredness generally means in religious thought, due to the complexity of the matter. The idea has been to point to the churches as religious communities themselves. When acquiring official status as a church or religious community under Finnish law, they may have presented what the core beliefs are that constitute their sacred beliefs. The legislation on religious freedom only applies to communities which possess such beliefs. This is thus a constitutive factor. Philosophical *Weltanschaungen* do not fall under beliefs held or having a relationship to something held as sacred. Nothing prevents the application in some cases of the ordinary penal code provisions on defamation and invasion of personal reputation, when the personal non-religious beliefs and convictions of people are being offended.

The case law on religious offences is rather limited, making it difficult to reach definite conclusions. As regards blasphemy, it is likely that all the cases so far have dealt with protection of the traditional core area of such provision, namely blasphemy of God.

The extension to protect also the religious feelings of other religious communities raises new problems. These were met for the first time more than a century ago when the penal code of 1889 was drafted. The main problems relate to defining what merits the status of being a sacred thing and thus falls under the provision. How would it be researched in the course of a criminal investigation, for instance? Do we need academic research and expertise on religions? Is it a matter of presenting "scientific" evidence, or should we simply give a voice to the religious communities themselves? How do churches deliver such opinions particularly in disputed cases? Do the churches vote? Will a clear answer always be given? Is there a problem of representation? What about factions, which are sometimes hurt more and are serious in their reactions? Should they also get a voice? It is likely that various smaller communities which might be affected by such behaviour have not been bringing cases to court.

Chapter 10 – *Breach of the sanctity of religion* (563/1998):
A person who
(1) publicly blasphemes against God or, for the purpose of offending, publicly defames or desecrates what is otherwise held to be sacred by a church or religious community, as referred to in the Act on the Freedom of Religion (267/1998), or

(2) by making a noise, acting threateningly or otherwise, disturbs worship, ecclesiastical proceedings, other similar religious proceedings or a funeral, shall be sentenced for a *breach of the sanctity of religion* to a fine or to imprisonment for at most six months.

It seems that there is no case law involving Finland as a respondent state at the ECtHR as concerns alleged violations of ECHR Art 9.

Freedom of religion is granted as a right under the Finnish Constitution of 2000. The provisions on fundamental rights were reformed in 1995, thereby adapting the Finnish constitutional provisions to the developing human rights law. The Supreme Court has in one case (SC 2001:9) dealt with this right. It concerned equality of the sexes in an employment situation involving the church.

Two cases in the 1960s (*Hannu Salama*) and 1970s (*Harro Koskinen*) led to convictions. Both concerned the limits of artistic expression. In the first, the author had described in a novel a priest's sexual fantasies. The second concerned a painting which showed a pig crucified.

As concerns agitation and discrimination, after provisions in Chapter 11 on war crimes and offences against humanity, the following are significant:

Chapter 11, Section 8 – *Ethnic agitation* (578/1995)
A person who spreads statements or other information among the public where a certain race, a national, ethnic or religious group or a comparable group is threatened, defamed or insulted, shall be sentenced for *ethnic agitation* to a fine or to imprisonment for at most two years.

Chapter 11, Section 9 – *Discrimination.* See below.

The following contains a general prohibition on public incitement to an offence:

Chapter 17 – Offences against public order (563/1998)
Section 1 – *Public incitement to an offence* (563/1998)
(1) A person who through the mass media or publicly in a crowd or in generally published writing or other presentation exhorts or incites anyone to the commission of an offence, so that the exhortation or incitement
(1) causes a danger of the offence or a punishable attempt being committed, or
(2) otherwise clearly endangers public order or security, shall be sentenced for *public incitement to an offence* to a fine or to imprisonment for at most two years.
(2) If the exhortation or incitement causes the commission of an offence or a punishable attempt, the provisions on participation in Chapter 5 also apply.

Chapter 5 Section 5 defines instigation as a form of participation in an offence:
A person who intentionally persuades another person to commit an intentional offence or to make a punishable attempt at such an act is punishable for incitement to the offence as if he/she was the offender.

Also, the sentencing rules recognize the significance of certain severely discriminatory motives:

Chapter 6, Section 5 – *Grounds increasing the punishment*
(1) The following are grounds for increasing the punishment…
(4) the offence has been directed at a person belonging to a national, racial, ethnic or other population group due to his/her membership in such a group.

2. Defamation or outrage against a church or religious community

See Part 1 above. The church is not protected as such.

3. Desecration of a place of worship or of sacred objects of any religion

See above.

4. Hindering or disrupting a religious meeting

Proof of intent is required. The relevant offences are as follows:

Chapter 17, Section 11 – *Prevention of worship* (563/1998)
(1) A person who employs or threatens violence, so as unlawfully to prevent worship, ecclesiastical proceedings or other similar religious proceedings arranged by a church or a religious community, as referred to in the Act on Religous Freedom, shall be sentenced for *prevention of worship* to a fine or to imprisonment for at most two years.
(2) An attempt is punishable.

Philosophical associations are not protected.

The following two offences included in Chapter 25 on offences against liberty might also be relevant:

Section 7 – *Menace* (578/1995)
A person who points a weapon at another or otherwise threatens another with an offence under such circumstances that the person so threatened has reason to believe that his/her personal safety or property or that of

someone else is in serious danger shall be sentenced, unless a more severe penalty for the act is provided elsewhere in the law, for *menace* to a fine or to imprisonment for at most two years.

Section 8 – *Coercion* (578/1995)
A person who unlawfully by violence or threat forces another to do, endure or omit to do something shall be sentenced, unless a more severe penalty for the act is provided elsewhere in the law, for *coercion* to a fine or to imprisonment for at most two years.

5. Menaces, violence or the application of force against another's freedom of religion or conscience

There are no specific rules on this matter: menace, assault or coercion. Assault, if not aggravated, may lead to imprisonment up to two years or fines. If aggravated, imprisonment up to ten years may be imposed.

6. Discrimination because of religion

For the general offence of discrimination, proof of intent is required. The relevant offences are as follows:

Chapter 11, Section 9 – *Discrimination*
A person who in his/her trade or profession, service to the general public, exercise of official authority or other public function or in the arrangement of a public amusement or meeting, without a justified reason
(1) refuses someone service in accordance with the generally applicable conditions;
(2) refuses someone entry to the amusement or meeting or ejects him/her; or
(3) places someone in an unequal or an essentially inferior position owing to his/her race, national or ethnic origin, colour, language, sex, age, family ties, sexual preference, state of health, religion, political orientation, political or industrial activity or another comparable circumstance shall be sentenced, unless the act is punishable as industrial discrimination, for *discrimination* to a fine or to imprisonment for at most six months.

A special provision concerns discrimination at work. Intent is required.

Chapter 47, Section 3 – *Work discrimination*
An employer, or a representative thereof, who when advertising for a vacancy or selecting an employee, or during employment without an

important and justifiable reason puts a job seeker or an employee in an inferior position
(1) because of race, national or ethnic origin, colour, language, sex, age, relations, sexual preference or state of health; or
(2) because of religion, political opinion, political or industrial activity or a comparable circumstance shall be sentenced for *work discrimination* to a fine or to imprisonment for at most six months.

7. Disrupting a funeral

There is no separate offence. See above.

8. Abuse of a corpse or desecration of a sepulchre

Intent is required. The relevant provisions are as follows:

Chapter 17 Section 12 – *Breach of the sanctity of a grave* (563/1998)
A person who
(1) unlawfully opens a grave or exhumes a corpse, a part thereof, a coffin or a burial urn,
(2) handles an unburied corpse in a manner giving offence, or
(3) damages or desecrates a grave or a memorial of the dead, shall be sentenced for a *breach of the sanctity of a grave* to a fine or to imprisonment for at most one year.

9. Proselytizing

This is not a known offence today. The provision on proselytizing was formally abolished as late as 1971. Chapter 10 Section 5 in the penal code of 1889/1894, however, set relatively strict conditions for punishable proselytizing. The fundamental right of religious freedom was established in 1922/1923. In that context, the original provision of Chapter 10 Section 5 was adjusted to this legislation on religious freedom.

10. Apostasy

This is not known offence today. The provision on heresy was abolished in 1889/1894. The fundamental right of religious freedom was established in 1922/1923.

In any event, Chapter 41 on breaches concerning church order provided for punishment by way of a fine for a member of the evangelical

Lutheran community who favoured heresy and tried to incite another to it, thus causing disorder and indignation. With the reform of the church law in 1964 the rules in Chapter 41 finally lost their significance.

11. Misuse of religious garment or impersonation of office

There are no express rules on this matter.

Offences by the ministers of religion

Some offences can only be committed by ministers of religion.

12. Revelation of a secret obtained in the exercise of ministry

Secrets obtained in confession are traditionally the most absolute of all secrets. The Church Law 1993 (Ch. 5 Sect. 2) regulates confession and pastoral counselling. A priest is not entitled to reveal a secret received in confession or in pastoral counselling. Priests are subject to special regulation. This provision only concerns priests under the Church Law, not priests in any other sense. The provisions of the Church Law are also applied to some so-called lecturers. The law on the Orthodox Church has a similar regulation on secrecy. There are no specific rules on religious secrecy for other religions and, thus, no protection against the duty to testify.

If the priest in a confession or in pastoral counselling learns that a serious offence is underway, he/she should encourage the person in question to inform either the authorities or the person under threat. If that person does not comply, the priest has the obligation cautiously and, if possible, not indicating the identity of the individual, to inform either the potential victim or the police about the crime in question. In criminal proceedings, the duty to keep this sort of information secret may in most cases be overridden, if the charges concern a sufficiently serious offence, that is, one carrying a punishment of at least six years maximum. As a sole profession the priests are under a more flexible rule, and the priest's duty to secrecy cannot be fully exempted.

PC Chapter 38, Section 1 – *Secrecy offence*, provides for a punishment of at most one year of imprisonment. This offence requires intent as also does the Section 2 offence, *Secrecy violation*. Crimes of office may also apply.

13. Celebration of religious marriage before civil marriage

Such a crime is unknown.

14. Offences against public order in a place of worship or during a religious practice

See, for example, Chapter 17, Section 1 – *Public incitement to an offence.*

Also the offences relating to intentional rioting should be mentioned.

Chapter 17, Section 3 – *Violent rioting*
When a crowd commits an offence referred to in Chapter 16, Section 1, employs violence against a person or causes significant damage to property, a person who actively participates in the acts of the crowd, shall be sentenced for *violent rioting* to a fine or to imprisonment for at most two years.

Chapter 17, Section 4 – *Leading a violent riot*

A person who incites or leads a crowd referred to in Section 3 shall be sentenced for *leading a violent riot* to imprisonment for at most four years.

Offences linked to acts of worship or to rites

Acts of worship or rites may be crimes *sui generis*, such as female genital mutilation or female circumcision. Ritual homicide is included only as an aggravation of homicide. Bigamy and polygamy (and ritual usage of drugs) are not included because their legal description is not linked to religion.

Ritual homicide could basically be regarded, because of this particular circumstance, either as a grave form of manslaughter, that is, murder, or as in minor form of it, that is, killing, depending on the point of view taken. It is likely that Finnish court practice would not emphasize the particular religious character of the activity when assessing it normatively.

15. Female genital mutilation/cutting

Normal provisions of assault are applicable here. Intent is required. Assault carries a punishment of up to two years' imprisonment. Aggravated assault carries a punishment of up to ten years' imprisonment. It is likely that the religious context of the offence would not be regarded as highly relevant when applying the general rules.

Religious motivation as a cause of aggravation or attenuation of the offence

Religious motivation is not mentioned in the law. Religious motivation would be relevant only if it substantiated one or several of the grounds listed in the legal provisions. The methodical nature of committing the act could in principle constitute an aggravating circumstance. Religious motivation could perhaps in some cases be regarded as a factor mitigating culpability because of the external pressure involved and convictions about the rightfulness of the acts. In any event, in Finnish law, the religious communities have to respect fundamental rights and freedoms, and in the case of harmful religious practice the authorities could take action to ban the community. Religious freedom is thus not unrestricted.

16. What are the offences aggravated by religious motivation?

See above.

17. What are the offences attenuated by religious motivation?

See above.

18. The criminal law and sects

The law provides nothing specific on this matter.

Literature

Backman, Eero: Rikoslaki ja yhteiskunta I. Teoreettinen erittely rikosoikeuden tieteenkäsityksistä 18000-luvulla ja sen konkretisointi moraalin, uskonnon ja rikoslain suhteisiin Suomessa vuosina 1894-1917. Suomalainen lakimiesyhdisty, Helsinki.

Ketola, Mikko: Vapaa Ajatus -lehti suomalaisen jumalanpilkan edistäjänä 1910-1917. Suomen kirkkohistoriallisen seuran vuosikirja 84-85 (1994-1995). Jyväskylä 1995.

Kircko-Laki Ja Ordningi 1686. Näköispainos ja uudelleen ladottu laitos. Suomalaisen kirjallisuuden seura, Helsinki 1986.

Lappi-Seppälä, Tapio et al: Rikosoikeus. WSOY, Helsinki 2009.

Leino, Pekka: Kirkkolaki vai laki kirkosta. Suomalainen lakimiesyhdistys, Helsinki 2002.

Prinen, Kauko: Schaumanin kirkkolain synty. Suomen kirkkohistoriallinen seura, Helsinki 1985.

Seppo Juha: Uskonnonvapaus 2000-luvun Suomessa. Edita, Helsinki.

Isabelle Riassetto

Agrégée des facultés de Droit,
Professeur à l'Université du Luxembourg

RELIGION ET DROIT PÉNAL EN FRANCE

I. Protection pénale de la religion

1. *Diffamation et injure à l'égard du contenu de la religion*

a) Quelles sont les infractions qui correspondent au blasphème ou qui l'ont remplacé dans l'histoire du droit?

Depuis 1791, il n'existe plus en France de délit de blasphème.

En revanche, en droit local alsacien-mosellan, qui concerne les trois départements de l'Est de la France (Bas-Rhin, Haut-Rhin et Moselle), la loi du 9 décembre 1905 concernant la séparation des Églises et de l'État n'est pas applicable, faute d'avoir été introduite. Il existe un délit de blasphème. L'article 166 du Code pénal local Alsacien-Mosellan prévoit que «*celui qui aura causé un scandale en blasphémant publiquement contre Dieu par des propos outrageants, ou aura publiquement outragé un des cultes chrétiens ou une communauté religieuse établie sur le territoire de la Confédération et reconnue comme corporation, ou les institutions ou cérémonies de ces cultes ou qui, dans une église ou un autre lieu consacré à des assemblées religieuses, aura commis des actes injurieux et scandaleux sera puni d'un emprisonnement de trois ans au plus*». Ce texte a vocation à s'appliquer aux quatre cultes reconnus en Alsace-Moselle (Catholicisme, Église réformée, Église de la confession d'Augsbourg, Judaïsme). Il n'a pas donné lieu à jurisprudence depuis la loi de séparation de 1905.

b) La provocation à la discrimination, à la haine ou à la violence à l'égard d'une personne ou d'un groupe de personnes en raison de leur religion, est-elle spécialement incriminée?

1° Provocation publique

L'article 24 alinéa 8 de la loi du 29 juillet 1881 sur la liberté de la presse, introduit par la loi n° 72-546 du 1er juillet 1972, réprime la provocation«*à la discrimination, à la haine ou à la violence à l'égard d'une personne ou d'un groupe de personnes à raison (…) de leur appartenance ou de leur non appartenance à (…) une religion déterminée*».

* *Champ d'application*

Le texte vise **une personne ou un groupe** de personnes à raison de leur appartenance ou leur non-appartenance à une religion déterminée.

Il s'applique sans distinction à toutes les religions.

La protection s'étend aux mouvements sectaires dès lors qu'ils se présentent comme ayant un caractère religieux.

La protection porte sur les croyances religieuses

* *Eléments constitutifs*

– une provocation (il importe peu qu'elle soit suivie d'effet);
– une provocation comportant une mise en cause d'une personne ou d'un groupe à raison de leur religion. La provocation doit être directe et fondée expressément sur le motif religieux;
– moyens et supports de la provocation: discours, cris ou menaces proférés dans des lieux ou réunions publics, écrits, imprimés, dessins, gravures, peintures, emblèmes, images ou tout autre support de l'écrit, de la parole ou de l'image, vendus ou distribués, mis en vente ou exposés dans des lieux ou réunions publics, placards ou affiches exposés au regard public, enfin tout moyen de communication audiovisuelle.

* *Répression*

– 1 an d'emprisonnement et amende de 45 000 euros ou l'une de ces deux peines seulement.
– Peines susceptibles d'être doublées en cas de récidive (Loi du 29 juillet 1881, art. 63).

2° Provocation non publique

Selon l'article R. 625-7 du Code pénal, la provocation non publique à la discrimination, à la haine ou à la violence à l'égard d'une personne ou d'un groupe de personnes à raison de leur origine ou de leur appartenance ou de leur non-appartenance, vraie ou supposée, à une ethnie, une nation, une race ou une religion déterminée est punie de l'amende prévue pour les contraventions de la 5e classe (1 500 euros), ainsi que des peines complémentaires prévues par le même texte.

2. *Diffamation et injures contre une église ou communauté religieuse*

Le droit pénal français de la presse distingue les diffamations et injures publiques et non publiques.

a) Diffamation

1° Diffamation publique
L'article 32 alinéa 2 de la loi du 29 juillet 1881 sur la liberté de la presse réprime la diffamation pour motif religieux.

Champ d'application

- Le texte vise «*une personne ou un groupe de personnes à raison de leur (...) appartenance ou non appartenance à une (...) une religion déterminée*». Il s'applique aux personnes physiques ainsi qu'aux personnes morales. S'agissant des groupes non dotés de la personnalité morale, la jurisprudence exige que le groupe soit identifié.
  Le texte a été appliqué à des «grandes religions» (Catholicisme, Protestantismes, Judaïsme, Islam), mais aussi à des mouvements présentés comme sectaires. A cet égard, si la simple allégation de l'appartenance à une secte n'est pas constitutive d'une diffamation (CA Paris, 15 mai 2002: Juris-data n° 180609), en revanche, le délit sera caractérisé toute les fois où la secte est accusée par exemple d'infiltration dans les «plus hautes sphères de l'État» (CA Paris, 3 juin 1997: Gazette du Palais 8-9 août 1997, *sommaire* p. 19).
- S'agissant des mouvements philosophiques, ils n'entrent pas à proprement parler dans le champ de la discrimination religieuse. En revanche, l'action en diffamation à leur encontre devra être fondée sur les articles 29 et 32 alinéa 1er de la loi de 1881 réprimant la diffamation sans considération d'un mobile religieux. Il en a été jugé ainsi de la franc-maçonnerie (Cass. crim., 17 janvier 2006, n° 05-83323; Cass. crim., 30 mai 2007, n° 0686326).
- L'article 31 de la loi de 1881 punit des mêmes peines la diffamation contre un ministre de l'un des cultes salariés par l'État (ministres des cultes reconnus d'Alsace-Moselle), à raison de sa fonction ou de sa qualité.
- La protection porte sur les **croyances**. Lorsque ne sont pas en cause les croyances mais les pratiques d'un groupement, en particulier d'un groupement sectaire, l'action devra être fondée sur les articles 29 et 32 alinéa 1er de la loi de 1881.

Eléments constitutifs

* Eléments matériels

– Un propos diffamatoire: constitue une diffamation (art. 29, al. 1er Loi 1881) «*toute allégation ou imputation d'un fait qui porte atteinte à l'honneur ou à la considération de la personne ou du corps auquel le fait est imputé*»;
– Caractère du propos: il doit s'agir d'allégations ou d'imputations. Il doit porter sur des faits précis ou déterminés (contrairement à l'injure);
– Le propos doit porter atteinte à l'honneur ou à la considération;
– Mobile discriminatoire religieux;
– Caractère public par l'un des moyens énoncés à l'article 23 (V° provocation, Question n° 1 b).

* Elément intentionnel

Les imputations injurieuses sont réputées faites avec intention de nuire, mais il s'agit d'une présomption simple.

* L'exceptio veritatis n'est pas applicable au délit de diffamation religieuse. Il en va de même de l'excuse de provocation.

Répression

– 1 an d'emprisonnement et amende de 45 000 euros ou l'une de ces deux peines.
– Peines susceptibles d'être doublées en cas de récidive (Loi du 29 juillet 1881, art. 63).

2° Diffamation non publique

La diffamation non publique est une contravention prévue par l'article R. 624-3 du Code pénal. Elle est «*commise envers une personne ou un groupe de personnes à raison de leur origine ou de leur appartenance ou de leur non-appartenance, vraie ou supposée, à une ethnie, une nation, une race ou une religion déterminée*».

Elle est punie de l'amende prévue pour les contraventions de la 4e classe (750 euros).

b) Injures

1° Injure publique

L'injure publique est un délit réprimé par l'article 33 alinéa 3 de la loi du 29 juillet 1881 sur la liberté de la presse.

Champ d'application
Même champ d'application que la diffamation (cf. a).

Eléments constitutifs
* Eléments matériels
– Une expression outrageante: tout propos qui, sans contenir d'imputation d'un fait précis, est de nature à porter atteinte à l'honneur ou à la délicatesse de celui auquel il s'adresse. Il peut s'agir d'une invective (poursuit le même but sous une forme violente) ou d'un terme de mépris (non respect de la dignité de la personne).
– Mobile discriminatoire religieux
– Caractère public.

* Elément intentionnel
Les imputations injurieuses sont réputées faites avec intention de nuire, mais il s'agit d'une présomption simple.

Si l'excuse légale de provocation est recevable, l'*exceptio veritatis* n'est pas applicable au délit d'injure.

Répression
– 6 mois d'emprisonnement et amende de 22 500 euros;
– Peines susceptibles d'être doublées en cas de récidive (Loi 29 juillet 1881, art. 63).

2° Injure non publique
L'injure privée est une contravention prévue par l'article R. 624-4 du Code pénal.

«L'injure non publique commise envers une personne ou un groupe de personnes à raison (...) de leur appartenance ou de leur non-appartenance, vraie ou supposée, à (...) une religion déterminée est punie de l'amende prévue pour les contraventions de la 4e classe» (750 euros). Tel est le cas de l'injure par lettre, à condition qu'elle ne soit pas confidentielle.

Sur les pénalités, cf. la diffamation non publique.

3. *Profanations de lieu ou d'objet sacré d'une religion. Les mêmes questions en relation à chaque infraction comme au n° 1*

* La loi du 9 décembre 1905 a rendu sans objet la protection spéciale des **lieux de culte** (sacrilège) qui figurait aux articles 385 et 386 de l'ancien Code pénal. L'article 385 a été abrogé par la loi du 23 novembre 1950,

l'article 386 de l'ancien Code pénal l'ayant été par la loi n° 81-82 du 2 février 1981.

* Aujourd'hui, l'article 322-3-1 du Code pénal punit de 7 ans d'emprisonnement et de 1000 euros d'amende, la destruction, la dégradation ou la détérioration portant sur:
1° Un immeuble ou objet mobilier classé ou inscrit en application des dispositions du code du patrimoine ou un document d'archives privées classé en application des dispositions du même code;
2° Une découverte archéologique faite au cours de fouilles ou fortuitement, un terrain sur lequel se déroulent des opérations archéologiques ou un édifice affecté au culte;
3° Un bien culturel qui relève du domaine public mobilier ou qui est exposé, conservé ou déposé, même de façon temporaire, soit dans un musée de France, une bibliothèque, une médiathèque ou un service d'archives, soit dans un lieu dépendant d'une personne publique ou d'une personne privée assurant une mission d'intérêt général, soit dans un édifice affecté au culte.

Les peines sont portées à dix ans d'emprisonnement et 150 000 € d'amende lorsque l'infraction est commise pour un mobile religieux.

L'article 311-4-2 du Code pénal punit de sept ans d'emprisonnement et de 100 000 € d'amende le **vol** lorsqu'il porte sur: «3° Un bien culturel qui relève du domaine public mobilier ou qui est exposé, conservé ou déposé, même de façon temporaire, (...) soit dans un édifice affecté au culte».

Les peines sont portées à dix ans d'emprisonnement et 150 000 € d'amende lorsque l'infraction prévue au présent article est commise en considération de l'appartenance religieuse de la victime.

4. *Empêchement ou perturbation d'une pratique cultuelle*

a) Droit général

Il existe en droit français une infraction spécifique d'entrave aux pratiques cultuelles. Elle est prévue par l'article 32 de la loi du 9 décembre 1905 qui punit «*ceux qui auront empêché, retardé ou interrompu les exercices d'un culte par des troubles ou désordres causés dans le local servant à ces exercices*».

Ce texte s'applique à tous les cultes. En vertu du principe d'autodétermination qui caractérise le régime de laïcité, ce texte a vocation à s'appliquer à tous les mouvements se reconnaissant comme religion.

En revanche, il ne trouve pas application aux mouvements philosophiques.

Eléments constitutifs
* Eléments matériels
- Conditions tenant aux victimes: les ministres du culte, mais également les fidèles. Peu importe que l'officiant se soit contenté d'inviter le perturbateur à interrompre son action ou encore qu'il n'ait pas été personnellement gêné dans l'exercice en question (CA Toulouse, 3e ch., 19 nov. 1868, *Franck Michet*: DP 1869, 2, p. 77; T. corr. Bar-le-Duc 2 juin 1982: Revue de sciences criminelles 1983, p. 76).
- Conditions tenant à l'auteur: il peut s'agir de toute personne, même l'officiant.
- Comportements: il doit s'agir de troubles, outrages ou voies de fait. Ces troubles ne doivent pas, en raison de leur nature ou des circonstances, donner lieu à de plus fortes peines d'après les dispositions du code pénal (L. 1905, art. 33).
  Les troubles doivent avoir entraîné un empêchement, retard ou interruption dans l'exercice d'un culte.
- Exercice du culte : l'expression vise tous les actes religieux accomplis par un ministre des cultes, qu'il s'agisse de l'administration d'un sacrement ou même d'une réunion de catéchèse dans la sacristie d'une église (Cass. crim., 6 nov. 1909, *Proc. gén, CA Amiens c/ Waguet*: DP 1910, 1, p. 377).
- Les troubles doivent avoir été causés dans le local servant à l'exercice du culte.

* Elément intentionnel: volonté d'entraver l'exercice du culte.

Répression
Amende de 1 500 euros (contravention de 5e classe) et/ou emprisonnement de 6 jours à 2 mois (art. 31 de la loi du 9 décembre 1905 auquel renvoie l'article 32).

b) Droit local alsacien-mosellan

En droit local, l'article 167 du Code pénal local réprime le trouble à l'exercice public du culte: «*celui qui, par voie de fait ou menaces aura empêché une personne d'exercer le culte d'une communauté religieuse établie dans l'État, ou qui, dans une église ou dans un autre lieu destiné à des assemblées religieuses, aura par tapage ou désordre volontairement empêché ou troublé le culte ou certaines cérémonies du culte d'une communauté religieuse établie dans l'État, sera puni d'un emprisonnement de trois ans au plus».* (CA Colmar, Ch. app. corr., 19 nov. 1954, *Pfertzer et Sobezak*: RJAL 1955, p. 24, note C.L; Cass. crim., 30 nov. 1999, *Fromm et a.* : RJE 2000 n° 2, pp. 47-48).

5. *Menaces, violences ou voies de fait contre la liberté religieuse ou de conscience de l'individu*

Il existe en droit français une infraction spécifique. Elle est prévue par l'article 31 de la loi du 9 décembre 1905 qui punit «*ceux qui par voie de fait, violences ou menaces contre un individu, soit en lui faisant craindre de perdre son emploi ou d'exposer à un dommage sa personne, sa famille ou sa fortune, l'auront déterminé à exercer ou à s'abstenir d'exercer un culte, à faire partie ou à cesser de faire partie d'une association cultuelle, à contribuer ou à s'abstenir de contribuer aux frais d'un culte*».

Champ d'application

Ce texte a vocation à s'appliquer à tous les cultes. En vertu du principe d'autodétermination, il doit pouvoir s'appliquer à des mouvements se définissant comme des religions.

La jurisprudence ne l'a pas appliqué aux mouvements philosophiques.

Eléments constitutifs

* Eléments matériels

– Un acte de violence (voie de fait, violences ou menaces);
– La crainte de perte d'emploi ou d'exposition à un dommage (pour sa personne, sa famille ou sa fortune);
– L'atteinte à la liberté de culte d'une personne: déterminer la personne à exercer ou s'abstenir d'exercer un culte, à faire partie ou à abandonner une association cultuelle, à contribuer ou à s'abstenir de contribuer aux frais d'un culte.

* Elément intentionnel: intention de vouloir attenter à la liberté de culte de la victime.

Répression

Amende de 1 500 euros (contravention de 5e classe) et/ou de 6 jours à 2 mois d'emprisonnement.

6. *Discrimination en raison de la religion*

a) Eléments constitutifs

Selon l'article 225-1 du Code pénal, discriminer consiste à opérer une distinction entre des personnes à raison notamment de leur appartenance ou de leur non-appartenance, vraie ou supposée, à une religion. Constitue également une discrimination toute distinction entre des personnes morales à raison de l'appartenance ou de la non-appartenance vraie ou supposée, à une religion déterminée des membres ou de certains d'entre eux.

La discrimination est pénalement sanctionnée (C. pén., art. 225-2) lorsqu'elle consiste:

1° À refuser la fourniture d'un bien ou d'un service;
2° À entraver l'exercice normal d'une activité économique quelconque;
3° À refuser d'embaucher, à sanctionner ou à licencier une personne;
4° À subordonner la fourniture d'un bien ou d'un service à une condition fondée sur l'un des éléments visés à l'article 225-1;
5° À subordonner une offre d'emploi, une demande de stage ou une période de formation en entreprise à une condition fondée sur l'un des éléments visés à l'article 225-1;
6° À refuser d'accepter une personne à l'un des stages visés par le 2° de l'article L. 412-8 du code de la sécurité sociale.

Le délit prévu est constitué même s'il est commis à l'encontre d'une ou plusieurs personnes ayant sollicité l'un des biens, actes, services ou contrats mentionnés à l'article 225-2 dans le but de démontrer l'existence du comportement discriminatoire, dès lors que la preuve de ce comportement est établie (testing) (C. pén, art. 225-3-1).

Ce principe de non-discrimination est repris et développé à l'article L. 1132-1 (ancien art. 122-45 du Code du travail), en vertu duquel «*Aucune personne ne peut être écartée d'une procédure de recrutement ou de l'accès à un stage ou à une période de formation en entreprise, aucun salarié ne peut être sanctionné, licencié ou faire l'objet d'une mesure discriminatoire, directe ou indirecte, telle que définie à l'article 1er de la loi n° 2008-496 du 27 mai 2008 portant diverses dispositions d'adaptation au droit communautaire dans le domaine de la lutte contre les discriminations, notamment en matière de rémunération, au sens de l'article L. 3221-3, de mesures d'intéressement ou de distribution d'actions, de formation, de reclassement, d'affectation, de qualification, de classification, de promotion professionnelle, de mutation ou de renouvellement de contrat en raison (...) de ses convictions religieuses (...)*».

b) Répression

– 3 ans d'emprisonnement et 45 000 euros d'amende.
– 5 ans d'emprisonnement et 75 000 euros d'amende:

* lorsque le refus discriminatoire de fourniture d'un bien ou d'un service est commis dans un lieu accueillant du public ou aux fins d'en interdire l'accès;

* lorsque la discrimination consistant à refuser le bénéfice d'un droit accordé par la loi ou à entraver l'exercice normal d'une activité économique quelconque est commise par une personne dépositaire de l'autorité publique ou chargée d'une mission de service public (par exemple un maire), dans l'exercice ou à l'occasion de l'exercice de ses fonctions ou de sa mission (C. pén., art. 432-7).

7. *Perturbation de cérémonie funèbre*

a) L'infraction de perturbation des cérémonies funèbres n'existe pas en tant que telle en droit français.
b) Toutefois, il existe des dispositions incriminant la perturbation de l'exercice d'un culte (V. question n° 4).

8. *Profanation de cadavre ou de sépulture*

L'article 225-17 du Code pénal, punit les atteintes au respect dû aux morts:

Eléments constitutifs
– Une atteinte à l'intégrité d'un cadavre par quelque moyen que ce soit (al. 1),
– «*la violation ou la profanation* (...) *de tombeaux, de sépultures ou de monuments édifiés à la mémoire des morts*» (al. 2) par quelque moyen que ce soit;

Répression
– 1 an d'emprisonnement et 15 000 euros d'amende.
– Le concours des deux infractions fait encourir à son auteur 2 ans d'emprisonnement et 30 000 euros d'amende (al. 3).
– Le Code pénal français a pris en compte le mobile religieux animant l'auteur de ces faits comme cause d'aggravation de la sanction, à la suite d'un certain nombre d'affaires de profanation de cimetières israélites, dans les années 1980. Lorsque les infractions des alinéas 1

et 2 de l'article 225-17 sont commises «*à raison de l'appartenance ou la non appartenance, vraie ou supposée, des personnes décédées à une ethnie, une nation, une race ou une religion déterminées*» (art. 225-18), la peine est portée à 3 ans d'emprisonnement et 45 000 euros d'amende; lorsque l'infraction de l'alinéa 3 de l'article 225-17 est commise pour le même motif la peine est portée à 5 ans d'emprisonnement et 75 000 euros d'amende.

9. *Prosélytisme*

a) Le prosélytisme n'est pas spécialement réprimé. Néanmoins, l'article 31 de la loi du 9 décembre 1905 (v. Question n° 5) punissant «*ceux qui par voie de fait, violences ou menaces contre un individu, soit en lui faisant craindre de perdre son emploi ou d'exposer à un dommage sa personne, sa famille ou sa fortune, l'auront déterminé à exercer ou à s'abstenir d'exercer un culte, à faire partie ou à cesser de faire partie d'une association cultuelle, à contribuer ou à s'abstenir de contribuer aux frais d'un culte*» est susceptibles de couvrir certains actes graves de prosélytisme.
b) Par ailleurs, l'article 19 de la loi n° 2001-504 du 12 juin 2001 tendant à renforcer la prévention et la répression des mouvements sectaires portant atteinte aux droits de l'homme et aux libertés fondamentales (JORF, 13 juin) tend à limiter la publicité en faveur des mouvements sectaires.

Eléments constitutifs

* Auteur de l'infraction
La personne morale doit répondre à la qualification de mouvement sectaire au sens de la loi de 2001: elle doit poursuive des activités ayant pour but ou pour effet de créer, de maintenir ou d'exploiter la sujétion psychologique ou physique des personnes qui participent à ces activités. Il faut de plus que la secte ou ses dirigeants de fait ou de droit ait fait l'objet à plusieurs reprises (au moins deux fois) de condamnations pénales définitives figurant sur la liste établie par l'article 19 qui comprend la plupart des infractions pénales.

* Eléments matériels:
– Message destiné à la jeunesse;
– Message faisant la promotion du mouvement ou invitant à rejoindre le mouvement;

– Diffusion par quelque moyen que ce soit (presse, tracs, Internet, radio etc.) des messages destinés à la jeunesse et faisant la promotion d'un tel mouvement.

* Elément intentionnel: dol général

Répression
Amende de 7 500 euros.

Elle est applicable à la personne morale et à ses dirigeants personnes physiques.

10. *Apostasie*

L'infraction n'existe pas en droit français.

11. *Usage incorrect des habits religieux ou de service. Y a-t-il des règles qui couvrent le cas où quelqu'un se fait passer comme un prêtre?*

Avant la loi du 9 décembre 1905 de séparation de l'Église et de l'État, le port illégal d'un costume ecclésiastique était pénalement sanctionné (C. pén., art. 259). Étaient concernés, aussi bien l'habit de ville que les habits sacerdotaux utilisés dans les cérémonies cultuelles.

Depuis la loi de 1905, en droit général, le port d'un costume ecclésiastique n'est plus pénalement sanctionné car ce costume n'entre pas dans le champ d'application de l'article 433-14 du Code pénal qui punit d'un an d'emprisonnement et d'une amende de 15 000 euros toute personne qui aura publiquement et sans droit «*porté un costume, un uniforme ou une décoration réglementés par l'autorité publique*». En revanche, ce texe s'applique dans les trois départements régis par le droit local alsacien-mosellan, le régime concordataire en vigueur faisant entrer le costume ecclésiastique dans la catégorie des costumes officiels.

II. Infractions des ministres du culte

12. *Révélation de secret obtenu dans l'exercice du ministère*

a) Quels sont les éléments matériels et psychologiques et quelle est la peine de l'infraction?

L'article 226-13 du Code pénal réprime «*la révélation d'une information à caractère secret par une personne qui en est dépositaire soit par état ou par profession, soit en raison d'une fonction ou d'une mission temporaire*».

1° Personnes punissables

En l'absence de texte, il est admis par la jurisprudence que les ministres du culte participent de la catégorie de ceux qui *«par état ou profession»* sont dépositaires des secrets qu'on leur confie (Cass. crim., 4 déc. 1891, *Fay*: Bull. Crim., n° 239; DP 1892, 1, p. 139). Admise pour le culte catholique, la solution vaut pour toutes les religions.

2° Eléments constitutifs

* Eléments matériels

– **Information confidentielle**

Un ministre du culte peut obtenir des informations susceptibles d'être couvertes par le devoir de secret de différentes manières.

Il peut y avoir accès **directement** par la confession ou bien par la confidence faite par la personne concernée, au ministre du culte ès-qualité. Ce secret présente un **caractère général et absolu**. (Cass. crim., 30 nov. 1810, *Lavaine*: Bull. crim., n° 151; Cass. crim., 4 déc. 1891, *Fay*: Bull. crim., n° 239; DP 1892, 1, p. 139): *«Attendu...* (énonce la chambre criminelle en 1891) *que pour les prêtres catholiques il n'y a pas lieu de distinguer s'ils ont eu connaissance des faits par la voie de la confession ou en dehors de ce sacrement, que cette circonstance en effet ne saurait changer la nature du secret dont ils sont dépositaires si les faits leur ont été confiés dans l'exercice exclusif de leur ministère sacerdotal et à raison de ce ministère; que cette obligation est absolue et d'ordre public; (...)»*.

Mais il peut encore se trouver **indirectement** dépositaire d'une information en liaison avec sa qualité de religieux, soit à raison de ses propres investigations (interrogatoire de la personne), soit en raison de ses propres constatations ou déductions (recoupements d'éléments), soit parce qu'il en a été informé par des tiers.

Un jugement du Tribunal correctionnel de Caen du 4 septembre 2001 (L. Leturmy, *Commentaire du jugement du tribunal correctionnel de Caen du 4 septembre 2001 (affaire Pican)*: Dr. pén. 2001, n° 46; O. Echappé, *Le secret professionnel de l'ecclésiastique*, interview par P. Rancé: D. 2001, p. 2606) a restreint le champ d'application du devoir de secret en limitant la notion d'information couverte par le secret pesant sur les ministres du culte. En l'espèce, un évêque a été mis en examen pour non dénonciation de crime et non dénonciation d'atteintes sexuelles sur mineurs dans une affaire qui concernait un prêtre de son diocèse condamné pour viol et agressions sexuelles sur mineurs. La connaissance qu'avait eu l'évêque des agissements ne résultait pas de la confession ni de confidences au sens strict obtenues du prêtre, mais d'informations divulguées par le vicaire général, auquel s'était adressée la mère d'une des victimes, ainsi que de ses propres investigations. Après avoir constaté que le prêtre n'était pas à l'origine de l'information recueillie par l'évêque, les juges ont estimé que cette information ne constituait pas un secret professionnel. Il ne s'agissait donc pas d'une confidence couverte par le secret professionnel. En conséquence, il avait l'obligation de dénoncer les faits en question et ne pouvait se retrancher derrière le secret. Faut-il en conclure que le secret est relatif? Une réponse négative s'impose car les informations litigieuses ne sont pas couvertes par le secret: elles n'entrent pas dans le champ d'application de l'article 226-13 C. pénal. En effet, pour parler de secret relatif, il faut que l'on soit en présence d'une information qui entre dans le champ du secret.

Enfin parce qu'il s'agit d'un secret «*professionnel*», les confidences faites à un ministre du culte en tant qu' «***ami ou parent***», ou «*médiateur*» ne sont pas couvertes par le secret.

– **Révélation de l'information**, même à une seule personne, quelle que soit les modalités de la communication.

* Elément intentionnel: dol général.

2° Répression

– 1 an d'emprisonnement et 15 000 euros d'amende.

b) Comment résoudre les conflits entre devoir de secret et devoir de dénoncer?

Le droit français connaît un certain nombre d'obligations de dénoncer pénalement sanctionnées, notamment celle de dénoncer la préparation ou la commission de crimes dont on aurait connaissance (234-1) et celle de dénoncer les privations, mauvais traitements ou atteintes sexuelles infligés à un mineur ou à une personne vulnérable (434-3).

Toutefois, le Code pénal exclut du champ de la répression de l'obligation de dénonciation ceux qui sont les dépositaires d'un secret professionnel (C. pén., art 434-1 al. dernier et 434-3 al. 2). Ce faisant, la décision de dénonciation est abandonnée, en conscience, au for interne des personnes soumises au secret (option de conscience).

Dans le même esprit, l'article 226-14 du Code pénal exclut l'application du délit de violation de secret professionnel de l'article 226-13 «*dans les cas où la loi impose ou autorise la révélation d'un secret»* ainsi qu'à l'égard de «*celui qui informe les autorités judiciaires, médicales ou administratives de sévices ou privations de soins dont il a eu connaissance et qui ont été infligés à un mineurs de moins de quinze ans ou à une personne qui n'est pas en mesure de se protéger en raison de son âge, ou de son état physique ou psychique* (...)». Même si les médecins et les travailleurs sociaux sont les destinataires privilégiés de ces prévisions légales, ces dernières sont assurément applicables aux ministres du culte.

c) Le secret de confession est-il plus protégé que d'autres secrets professionnels?

Le secret de la confession n'est pas plus protégé que d'autres secrets professionnels en droit pénal français.

13. *Célébration de mariage religieux antérieur au mariage civil*

L'article 433-21 du Code pénal sanctionne «*tout ministre d'un culte qui procédera, de manière habituelle, aux cérémonies religieuses de mariage sans que ne lui ait été justifié l'acte de mariage préalablement reçu par les officiers de l'état civil*».

a) Eléments constitutifs

* Ministre d'un culte: toutes religions.

* Elément matériel
– Célébration d'un mariage religieux (et non d'une simple bénédiction), valable ou non (pourvu que l'officiant ait cru qu'il l'était). Il importe peu qu'il ait été célébré entre deux étrangers dont la (ou les) lois personnelle(s) reconnaît(ssent) la valeur juridique de l'union religieuse. Peu importe enfin que le ministre du culte ait dû célébrer un mariage *in extremis* en raison du danger de mort d'un des futurs époux. En revanche, si les époux avaient produit à l'officiant un faux acte de mariage civil, l'infraction ne serait pas constituée puisqu'il aurait satisfait à son obligation formelle de contrôle de l'existence préalable du mariage civil.
– Circonstance d'habitude.
– Absence de mariage civil antérieur.

* Elément intentionnel: Intention délictueuse.

b) Répression

- Le délit est puni de six mois d'emprisonnement et de 7 500 euros d'amende. Le texte n'a plus été appliqué depuis les années 1970.
- Il est possible de poursuivre comme complices les époux ou des tiers (parents, autre ministre du culte) qui auraient provoqué ou aidé le ministre du culte à célébrer le mariage irrégulier.

14. *Atteinte à la paix publique dans un lieu de culte ou à l'occasion de l'exercice du culte*

a) Droit général

Outre les délits d'outrage (C. pén., art. 433-5) et de diffamation publique de l'autorité publique (L. 29 juillet 1881, art. 31), il existe deux infractions spécifiques prévues par la loi du 9 décembre 1905.

1° L'article 35 de la loi du 9 décembre 1905 sanctionne la **provocation à la résistance aux lois**: «*Si un discours prononcé ou un écrit affiché ou distribué publiquement dans les lieux où s'exerce le culte contient une provocation directe à résister à l'exécution des lois ou aux actes locaux de l'autorité publique, ou s'il tend à soulever ou à armer une partie des citoyens contre les autres, le ministre du culte qui s'en sera rendu coupable sera puni d'un emprisonnement de trois mois à deux ans, sans préjudice des peines de la complicité, dans le cas où la provocation aurait été suivie d'une sédition, révolte ou guerre civile*».

Cette infraction participe de la catégorie des infractions politiques.

Eléments constitutifs

* Auteur: ministre du culte.

* Eléments matériels
- Une provocation: écrit ou discours.
- Une provocation directe à la résistance aux lois ou actes locaux de l'autorité publique. Il n'est pas «*nécessaire que ces actes de résistance soient nettement spécifiés dans le discours ou l'écrit contenant cette provocation*» (Cass. crim., 17 mai 1907: DP 1907, 1, p. 273). L'infraction est formelle, constituée même si la provocation n'est pas suivies d'effet. Dans l'hypothèse où elle serait suivie d'effet et

notamment, précise le texte, en cas de «*sédition, révolte ou guerre civile*», l'auteur de la provocation serait également poursuivi comme complice des crimes commis à l'issue de ses faits de provocation.

* Elément intentionnel
L'auteur doit être animé par le but «*d'exciter à résister à l'exécution des lois ou d'armer une partie des citoyens contre l'autre*» (Cass. crim., 4 janv. 1912: Bull. crim., n° 2; Cass. crim., 5 août 1915: Bull. crim., n° 168).

Répression
– Emprisonnement de 3 mois à 2 ans, sans préjudice des peines de la complicité, dans le cas où la provocation aurait été suivie d'une sédition, révolte ou guerre civile.

2° Par ailleurs, selon l'article 34 de la loi de 1905, «*Tout ministre d'un culte qui, dans les lieux où s'exerce ce culte, aura publiquement par des discours prononcés, des lectures faites, des écrits distribués ou des affiches apposées,* ***outragé ou diffamé un citoyen chargé d'un service public****, sera puni d'une amende* de *25 000 F.* (37 500 euros) *et d'un emprisonnement d'un an, ou de l'une de ces deux peines seulement. La vérité du fait diffamatoire, mais seulement s'il est relatif aux fonctions, pourra être établi devant le tribunal correctionnel dans les formes prévues par l'article 52 de la loi du 29 juillet 1881*».

b) Droit local

L'article 130 a) du Code pénal local applicable en Alsace et en Moselle sanctionne l'**atteinte à la paix publique**.

«*Tout ecclésiastique ou autre ministre du culte qui, soit dans l'exercice ou à l'occasion de l'exercice de ses fonctions, publiquement ou devant une foule, soit dans une église ou tout autre lieu affecté à des assemblées religieuses, devant plusieurs personnes, se sera livré, au sujet des affaires de l'État, à des déclarations ou discussions de nature à porter atteinte à la paix publique, sera puni de l'emprisonnement ou de la détention dans une forteresse, pendant deux ans au plus.*

Sera puni de la même peine tout ecclésiastique ou autre ministre du culte qui, dans l'exercice ou à l'occasion de l'exercice de ses fonctions, aura émis ou répandu un écrit contenant, au sujet des affaires de l'État, des déclarations ou discussions de nature à porter atteinte à la paix publique».

Cette infraction est un délit intentionnel. Il n'en a été trouvé aucune application jurisprudentielle.

III. Infractions liées à des actes de culte ou à des rites

15. *La mutilation génitale féminine. Est-elle considérée comme un crime particulier, comme une offense ou violence corporelle qualifiée ou aggravée ou comme une simple offense corporelle? Dans les deux premiers cas, quels sont les éléments matériels et psychologiques et quelle est la peine de l'infraction?*

La mutilation génitale féminine ne constitue pas une infraction spécifique en droit français.

Sa qualification relève des **violences volontaires** qui tombent sous le coup:

- soit du délit aggravé de l'article 222-9 du Code pénal lorsqu'il y a mutilation ou plus généralement infirmité permanente. La peine encourue est alors de 10 ans d'emprisonnement et de 150 000 euros d'amende;
- soit du crime prévu par l'article 222-10 1° lorsque la victime est âgée de moins de 15 ans au moment des faits. La peine encourue est alors de 15 ans de réclusion criminelle. Elle peut atteindre 20 ans si l'auteur des faits est un ascendant légitime, naturel ou adoptif, ou toute autre personne ayant autorité sur l'enfant (C. pén., art. 222-10 al. 2).

La mort non voulue de la victime des violences volontaires aggrave encore les qualifications:

- si la victime a plus de 15 ans, l'article 222-7 du Code pénal prévoit une peine de 15 ans de réclusion criminelle;
- si la victime a moins de 15 ans, l'article 222-8 1° édicte une peine de 20 ans de réclusion, peine que l'article 222-8 alinéa 2 porte à 30 ans lorsque l'auteur des faits est un ascendant légitime, naturel ou adoptif ou toute autre personne ayant autorité sur le mineur.

En cas de décès accidentel, on peut encore songer à retenir le délit d'homicide involontaire (C. pén., art. 221-6 prévoyant une peine d'emprisonnement de 3 ans et une amende de 45 000 euros), voire celui d'omission de porter secours (C. pén., art. 223-6 al. 2 prévoyant une peine de 5 ans d'emprisonnement et de 75 000 euros d'amende).

Par ailleurs, lorsqu'ils ne sont pas les auteurs de l'infraction, les parents peuvent être condamnés pour complicité.

IV. La motivation religieuse en tant que cause d'aggravation légale (ou qualification) ou, inversement, cause d'atténuation de l'infraction

16. *Quelles sont les infractions qualifiées par la motivation religieuse?*

Selon l'article 132-76 du Code pénal, dans les cas prévus par la loi, le fait que l'infraction est commise en raison de l'appartenance, vraie ou supposée, de la victime à une religion déterminée est une circonstance entraînant l'aggravation de la peine encourue pour un crime ou un délit. La circonstance aggravante est constituée lorsque l'infraction est précédée, accompagnée ou suivie de propos, écrits, images, objets ou actes de toute nature portant atteinte à l'honneur ou à la considération de la victime ou d'un groupe de personnes dont fait partie la victime à raison de leur appartenance ou de leur non-appartenance, vraie ou supposée, à une religion déterminée (C. pén., art. 132-76 al. 1).

Tel est le cas:

- du meurtre (C. pén., art. 221-4 6 °): réclusion criminelle à perpétuité (au lieu de 30 ans de réclusion criminelle);
- du vol (C. pén., art. 311-4 9°): 5 ans d'emprisonnement et 75 000 euros d'amende (au lieu de 3 ans d'emprisonnement et de 45 000 euros d'amende);
- de l'extorsion (C. pén., 312-2 3°): 10 ans d'emprisonnement et 150 000 euros d'amende (au lieu de 7 ans d'emprisonnement et 100 000 euros);
- des destructions, dégradations ou détériorations d'un bien appartenant à autrui (C. pén., art. 322-2 al. 2): 3 ans d'emprisonnement et 45 000 euros d'amende (au lieu de 2 ans et 30 000 euros);
- des destructions, dégradations ou détériorations d'un bien appartenant à autrui par l'effet d'une substance explosive, incendie ou de tout autre moyen (C. pén. 322-8): 20 ans d'emprisonnement (au lieu de 10 ans prévus par l'article 322-6) et 150 000 euros d'amende;
- de l'atteinte à l'intégrité du cadavre et la violation de sépulture (C. pén., art. 225-18, v. Question n° 8);
- des infractions en matière de presse: injure et diffamation (V. Question n° 2).

17. *Quelles sont les infractions à l'égard desquelles la motivation religieuse est une excuse atténuante?*

Il n'en existe pas en droit français.

V. Le droit pénal des sectes

18. *Quels sont les infractions pénales ayant pour cadre les sectes?*

Il existe en France de nombreuses dispositions pénales permettant de sanctionner les infractions commises au sein des mouvements sectaires. Mais ces textes ne sont pas spécifiquement applicables aux groupements sectaires, ainsi qu'à leurs dirigeants et à leurs membres. Tel est le cas par exemple, de l'escroquerie, de l'exercice illégal de la médecine ou de la pharmacie, du viol, des violences, etc…. Les parents peuvent également être sanctionnés en cas de refus de satisfaire aux vaccinations obligatoires de leurs enfants (C. Santé publique, art. L. 3111-1 à L. 3111-11 et articles L. 3112-1 à L. 3112-5) ou en cas d'infraction à l'obligation de scolarisation de leurs enfants (C. pén., art. 227-17-1 et art. 227-17-2).

Afin d'appréhender de manière plus ciblée les infractions commises dans le cadre des sectes, le législateur est intervenu par la loi n° 2001-504 du 12 juin 2001 tendant à renforcer la prévention et la répression des mouvements sectaires portant atteinte aux droits de l'homme et aux libertés fondamentales, dite loi «About-Picard». Cette loi a défini la notion de «mouvement sectaire» comme un mouvement «*qui poursuit des activités ayant pour but ou pour effet de créer, de maintenir ou d'exploiter la sujétion psychologique ou physique des personnes qui participent à ces activités*» (art. 1er). Mais elle ne fait pas précisément référence à la dimension religieuse du mouvement sectaire.

a) Cette loi a introduit deux **infractions spécifiquement applicables** aux mouvements sectaires;

– la diffusion par quelque moyen que ce soit des messages destinés à la jeunesse et faisant la promotion d'un mouvement sectaire (V. Question n° 9).
– le fait pour toute personne physique (dirigeants de droit ou de fait, membres du groupement) de participer au maintien ou à la reconstitution, ouverte ou déguisée, d'une personne morale qui poursuit des activités ayant pour but ou pour effet de créer, de maintenir ou d'exploiter la sujétion psychologique ou physique des personnes qui participent à ces activités et dont la dissolution a été prononcée (C. pén. art. 434-43). Peine encourue: trois ans d'emprisonnement et de 45 000 euros d'amende. En récidive, la peine est portée à cinq ans d'emprisonnement et 75 000 euros d'amende.

b) La loi de 2001 a, par ailleurs, élargi le champ d'application de **l'abus frauduleux de l'état d'ignorance ou de faiblesse encore appelé «abus**

de faiblesse». L'article 223-15-2 punit «*l'abus frauduleux de l'état d'ignorance ou de la situation de faiblesse, soit d'un mineur, soit d'une personne dont la particulière vulnérabilité, due à son âge, à une maladie, à une infirmité, à une déficience physique ou psychique ou à un état de grossesse, est apparente et connue de son auteur,* ***soit d'une personne en état de sujétion psychologique ou physique résultant de l'exercice de pressions graves ou réitérées ou de techniques propres à altérer son jugement, pour conduire*** *ce mineur ou* ***cette personne à un acte ou à une abstention qui lui sont gravement préjudiciables***». Il convient toutefois d'observer que le terme «secte» n'est pas mentionné dans ce texte.

1° Eléments constitutifs

* Condition tenant à la victime
Les victimes de sectes sont concernées moins par l'état d'ignorance ou de faiblesse que par l'«*état de sujétion psychologique ou physique résultant de l'exercice de pressions graves ou réitérées ou de techniques propres à altérer son jugement*». La notion d'état de sujétion est difficile à cerner en particulier dans sa dimension psychologique dans laquelle entre une part de subjectivité. Cela renvoie à l'état de soumission, d'allégeance de l'individu. La formule a pu être critiquée par la doctrine en raison de son caractère flou.

* Condition tenant à l'auteur
Il peut s'agir de toute personne, physique ou morale, de dirigeants de fait ou de droit du groupement, ou de membres d'une secte.

L'auteur doit avoir, par son comportement, conduit la personne en état de sujétion à commettre «*un acte ou une abstention qui lui soit gravement préjudiciable*». La formule est large et non limitée à un préjudice d'ordre patrimonial.

L'infraction comporte un **élément intentionnel** (fraude): conscience de l'abus accompli de mauvaise foi et volonté de tromper pour atteindre le résultat contraire à l'intérêt de la victime.

2° Répression

* Personnes physiques
- 3 ans d'emprisonnement et 375 000 € d'amende (C. pén., art. 223-15-2), et peines complémentaires (C. pén., art. 223-15-3).
- 5 ans d'emprisonnement et 750 000 € d'amende (C. pén., art. 223-15-2 al. 2) pour le dirigeant du mouvement sectaire.

* Personne morale
Il existe également des sanctions pénales à l'encontre du groupement lorsque l'abus de faiblesse a été commis pour son compte (C. pén., art. 223-15-4) L'on observera qu'aucune aggravation de la sanction n'a été envisagée pour la personne morale répondant à la définition du mouvement sectaire. Elle encourt:

- une peine d'amende (C. pén., art. 131-38): 375 000 euros;
- des peines complémentaires (C. pén., art. 131-39), dont la mise sous contrôle judiciaire pour une durée qui ne peut excéder cinq ans (C. pén., art. 131-39, 131-46; CPP, art. 706-45), et la **dissolution judiciaire** prononcée par le juge répressif.

Cette dissolution ne doit pas être confondue avec la **dissolution civile** prononcée par le juge civil (tribunal de grande instance), spécifique aux groupements sectaires créée par la loi du 12 juin 2001 (art. 1er). Il s'agit ne s'agit pas d'une dissolution de plein droit, mais d'une simple faculté. Cette dissolution ne peut être prononcée que si le mouvement religieux, personne morale, ou ses dirigeants a fait l'objet de condamnations pénales définitives. Compte tenu des ramifications et la logique de groupe qui anime certains mouvements sectaires, l'article 1er alinéa 6 de la loi de 2001 autorise le tribunal, saisi d'une demande de dissolution, à prononcer au cours de la même instance la dissolution de plusieurs personnes morales liées entre elles, à défaut de pouvoir dissoudre le groupe qui n'a pas la personnalité morale.

Richard Puza

RELIGION IN CRIMINAL LAW: GERMANY

The change in the passage from state religions to separation of state and religion in Germany begins in the nineteenth century and becomes definitive with the Constitution of Weimar. Today we speak of the positive neutrality of the state in relation to the churches, religious communities and philosophical communities in a plural, multicultural society.

The Criminal Code (CC), whose English translation, provided by the German Federal Ministry of Justice, was utilised for this study, speaks of the general protection of religion in Chapter Eleven, which has the title "Crimes Which Relate to Religion and Philosophy of Life" in four paragraphs: 1) Para. 166, Insulting Faiths, Religious Societies and Organizations dedicated to a Philosophy of Life; 2) Para. 167, Disturbing the Practice of Religion; 3) Para. 167a, Disturbing a Funeral Service; and 4) Para. 168, Disturbing the Peace of the Dead. But we find norms of protection of religion also in other parts of the CC.

General protection of religion

1. *Defamation or outrage of religion: "Insulting Faiths" (CC para. 166.1)*

Paras. 166 ff. CC were re-formulated by Art 1. StRG of 25.06.1969 (BGBl 1 645) and completely changed.[1] The crimes of blasphemy and hindering church services were abolished. The concept of blasphemy (gr. ἡ βλασφημία, τῆς βλασφημίας – blasphêmía – disrepute; made up of βλάπτειν – bláptein – harm, injury and attack ἡ φήμη – phêmê and dorich ἡ φάμα – pháma – reputation) referred initially to an insult addressed to the Gods, i.e. to an open denial, insult, or derision of certain belief contents of a religion. Blasphemy was replaced by new, corresponding offences. Courts and lawyers are required to analyse the legal values

[1] Söhnke /Schröder, Strafgesetzbuch, Kommentar 42. Auflage, München1991, 1274ff. Albin Eser, Schutz von Religion und Kirchen im Strafrecht und im Verfahrensrecht, in: Handbuch des Staatskirchenrechts der Bundesrepublik Deutschland (Hg. Josef Listl und Dietrich Pirson), 2. Aufl., Bd. II, Berlin 1996, 1019-1045.

underlying the relevant crimes through these paragraphs. A protected legal good is the maintenance of public freedom and not a confession as such.

Philosophical movements were included in the stipulations. The early necessary public status of religious communities was no longer mentioned. The lay state (or more accurately, the neutral state[2]) in Germany brings into question differences between the general limits to the liberties of expression, manifestation, association and action and those related to religion. Judicial decisions are confronted with such difficulty and often only they reveal the true limits of the conflicting liberties.

CC Paragraph 166.1 provides: Whoever publicly or through dissemination of writings (Para. 11 section [3]) insults the content of others' religious faith or faith related to a philosophy of life in a manner that is capable of disturbing the public peace, shall be punished with imprisonment for not more than three years or a fine.

Judgements on "blasphemy"[3]

The "paragraph on blasphemy" justified in 1994 a prohibition on the representation of crucified pigs in the musical "The Maria-Syndrome". The musical depicted a modern Maria who became pregnant by using an unclean toilet seat. This is the way in which the virgin birth is described. The debut performance should have taken place on May 28, 1994 in Trier. One day before the scheduled first night the show was forbidden by the local authorities who responded to a request by the diocese of Trier. Even showing the musical before a "non-religious" public was forbidden. The court case which followed took place at several levels. The Federal Administrative Court confirmed the lawfulness of the ban and accepted by its judgement the decision of the High Administrative Court Koblenz. The Federal Administrative Court did not analyse the case further and gave no reasons for its decision.

Another well-known case is that of a woman who has been convicted in many courts for the creation of a sticker in which Jesus was represented with the following text: "masochism can be cured." At a theatre at Köln in the carnival a crucifix carried the blasphemous inscription "TÜNNES" instead of "INRI". The sign was confiscated by the police

[2] See Richard Puza, *La loi francaise de 1905 et la séparation Église-État en Allemagne*, in: Revue des Sciences Religieuses 79 (2005) 511-524.

[3] See Schönke/Schröder a.a.O.

after a complaint of blasphemy. The director of the session was convicted with a fine of 6000 DM which he did not pay because the court accepted the argument that the artist had created a new symbol on the basis of his freedom of creativity. Objects of another sketch at a carnival session in 2006 were Pope Benedict XVI and Cardinal Meisner. The WDR-TV-station refused to cut the sketch from its broadcast.

In February 2006 a pensioner was sentenced to 12 months' imprisonment with release on licence and 300 hours of social work for insulting a religious confession and disturbance of public freedom. He printed toilet paper with the inscription "The Quran, the holy Quran"; he sent it with insulting letters to several mosques and TV-stations and offered it for sale.[4]

2. *Defamation or outrage against a church or religious community: "Insulting Religious Societies and Organizations Dedicated to a Philosophy of Life" (CC para. 166.2)*

Insulting religious societies and organisations and of organisations dedicated to a philosophy of life is liable to prosecution in Germany according to §166 StGB (the old paragraph on blasphemy) if it leads to the disturbance of public peace. There is equal protection regarding all religions.

Para. 166.2 provides: Whoever publicly or through dissemination of writings (Para. 11 section (3]) insults a church, other religious society, or organization dedicated to a philosophy of life located in Germany, or their institutions or customs in a manner that is capable of disturbing the public peace, shall be similarly punished.

Para. 166 CC not only protects the religions as such and religious feelings but also the content of the religious confession (166.1) and the institutions of a church or other religious organisation or organisation promoting a philosophy of life (166.2). According to Para. 166.2 CC a religious community or a church as such must be insulted.

Judgements

Is it permissible to call Christian churches "criminal organisations"? The judgement of the Local Court in Göttingen answered this question negatively in 1985. In 1984 a medical student from Bochum distributed

[4] See II.

several flyers which presented the activities of the so-called "committee for abolishing para. 166 CC". One flyer presented the case of a member of the "International Association for the Promotion of a Joyful Life" who spread pamphlets containing the following: "It is better to have a maculate birth control than an immaculate conception", "masochism can be cured". The flyer also stated: "The critics of the policies of dominance of the church which is the biggest criminal organisation of all times, which has the highest number of victims of terror and crimes (22 million people during the crusades), are prosecuted by state law". He was prosecuted with a fine of 400 DM.

Heinrich Heine, George Grosz, Kurt Tucholsky, the Drei Tornados, Walter Moers, Titanic, the TAZ-newspaper and satirists have been accused of blasphemy. They have all been subject to judicial proceedings for blasphemy or insulting a religious organisation.

Until February 2006 only one person had been accused of insulting Islam. Following the attacks in London (2005), he printed toilet paper with the words: "Quran, the Holy Quran". As outlined above, he sent this to 20 mosques, and several magazines and TV stations to be sold in order to fund the construction of a monument to the victims of Islamic terror.

In past decades, sentences for blasphemy against the Christian religion have not been very severe. However, one judgement of the Land court was rather harsh. The person was given a punishment of one year on release and 300 hours of social work. In the case of the Titanic there were eight charges – four for an insult addressed to the pope, three for insulting religion and one for insulting the bishop of Fulda, Dyba; but they were unsuccessful. Neither the crucifix with the inscription "I was also a tin" nor a depiction of Jesus on which was written "Does Jesus still play a role?" led to convictions.

Defamation may be committed in oral (speech, remarks), written (flyers, books), or graphic (poster, commercial) form, or by gesture (parody). Proof of intention is required. Moreover, the act of defamation must be carried out publicly or its results must be known to the public, and it can refer to items or goods which are of particular importance to the denomination in question: a cross, pictures of saints, etc. The protected value is God or a god, but not the object itself (idolatry). Criticisms of a religious community or of the statements and opinions of religious leaders are not punishable.

According to Article 6 of the Basic Law on freedom of conscience and religion, the citizens of other states and stateless persons have the same rights as German citizens.

The cartoons case

What follows discusses the cartoons case. Once more, one has to pose the question: what goods are protected by German legal norms? On a Friday morning two years ago several German, Italian, and French TV-programmes showed the caricatures of Mohamed which not only hurt the feelings of fundamentalist believers but also the religious feelings generally of Islamic European citizens. Journalists talked about the value of freedom of speech. The question is which values are protected by a secular, religiously neutral democracy like Germany? The religious and Christian foundations of state laws disappeared a long time ago. Sunday is a guaranteed day of rest and not a day in which one remembers that God rested on the seventh day of creation. But let us go further in our analysis.

What happened during that Friday morning could be subsumed under blasphemy according to para. 166 CC and could be punished accordingly with a suspension of liberty of up to three years and a fine. The same regulation applies when one propagates writings against a substantive religious belief or a religious organisation or an organisation dedicated to a philosophy of life which leads to the disturbance of public freedom. The Paragraph mentions clearly that public freedom should be protected by law. This also underlines that one is obliged to show a minimum of reciprocal respect and tolerance. If journalists make critical statements on the reactions of Muslim citizens on grounds of freedom of speech and freedom of the press one can no longer argue against them. What one can criticize is their publishing and re-publishing of such insulting caricatures. By such publications they endanger the maintainance of public freedom which is a legal good of our democratic state, with possible consequences on the international level.

Certainly para. 166 CC is questionable. Kurt Tucholsky called the earlier versions of the law a "dictatorial paragraph of the Middle Ages." He considered it an unreasonable demand that churches be protected by the law. In the case of the crucifix with the inscription "TÜNNES" (see above), freedom of art was considered to be of higher importance than the religious representation. The paragraph has been applied successfully in the following cases: in judging a film which insulted the virgin birth (this film could not even be shown to a religiously neutral public), in the representation of crucified pigs or in the case of a Jesus-sticker with the message "masochism can be cured".

In the case of the caricatures we face another challenge: the peace in our country and peace in the world. The persons who support freedom of the press have at least the moral obligation not to endanger peace in our country.

3. and 4. *Desecration of a place of worship and hindering or disturbing a religious meeting: "Disturbing the Practice of Religion" (CC para. 167)*

Whoever (1) intentionally and in a gross manner disturbs a religious service or an act of a religious service of a church or other religious society located in Germany; or (2) commits insulting mischief at a place dedicated to the religious services of such a religious society, shall be punished with imprisonment for not more than three years or a fine.

Corresponding celebrations of an organization dedicated to a philosophy of life located in Germany shall be the equivalent of religious services.

5. *Menaces, violence or application of force against freedom of religion or conscience*

Not applicable in Germany.

6. *Discrimination on grounds of religion*

Not applicable in German penal law.

7. *Disturbing a funeral service (CC para. 167)*

Whoever intentionally or knowingly disturbs a funeral service shall be punished with imprisonment for not more than three years or a fine. This provides that anybody who maliciously disturbs a funeral, mourning ceremony or rites, shall be punished. The ceremony does not have to be a religious one; it may be performed in public or in private. The protected good is the honour of a deceased person and the religious feelings of the participants. The provision states clearly that the object of punishment is "malicious" disruption; thus behaviour resulting from a lack of knowledge concerning a given religion or behaviour caused by the excessive consumption of alcohol is regarded in the commentaries as *faux-pas*, but not as a malicious disruption.

8. *Disturbing the peace of the dead (CC para. 168)*

Whoever, without authorization, takes away the body or parts of the body of a deceased person, a dead foetus or parts thereof or the ashes of a deceased person from the custody of the person entitled thereto, or whoever commits insulting mischief thereto, shall be punished with imprisonment for not more than three years or a fine.

Whoever destroys or damages a place for lying-in-state, burial site or public place for remembering the dead, or whoever commits insulting mischief there, shall be similarly punished. An attempt is also punishable.

Whoever defames a corpse or any of its part or "the place of inhumation", shall be punished by fine, limitation of freedom or withdrawal of freedom up to three years. Despoiling a corpse or sepulchre is also penalized. These crimes do not have to be committed in public, as the human corpse itself is legally protected from the moment of the death.

9. and 10. *Proselytism and apostasy*

Not applicable in Germany.

11. *Misuse of religious garments or falsification of office*[5]

(1) The penal protection of the titles of ecclesial office

The titles of ecclesial office, administrative office and other titles are protected in German penal law. Ecclesiastical titles are also protected in canon law. Para 132a sect. 1 CC on the misuse of titles, names of professions and emblems forbids a person to hold titles of office, administrative office, academic degrees or public dignities obtained in Germany or outside Germany without authorisation. Persons who wear without authorisation uniforms, administrative clothing or emblems are punished by a custodial sentence for up to one year or by a fine. According to para. 132a sect. 2 academic titles, dignities, habits or emblems that have a similarity with those protected by the state are also protected. The provision also forbids the holding of a domestic or foreign office or professional titles without authorisation. Paragraphs 1, 2 and 3 apply also to office names, titles, dignities, emblems or habits belonging to all churches or religious communities which function as corporations for the purposes of public law. Churches are the traditional christian religious communities, i.e. the Protestant Church, Roman Catholic Church, Old Catholic Church, Methodist Church, Baptist Church, Greek Orthodox Church,

[5] Richard Puza (Hg.), Lexikon kirchlicher Amtsbezeichnungen der katholischen, evangelischen und Orthodoxen Kirchen, Stuttgart 2007, Einführung XX-XXII.

Romanian Orthodox Church and Russian Orthodox Church. The other religious communities are the Jewish Communities, Salvation Army but not Yehovah's Witnesses or Buddhists.

I believe that the styles 'pater' or 'frater' are also included in this category, especially when that particular person considers himself the pater or frater of a certain religious community.

Judgements

According to judgements on para. 132a CC ecclesial titles of 'pastor' or 'Pfarrer' are protected. However, 'Konsistorium' or 'Oberkirchenrat' are not protected. The argument for this decision was the fact that the Protestant church in Germany is no longer a state church and has no special position in the state compared to other religions or religious communities.

In a judgement of 24.3.1983 from Mainz the ecclesial title of 'Generaldekan' was debated. The accused added to the title 'of the Protestant Church X'. This title does not exist in this form in any of the Protestant churches in Germany recognised as corporations in public law. The title 'Dekan' is protected under para 132a CC. The court held that: (1) The ecclesial titles issued by a particular church in the sense used in para. 132 sect. 1 n. 1 and sect. 3 CC name only the person who can hold a title of an ecclesial office which is recognised by the Church which itself is recognised as a coporation in public law; (2) The administrators of a newly erected church in the sense of para. 132a sect. 2 CC which holds a title similar to one already held by an existing church can be prosecuted only when it is not recognisable that this new title is connected to the newly erected church; and (3) There is no protection for titles which are in use in already existing churches.

One cannot talk about 'holding a title' if a person uses that title only once or twice before individual persons. An unauthorised holding of a title occurs only when this title violates the interests of a community. A person who holds an unauthorised title only in the private sphere without endangering the interests of the community (BGH vom 13.05.1982) is not liable to prosecution.

The unauthorised holding of the title 'archbishop' was discussed in a judgement of OLG Köln of 10.8.1999. In the case of the title 'archbishop' one is faced with an ecclesial office of the Roman Catholic Church which is recognised as a corporation for public law purposes in Germany and which is protected under para. 132a sect. 3 CC. This paragraph talks about the constitutional privilege of a religious community organised on the basis of public law. Therefore the holding of an ecclesial title of such a type is protected by law.

(2) Protection of identities attributable to a title

Identities attributable to a title are mentioned in para. 12 BGB. Churches may also rely on this provision. Protection is enjoyed by names or parts of names and abbreviated names deriving from them which symbolise a particular function attirbuted to that name. The law is applicable when there is a danger of mistaking the names.

(3) Protection of ecclesiastical garments

Reichskonkordat Art. 10: The protection of ecclesial apparel is granted by the German Reichskonkordat Art. 10. This article protects the wearing of ecclesiastical garments only by people who are authorised by the church to wear them. The unauthorised wearing of such garments may be prosecuted by the state in the same way in which it prosecutes someone who wears uniforms in an unauthorised way. This specification is not a penal norm but it implies that the state has the obligation to punish the unauthorised wearing of ecclesiastical garments according to the provisions of §132 a par. 3 StGB geschehen ist.

The law on administrative offences (OWiG) para. 126: According to para 126 1 OwiG an administrative fine may be imposed when a person wears without authorisation a habit or an emblem of a particular religious organisation which is recognised by another religious organisation of public law. Habits or emblems which are similar to the ones mentioned above fall under the same law. The administrative offence can be punished with a fine.

The aim of this prescription is to protect not only those institutions which are represented by certain habits and emblems but also to protect the community against the misuse of trust arising when people wear these habits or emblems without authorisation. Religious communities recognised by the Catholic Church are for instance religious orders or institutes of the Roman Catholic Church. Their habits are protected under para. 126 OWiG geschützt. The habits and emblems of churches and religious communities which are recognised as corporations of public law are under the penal protection of para. 132 (3) CC.

The violation of the OwiG-law consists in the unauthorised wearing of a professional habit or a professional emblem. The simple possession of a professional habit or of a professional emblem is not punished with a fine. The prosecution process starts when the person in question appears in public with the habit or the emblem or when he gives the impression that he belongs to the group of persons entitled to wear them.

Offences by ministers of religion

12. *Disclosure of a secret obtained in the exercise of ministry*[6]

Secrets of the confessional are protected in the code on criminal procedure. Para. 53 of the German Strafprozessordnung (CCP) regulates the "Right to Refuse Testimony on Professional Grounds". The following persons may refuse to testify: (1) Geistliche (clergymen, priests), concerning information entrusted to them or which became known to them in their capacity as spiritual advisers (para. 53 sect. 1 n. 1); (2) Berufshelfer eines Geistlichen (assistants and persons being trained for their profession who participate in their respective professional activities) – these shall be considered equivalent to the persons specified in para. 53 sect. 1, n. 1. to 4. The persons specified in para. 53 sect. 1, n. 1 shall decide whether these assistants should exercise their right to refuse to testify, except when such a decision cannot be obtained within a foreseeable period.

It is forbidden to hear a clergyman as a witness concerning facts received while listening to a confession or as a Seelsorger (spiritual adviser). This ban is absolute and cannot be lifted, either by the priest himself or by anybody else. Such evidence is null and void, and cannot be used at trial. There is no punishment for a priest who reveals such secrets. Nevertheless, a couple of comments may be offered here. This rule applies only when the priest is to be heard as a witness; it is not applicable when the priest is accused or is a suspect, and it is applicable only to the questions which were entrusted to the priest while listening to the confession – thus he can be a witness in all other situations.

However, the rule applies not only to a priest of the Catholic Church but also to a clergyman of another church or religious community, with

[6] Diese Frage ist in diesem Jahr durch eine Gesetzesnovelle des Innenministerium (Minister Schäuble) aktuell geworden. Es gibt Arbeiten dazu und jetzt ein Heft der Deutschen Bischofskonferenz: Arbeitshilfe Nr.222. Zeugenaussage, Zeugnisverweigerungsrecht und Schweigepflicht. Ein juristischer Leitfaden für Seelsorger zum Schutz des Beicht- und Seelsorgegeheimnisses, 1. Januar 2008.

Judgements: Beschluss des Bundesgerichtshofes (BGH) vom 15. November 2006 – StB 15/06 – und Entscheidung des Bundesverfassungsgerichtes (BVerfG) vom 27. Januar 2007 – 2 BvR – 26/07.

a special role in that community, when he is appointed for the regular performance of such celebrations. The law does not distinguish secrets of confession (Beichtgeheimnis) and those of spiritual advice (Seelsorgegeheimnis). Thus, confessional secrets are protected equally with those entrusted to an attorney.

Secrets of the confession and spiritual advice: actual questions

The Protestant and the Roman Catholic Church in Germany have criticised the plans of the Federal Office of Criminal Investigation (BKA) according to which it would be possible under special circumstances to monitor conversations of ministers of religion. The secrecy of confession should not be breached, but it should be legally protected, said the director of the Catholic Bureau in Berlin. The deputy director of the Permanent Council of the Protestant Church in Germany (EKD) in Berlin said that the Constitutional Court considers that confessions and counselling lie at the core of private life, which cannot be controlled. The counselling which takes place in confessional discussion can only achieve its aim if there is absolute confidence and absolute discretion between the two partners of such conversation, affirmed the Church President of the Protestant Church in Hessen and Nassau. If one looses this confidence one cannot gain a sense of "security". Church counsellors can identify the development of negative behaviour through their counselling, only if trusted by the person who seeks advice. The right of priests to maintain the secrecy of the confession is put into question by these new developments. The Church President of the Protestant Church in the Palatine stressed that the secrecy of counselling and confession must remain obligatory, under the same category as telephone conversations and private mail.

The secrecy of the confessional should be also maintained. Richard Puza, Professor of Canon Law at the Faculty of Catholic Theology at the University of Tübingen said that neither from the point of view of canon law, nor from the point of view of state law is it acceptable to breach the secrecy of confession. From the perspective of canon law the breaking of confession can lead to excommunication. According to Article 9, Reichskonkordat, which still regulates the relationship between the Catholic Church and the state, the secrecy of confession is also protected. Prelate Jüsten points out that the Minister of Home Affairs, Wolfgang Schäuble (CDU), has not supported this legal draft until now. Conservative politicians have also stressed their doubt as far as this draft law and its consequences in religious law are concerned. A spokesman for the Home Office has confirmed information in the media that the BKA is preparing a law which would enable MPs, prosecutors and ministers to be monitored in the future. According to the present German law these professional groups are protected from being monitored. According to reports in the media the immunity for these groups should be lifted if the life of somebody is under threat.

13. *Celebration of religious marriage before civil marriage*[7]

From 2009 it will be possible to conclude a religious marriage prior to a civil marriage. Clerics solemnising such marriages will no longer commit an administrative offence. The new law on civil status no longer contains the restrictions of the former law. Thus religious marriages can be concluded without a previous civil marriage in Germany. Still, persons who enter only a religious marriage do not enjoy the benefits of a civil marriage, and they will therefore have to inform themselves very well about the consequences of such a marriage.

Nevertheless, one has to welcome the new provisions, because they sanitise the public image of a religious marriage. For catholics marriage is a sacrament. It was high time that freedom of religion was accomplished also in marriage law. Those who want only to conclude a religious marriage should be allowed to do so.

However, the Protestant and Catholic Churches seem to have problems with the new situation. There is considerable criticism of the new law from different perspectives. The Catholic church has its own marriage law, and the Protestant Church should also develop its own marriage law. The German Conference of Bishops has set up a commission to work on a statement or regulation on religious marriage without a civil marriage, but it gives the impression that it is still sceptical about the change since the legal consequences of such a decision are not yet very clear. The persons who get married only in church are living according to civil law in a non-marital relationship. Nevertheless one has to understand that certain civil rights can be also attained through contracts (on inheritance, on mutual representation etc.) which the partners can conclude themselves after the religious marriage.

The negative consequences of the change are always mentioned and extreme cases are postulated: some persons decide only to get married

[7] R. Puza, Resümee: Beginn und Ende der Ehe – alte und neue Gesichtspunkte, in: Richard Puza, Abraham Peter Kustermann (Hrsg.), Beginn und Ende der Ehe und Zivilrecht, Heidelberg 1994, 121-126.

in church so that they save divorce money in the case of marriage failure. The intention of polygamy is also mentioned, hinting in this way at Islamic believers who are allowed to marry more than one woman. One has to say that all these fears can be overcome by elaborating definite rules for church (or religious) marriages.

I am convinced that the new regulation should be viewed in a positive way. One should be grateful to the legislator for this late development. It would have been much better if these changes had occured 30 years ago. This new regulation makes an old dream come true.

The former regulation on obligatory civil marriages, introduced by the Reichchancellor Bismarck as a means of combatting the Catholic Church as a result of the 'Kulturkampf' (clash of cultures), has not always been viewed as consistent with the German Constitution. Obligatory civil marriage could be seen to contravene freedom of religion guaranteed by the German Constitution as well as by Article 9 of the European Convention on Human Rights.

In Austria, after 1945, because of the incorporation of laws, promulgated during the German occupation, in the Second Republic the German Civil Law on Persons of 1938 was valid. According to this law it was compulsory that the religious marriage was concluded after a civil marriage and any cleric who did not respect this was prosecuted. This has for a long time been seen to oppose the constitution and the principle of freedom of religion. Nevertheless the system of obligatory civil marriage was maintained. Because of this Austrian Dioceses have issued their own norms for religious marriages. The quintessence of these norms is that to conclude religious marriages the *nihil obstat* of the diocesan bishop is required. People decide to conclude only a religious marriage mainly for financial reasons, because in the case of a civil marriage the partners could loose their pensions. This affects not only older but also younger people – for instance when a church employee could not conclude a civil marriage for financial reasons but wants to live in a valid sacramental marriage. I have seen such cases from my long-standing practical experience. The Austrian Dioceses recognize explicitly financial reasons for the acceptance of religious marriages without civil marriages. At the same time the Catholic Church takes into consideration the church-state relationship in Austria in order not to jeopardize the system of obligatory civil marriage there. If there are no acceptable financial reasons for the conclusion of only a religious marriage then the couple is advised also to conclude a civil marriage.

This possibility offered by the Austrian Dioceses has been invoked by many German couples. One can talk about a kind of 'marriage tourism' to Austria. German citizens must nevertheless bring with them the *nihil obstat* of their own Ordinary if they want to get married in Austria. The Ordinaries (the Diocesan Bishop and the Vicar General) issue the *nihil obstat* after a thorough analysis of the case. In this way it is guaranteed that the German system of an obligatory civil marriage, established by the Reichskonkordat, is not violated and that polygamous marriages are avoided.

The new regulation makes it possible for Germans to have a religious marriage in Germany if they want their relationship to be legitimated in the eyes of God and the Church. This should be sufficient reason for the German Conference of Bishops to appreciate the new regulation. The new regulation can also benefit other religious organisations and I am sure they will take the opportunity and make use of it within their religious legal systems.

Moreover, these legal innovations, allowing a religious marriage without a prior civil marriage, could be viewed as an opportunity for the system of obligatory civil marriage to be replaced with a system of facultative civil marriage. The introduction of a facultative civil marriage could be the next step towards a radical change of marriage law in Germany which could serve the interests of churches, religious institutions and philosophical institutions. The manner in which this could be achieved can be seen from recent developments in Poland and Italy. Poland is a classical example of the replacement of the system of obligatory civil marriage with a modern system of religious marriage with civil recognition of the state against the background of civil, ecclesiastical and covenantal configurations of the law. Italy provides on the other hand an example of the covenantal renewal of the system of facultative civil marriage. In Italy and in Poland there are also a number of smaller religious communities whose clerics are permitted to conclude religious marriages. Noteworthy are: the Tavola valdese, Adventists, Assemblee di Dio, Unione delle Comunità ebraiche, Baptists and Chiesa Evangelica Luterana in Italia (CELI). In order to achieve this it is necessary to conclude an agreement (*intesa*) between the religious community and the state.

In Germany concordats and other agreements between church and state are constantly concluded. Why should not marriage law be included in these agreements? In this way marriage law could be settled on new foundations which would correspond to the legal prescriptions of many countries in the world, which offer their citizens a high degree of freedom in this matter. It is high time that Christians, Jews and Muslims, and others, stopped getting married twice if they want their marriage to be recognized by the state.

A *conditio sine qua non* of the introduction of the facultative civil marriage must be the fact that the state should not abandon its own marriage law. This is necessary for the maintainence of positive neutrality, freedom of religion and maintaining the principle of equality in religious matters. The latter principle underlines that churches and several other religious organisations or institutions of philosophical orientation are only given the right to conclude marriages. At the same time the state should have the authority to terminate all marriages – no matter whether they were concluded in a religious or in a civil way. Marriages annulled through church courts or dissolved in the Catholic Church because of disparity of religion, or non-consummation, should not be recognized by the state. One should not follow the Italian way according to which the judgements of church courts are ratified by the civil courts of appeal. When a religious marriage is recognised by the state or is registered by the state, one needs a civil divorce if this marriage fails and before that particular person is allowed to conclude a new, civil or ecclesial valid marriage.

14. *Offences against public peace in places of worship or during religious practice*

See 4 above.

Offences linked to acts of worship and rites

15. *Female genital mutilation*

Female Genital Cutting (FGC) is a term used to refer to any practice which includes the removal or alteration of female genitalia. There are three main types of FGC practised throughout the world: Type I or circumcision, Type II or excision, and Type III or infibulation. These three operations range in severity, from the 'mildness' of Type I, to the extreme Type III. Type II is a recent addition to FGC. Each practice may have short-term and long-term effects. Female circumcision is not just a problem in African countries. In Germany, as many as 6,000 girls of African origin are also threatened with the ritual, e.g. Somalian women. The practice is a culturally sanctioned tradition in about 30 African countries. No religion requires female circumcision, and its practice goes against every person's right to bodily integrity. According to the United Nation's

Declaration on Human Rights, female circumcision is both a form of child abuse, as well as an infringement of a person's basic rights.

Female genital mutilation is considered as dangerous bodily harm, not as grievous bodily harm. Consent does not justify the infringement of rights. The human right of bodily integrity has priority over religious freedom. Finally, the legal regulations on personal data exist, but compulsory registration does not.

Religious motivation: aggravation and attenuation

16. *Offences aggravated by religious motivation*

Chapter 19 CC (Theft and Misappropriation) para. 243 provides that theft is committed by "Whoever takes moveable property not being his own away from another with the intent of unlawfully appropriating the property for himself or a third person". It is a serious case (sect. 4) if the perpetrator steals property, used in religious services or for religious veneration, from a church or other building or space used for the practice of religion. In this case theft shall be punished with imprisonment from three months to ten years. Such cases shall be excluded if the act relates to property of slight value.

According to Chapter 28 CC (Crimes Dangerous to the Public) para. 306a (Serious Arson): whoever sets fire to, or, as a result of setting a fire, destroys, in whole or in part...a church or another building which serves for the practice of religion; shall be punished with imprisonment for not less than one year.

17. *Offences attenuated by religious motivation*

Not applicable in Germany.

Criminal law and sects

18. *Offences linked to the sectarian milieu*

Church advisers in the activity of sects were criticised in a judgement of the 3rd Civil Senate of the Federal Court of Justice of February 14, 2003. The Court decided that specialists in sectarian phenomena should be more careful in their disclosure of the activities of so-called sects. If these specialists do not show a high degree of respect to the sects they analyse, consequences may follow.

In the annual human rights report of the US Department of Foreign Affairs for 2002, Germany was criticised because of its discriminatory treatment of religious minorities. The Church of Scientology was offered as an example. Germany has reacted to this criticism and the US Government stated in its report for 2003 that Germany has overall reacted positively to the questions raised by the Scientology Church. Yet the provinces of Bavaria and Hamburg were still strongly criticised for their discriminatory approach to the Scientology Church. The report refers to the measures taken by these two provinces against a world-wide recognized church. These measures constitute an infringement on freedom of religion and conscience.

State warnings have been issued about the Church of Scientology.[8] Even if allowed to inform and counsel its citizens about certain organizations, the state finds itself in a situation of having at the same time the obligation to protect its citizens and to respect their freedom of conscience and religion. The Scientology Church has opened a European Bureau for Public Relations and Human Rights in Brussels. Moreover, the Administration in Berlin has issued a written statement for the Administrative Court of the Land Berlin in which it states that the Scientology Church is no longer supervised by the Office for Constitutional Protection. The Federal Office for Finances in Bonn has issued an allowance to the Scientology Church in Germany to operate without tax payments. This allowance implies that the Scientology Church in Germany and its American Source Organisation, the Church of Scientology International (CSI), were recognized as religions.

The 2004 Report on International Religious Freedom mentions the generally amicable relationships among religions in Germany, thereby contributing to religious freedom in society. Members of minority religions, including Scientologists, reported an improving climate of tolerance. However, senior government officials continued to refuse to enter into direct dialogue with the Church of Scientology. The Lutheran Church and the state governments of Bavaria, Baden-Wuerttemberg and Hamburg have continued their information campaign against Scientology and other alleged 'cults'. These actions have contributed to persistent negative public attitudes toward members of minority religions.

The US Government discusses religious freedom as part of its overall policy to promote human rights. It placed particular emphasis on support

[8] OVG Hamburg, 17.06.2004, Az.: 1 Bf 198/00.

for direct dialogue between representatives of minority religions and relevant government officials.

In a report of the European Parliament on the situation of respect for fundamental rights in the countries of the European Union, Germany is criticised for its attitude of intolerance and discrimination towards the so-called unrecognised religious organisations, such as the Scientology Church and Jehovah's Witnesses.

However, there are no special offences linked to the sectarian milieu.

Constantinos G. Papageorgiou

Lecturer of Ecclesiastical Law, Aristotle University of Thessaloniki, Attorney-at-Law

THE SPECIAL TREATMENT OF RELIGIONS IN THE CONTEXT OF GREEK PENAL LAW

Greek Penal Law contains the following regulations with respect to the protection of religions in the Greek territory:

Proselytism

The offence of proselytism is contained in Laws 1363/1938 and 1672/1939. Article 4 (2) of Law 1363/1938 (as amended by article 2 of Law 1672/1939) stipulates that proselytism is, mainly, the direct or indirect attempt to penetrate the religious conscience of people of a different creed or religion, in order to modify its contents, provided that, to this end, various unlawful or immoral benefits or promises are employed, by taking advantage of a person's material needs or intellectual weakness or lack of experience.

According to the Greek courts, in judgments issued pursuant to the aforementioned provision, even a parent can commit the offence of proselytism against his/her underage child;[1] and, where proselytism occurs between spouses, it can be grounds for divorce.

The aforementioned provisions contemplate the imposition of very serious penalties on anyone found guilty of proselytism. In particular, a prison sentence is foreseen, without specifying its upper limit, as well as a pecuniary penalty. In addition, where the perpetrator is a Greek citizen, police supervision is also imposed, and where the perpetrator is an alien he/she is extradited (article 4 of Law 1363/1938, as amended by article 2 of Law 1672/39, in conjunction with article 466 of the Penal Code).

However, the consequences of proselytism are not limited to the aforementioned penalties, but also extend to the area of freedom to worship.

[1] However, it has been correctly pointed out that such an act constitutes proselytism only where there is abuse in the exercise of the parents' religious education right towards their children, S. Troianos-G. Poulis, *Ecclesiastical Law* [in Greek], Athens 2003, p. 123.

The absence of any proselytism activity on behalf of a religion's followers is, according to the Council of State case-law, one of the conditions of the individual right for unimpeded exercise of the freedom to worship. Thus, the Administration examines the absence of any acts of proselytism before issuing any authorization to build a temple or a house of prayer.[2]

Following the adoption of the 1975 Constitution, the Administration does not limit itself to ascertaining the absence of any acts of proselytism against the prevailing religion, but also examines whether, in general, the followers of any religion or creed commit acts of proselytism, regardless of whom such acts are directed at. Furthermore, the Administration is entitled to take any other preventative measure deemed appropriate to prevent proselytism, provided such measure is intended to protect the followers of any known religion.

It is true that the prohibition of proselytism is the most particular restriction in the exercise of religious worship. Man, as a spiritual and social being, has the tendency to make others partake of his beliefs often acting, while pursuing such goal, in an uncontrollable and pushy manner, which entitles the state authority to establish limits to the exercise of religious worship.

Offences against religious peace (Articles 198-201 of the Penal Code)

In this case, the object of protection is religious peace and the citizens' religious feelings.

Article 198 (1) of the Penal Code contemplates punishment of the offence of blasphemy, i.e. insulting God, publicly and with a malicious intent. "Insulting" includes all manifestations of lack of respect and contempt in a particularly offensive manner, due either to its form or its content. Thus, decent conversations questioning the existence of God are not considered insulting. Insulting may take place orally, in writing, through gestures, pictures, etc. "God" means any deity, according to the creed of any religion. An insult is considered to take place in public when blasphemy can be noticed by an indefinite number of persons, beyond those to whom it is directed. Blasphemy must be malicious, i.e. the law requires awareness of the significance of the act and a will to commit the offence.

Article 199 of the Penal Code refers to "insulting religions", i.e. insulting the Eastern Orthodox Church or any other known religion. The

[2] Council of State judgment No 995/1970.

object of such insult can be any person considered "sacred" by any religion as well as any ceremony of worship.

Preventing or disturbing religious gatherings is an offence punishable under Article 200 (1) of the Penal Code. This provision aims at protecting freedom, by punishing any act preventing the preparation, commencement or continuation of a gathering of believers for the purposes of worship. Any such gathering shall be protected, regardless of whether it takes place in a private or public, indoors or outdoors (e.g. litany).

Article 200 (2) of the Penal Code provides for punishment of insulting acts taking place in the places of worship of known religions. A "place of worship" is defined in accordance with the rules of law of the relevant religion or creed, without requiring the performance of any act of worship at the time the unlawful act is committed. Moreover, it is not necessary that the act be committed inside the place of worship. It is clear that this provision also protects private places of worship. All acts demonstrating such contempt for the sacred character of the place of worship in such a way that they may offend the religious feelings of the faithful are punishable.

Lastly, in accordance with Article 158 of the Military Penal Code, any officer arbitrarily preventing the reasonable exercise, within the limits imposed by the defined measures of order adopted by the military authority, of the religious duties of any prisoner, or insulting the religion of such prisoner in his/her presence, shall be sentenced to imprisonment for a maximum of one year. It is evident that this provision also protects any known religion (Article 13 of the Constitution).

Aggravated theft

Among the cases of aggravated theft provided for by Article 374 of the Penal Code, it is important to mention, as a means to protect religions, the removal of objects dedicated to divine worship from a place intended for such worship. The objects dedicated to divine worship and the places (not necessarily buildings) intended for such worship shall be determined in each particular case on the basis of the rules of law governing the relevant "known" religious community. Temples of all kinds, as well as temples inside monasteries, etc., are considered places of worship.

The offence is considered to have been committed when the object is removed from the authority of any person entitled to possess it, without requiring that such object be moved outside the place of worship.

It should be noted, however, that where such removal happens in another place (e.g. from a goldsmith's workshop, where a sacred object has been under repair, or in the street during a litany), then it is a case of simple theft. Aggravated theft is punishable by imprisonment for a maximum of ten years.

Usurping the functions of a religious official

The offence is provided for by Article 175 (2) of the Penal Code and refers to officials of any known religion in Greece. Such usurpation is punishable by imprisonment for up to one year or by a pecuniary penalty. The validity of the status of a religious official shall be determined on the basis of the law of the relevant religion or creed, without requiring that the conditions for priesthood determined by the Orthodox Church be met. The offence is committed when the functions of a religious official are exercised by someone upon whom such status has not been conferred or who has been deprived of such status. In addition, it is possible that the acts foreseen in Articles 175 and 176 of the Penal Code might also be used as means of proselytism.

Any person wearing, without being entitled to, the robe of a religious official of the Eastern Orthodox Church or any other known church in Greece shall be sentenced, in accordance with Article 176 of the Penal Code, to prison for up to six months or to a pecuniary penalty. Such act is punishable when committed in public, i.e. in a public space or at a public gathering. The type of robe protected shall be determined on the basis of the provisions of each known religion. In particular, with respect to the Church of Greece, the clergy's robe is described in the Presidential Decree dated 21.01.1931.

The ecclesiastical courts

Lastly, Law 5383/1932 "*On the procedure before Ecclesiastical Courts*" contains procedural arrangements, providing for special Church judicial bodies to punish the offences of clergymen and monks and impose appropriate sanctions. Such bodies include Diocesan Courts, Synodal Courts and Courts for prelates and members of the Sacred Synod. However, both doctrine and case-law agree, with few exceptions, that the organization and functioning of ecclesiastical courts do not respect the fundamental procedural guarantees provided for by the Constitution, in order to ensure impartial dispensation of justice and protection of the defendant clergyman's rights. Such criticism focuses on the following provisions of Law 5383/1932:

(aa) The constitution of Diocesan Courts is presided over solely by the corresponding eparch of the defendant clergyman and not by regular and independent judges appointed for life (Articles 87 (1) and 88 (1) of the Constitution). Clergymen participating as members in this *sui generis* court only have an advisory vote, while the only decisive vote is that of the eparch-president, who is the administrative chief of both the other "judges" and the defendant. To the above, one should also add the frequent lack of basic, or any, legal knowledge on behalf of the eparch-judge;

(bb) the lack of public character of the hearings (Article 93 (2) of the Constitution);

(cc) the non-provision to the defendant of an opportunity to defend himself fully (Article 20 (1) (2) of the Constitution).

The aforementioned deficiencies of Law 5383/1932 have given rise to intense criticism not only by jurists, who often refuse even to characterize such bodies as "courts", but also by clergymen, and particularly by those who have been tried by them. Many of these clergymen, considering that they had been injured by the decisions of Church judicial bodies, have appealed to the Council of State, challenging, through an application for annulment, the decisions of ecclesiastical courts,[3] a situation which has generated a particularly interesting case-law on annulment.

The implementation of Article 11 of Law 1700/1987 regarding the "*Regulation of ecclesiastical property matters*" has allowed defendant clergymen or monks to appear before the ecclesiastical courts "*with a clergyman counsel or an attorney*", and the sittings of such courts may now be attended by clergymen or monks (only). Nevertheless, it is imperative that the anachronistic Law 5383/1932 be replaced by a modern instrument, which will be in line with the Constitution,[4] and the European Convention for the Protection of Human Rights and

[3] It should be noted that, in its very important judgment No 825/1988, the Council of State Plenary Session admitted that, when ecclesiastical courts impose penalties affecting the administrative status of a clergyman (such as deprivation of pay, pecuniary penalty, suspension, etc.), they have a character of "*disciplinary boards*" (and not courts).

[4] It should not be forgotten that clergymen retain the quality of citizens, even after their ordination, together with all rights and obligations recognized by the Constitution and conferred by such quality.

Fundamental Freedoms. Such an instrument[5] could contain the following provisions:

(i) Constitution of a special body of ecclesiastical judges by clergymen, not necessarily eparchs;
(ii) The investigating eparch should not participate in the court judging the particular clergyman;
(iii) An ordinary judge, to be appointed by joint decision of the Church and the President of the Supreme Court, should participate in all ecclesiastical courts;
(iv) The defendant's counsel (attorneys, from any judicial district of the country, and clergymen) should be allowed to attend all stages of the proceedings (pre-trial proceedings and main proceedings);
(v) Attendance of clergymen, monks and relatives of the defendant (limited publicity) should be allowed in ecclesiastical trials during hearings;
(vi) Imposition of pecuniary penalties on presbyters, deacons and monks should be completely abolished;
(vii) Defendants in ecclesiastical courts should enjoy all guarantees and rights provided for by the ordinary procedural law before the state's penal courts.

[5] See the «*Draft Law on Ecclesiastical Justice*» prepared in 1987 by Ch. PAPASTATHIS, Professor of Ecclesiastical Law at the Faculty of Law of Thessaloniki, in *Armenopoulos, Epistimoniki Epetirida Law Bar of Thessaloniki*, vol. 19 (1998), p. 49-77. The draft was submitted to be further elaborated, on May 5, 1987, to the "Study Group on the Relationship between State and Church", which had been established by decision of the then Minister of National Education and Religious Affairs, Antonis Tritsis. However, the Committee did not have the time to complete its work and the elaboration of said draft.

Balázs Schanda

RELIGION IN CRIMINAL LAW: HUNGARY

Hungary has a long historical tradition of the tolerant coexistence of different denominations. Criminal law in general is hardly regarded as a tool to maintain or to promote this tolerance or religious freedom in general. The key legal provisions outlined in this paper may be found in the Annex.

1. Penal protection of religion

Blasphemy – defamation of communities: Blasphemy – when causing public scandal – used to be a crime under the first criminal code (1878).[1] The provision, however, was abolished in the early years of the communist regime. At the moment there is no offence similar to blasphemy; only the protection of national symbols has any vestigial similarity to blasphemy.[2] Neither God, nor religion, enjoy the protection of criminal legislation. What criminal law protects is freedom of religion, enjoyed by any person having a religious conviction and religious communities themselves. Freedom of expression enjoys special protection. Only incitement to hatred is criminalized: whoever incites to hatred publicly against the Hungarian nation, any national, ethnic, racial group or certain prescribed groups of the population is guilty of a misdemeanor punishable by imprisonment for up to three years.[3] Incitement to hatred towards a religious community (or a non-religious or anti-religious community) would fall under this provision. The religious sentiments of the population, or certain groups of the population, however, enjoy no protection under criminal law. Since 1992 mere defamation no longer qualifies as a criminal offence, as the Constitutional Court has found that this would be a disproportionate limitation of freedom of expression.[4] Since then Parliament has several times considered proposed amendments that

[1] Act V/1878. §190.
[2] Act IV/1978 (Criminal Code) §269/A.
[3] Criminal Code §269.
[4] Decision 30/1992. (V. 26.) AB.

would have penalized hate speech, but the Constitutional Court has consistently upheld its liberal approach to free speech.

Desecration of a place of worship or of sacred objects of any religion: The "Violation of the Right to Worship" is penalized as a misdemeanour. Thus:

> "A fine not exceeding HUF one hundred thousand may be imposed on whoever causes a public scandal on premises designated for the purposes of the ceremonies of a registered church or desecrates the object of religious worship or an object used for conducting the ceremonies on or outside the premises designated for the purposes of ceremonies."[5]

Hindering or disrupting a religious meeting may be covered by the same provision. In a more serious case the matter may be covered by the provisions on menaces (see below). In any event, in a case when a procession was disrupted by a driver forcing believers to let his car pass along the road the criminal offence of the "violation of the Freedom of Conscience and Religion" has been applied.[6]

Menaces, violence or application of force against freedom of religion or conscience: The Criminal Code has a provision on "the Violation of the Freedom of Conscience and Religion".[7] This was incorporated into the Code by the Act IV/1990:

> "Whoever
> a) restricts another person by violence or by threats in his freedom of conscience,
> b) prevents another person from freely exercising his religion by violence or by threats, commits a crime, and is punishable by imprisonment up to three years."

Crimes of this nature have to be intentional; the intent, however, may be indirect.

Discrimination because of religion: The Constitution contains a general prohibition against discrimination, amongst other things on the basis of religion (Art. 70/A.). Discrimination, however, as such is not a criminal offence. Nevertheless, abuse of a person because of his or her actual or assumed membership of a national, ethnic, racial or religious group is punishable by five years' imprisonment.[8] However, it is difficult to prove

[5] Act 69/1999 (on misdemeanors), §150.
[6] BH 1999.292.
[7] Criminal Code §174/A.
[8] Criminal Code §174/B.

that a person was attacked because of his or her membership of a religious group.

Disrupting a funeral: There is no offence that would correspond to the disruption of a funeral. It could be regarded as a public nuisance (*rowdyism*),[9] or as an impiety.[10]

Abuse of a corpse or desecration of a sepulchre: The abuse or desecration of a sepulchre could be punished as an impiety.

Proselytizing and apostasy: Proselytism and apostasy are not criminal offences – the terms do not appear in the Hungarian legal vocabulary. Apostasy, in the sense of leaving a religious order or the membership of the clergy, has not been a criminal offence in state law (local penal regulations in the Middle Age may have contained such provisions, when canon law of course had not been separated from state law). Apostasy in the original sense (leaving Christianity for paganism) had been penalized by royal acts in the early stages of Christianity in medieval Hungary.

Today, it is difficult to define what apostasy means in a multidenominational society. Changing denomination (becoming a Protestant) was criminalized (without success) only in the early years of the Reformation.[11] Protestants (Lutherans and Calvinists) first acquired religious freedom in 1606. After a series of restrictions – a Catholic becoming a Protestant made himself punishable according to decrees from 1731 (Carolina Resolututio) and 1751 (Maria Theresia) – the freedom of these denominations was reaffirmed in 1791. The right to convert from Catholicism to Protestantism was reaffirmed in 1844.[12] Since 1848, religion (and up to the mid-20th century very rarely lack of religion) had no relevance in the public standing of the individual (with the exception of anti-Jewish legislation that was in force between 1938 and 1945).

The misuse of religious garments or impersonation of office: The misuse of religious garments is not regarded as a criminal offence. Ultimately, the very general offence of fraud could be applied – certainly only if misleading someone or keeping them in error was intended to achieve an unlawful profit and damage has been caused.[13]

[9] Criminal Code §271.

[10] Criminal Code §181.

[11] Act 54/1523, Act 4/1525 ("Lutherani omnes de regno extirpantur (...) et comburantur!"; the legislator intended to gain the support of Catholic powers to resist the Ottoman invasion).

[12] Act III/1844.

[13] §318.

2. Offences by ministers of religion

Disclosure of a secret obtained in the exercise of ministry: Protection of the seal of the confessional is no different from the protection of other "vocational" secrets, such as secrets entrusted to medical doctors or advocates. There is no general duty of denunciation. With crimes (like terrorism) where the duty to denounce does exist, the seal of confession – on the basis of freedom of religion – would prevail. Disclosure of a secret obtained in the exercise of ministry may constitute "violation of privacy".[14]

Celebration of religious marriage before civil marriage: Due to the strict separation of church and state, religious marriages have no civil effect. Celebrating a religious marriage before (or without) a civil marriage has not been a criminal offence since 1962. Introducing such a crime would be a blatant violation of religious freedom and of the separation clause of the Constitution. From the legal point of view, a wedding at church is merely a church service; eventually it can serve as evidence of cohabitation.

Offences against public peace in a place of worship or during a religious practice: Religious communities would fall under the same legal regime as any other entity with regard to offences against public peace. The religious nature of the group or the place would not prevent prosecution – but it would certainly make the issue very delicate.

Clergy enjoy protection under criminal law as persons "performing public duties", such as lawyers, teachers, medical doctors on duty, or firemen.[15]

3. Offences linked to acts of worship or to rites

Female genital mutilation: Female genital mutilation is not mentioned in the Hungarian criminal code and has not been an issue so far with Hungarian criminal law. If such a case was to happen, it could qualify as an aggravated assault.

4. Religious motivation as a cause of aggravation or attenuation of the offence

Religious motives are not mentioned in the Criminal Code, either as aggravating or as attenuating circumstances. A religious motivation could

[14] §177.

[15] Act 4/1978, 137, 2. j.

eventually be a "base reason purpose" but the contrary might also apply – it depends on the circumstances of the case. No offence would be attenuated by religious motivation in general.

5. Criminal law and sects

There are no offences linked to sects or sectarian activities. These would fall under the general criminal law.

Summary

Hungarian criminal law seems to lack specialized criminal offences with regard to religion. Religion has been 'privatized' to a high degree. Special offences – such as that on the violation of freedom of conscience and religion – are hardly ever applied.

ANNEX
Violation of the Freedom of Conscience and Religion

§174/A. Any person who:

a) restricts another person in his freedom of conscience by applying violence or duress;

b) prohibits another person from freely exercising his religion by applying violence or duress;

is guilty of a felony punishable by imprisonment for up to three years.

Violence Against a Member of a National, Ethnic, Racial or Religious Group

§174/B. (1) Any person who assaults another person for being part, whether in fact or under presumption, of a national, ethnic, racial or religious group, or compels him by applying coercion or duress to do, not to do, or to endure something, is guilty of a felony punishable by imprisonment for up to five years.

(2) The punishment shall be imprisonment between two to eight years if the act of crime is committed:

a) by force of arms;

b) with a deadly weapon;

c) causing a considerable injury of interest;

d) with the torment of the injured party;

e) in groups;

f) in criminal conspiracy.

Violation of Privacy,

§177. (1) Any person who reveals any private secret he has obtained in a professional or official capacity without due cause is guilty of a misdemeanor punishable with a fine.

(2) The punishment shall be imprisonment for up to one year, community service work, or a fine, if the crime results in a considerable injury of interest.

Defamation

§179. (1) Any person who engages in the written or oral publication of anything that is injurious to the good name or reputation of another person, or uses an expression directly referring to such a fact, is guilty of a misdemeanor punishable by imprisonment for up to one year, community service work, or a fine.

(2) The punishment shall be imprisonment for up to two years, if the defamation is committed:

a) for a malicious motive or purpose;
b) in broad public;
c) causing considerable injury of interest.

Libel

§180. (1) Any person who, apart from what is contained in Section 179, makes a false publication orally or any other way:

a) tending to harm a person's reputation in connection with his professional, public office or public activity;
b) in broad public;

shall be punishable for a misdemeanor by imprisonment for up to one year, community service work, or a fine.

(2) Any person who engages in an act to defame someone by physical assault shall be punishable in accordance with Subsection (1).

Desecration

§181. Any person who violates the memory of the dead by the means defined in Section 179 or Section 180 is guilty of a misdemeanor punishable as defined therein.

Justification

§182. (1) A person charged with the crimes defined in Sections 179-181 shall not be liable for prosecution if there is conclusive evidence that the publication claimed as defamatory is proven to be accurate.

(2) Justification shall apply where the statement, publication or expression was communicated for reasons of public interest or by the lawful interest of any person.

Public Nuisance

§271. (1) Any person who displays apparently anti-social and violent conduct aiming to incite indignation or alarm in other people is guilty of a misdemeanor punishable by imprisonment for up to two years, community service work, or a fine, if such act does not result in a criminal act of greater gravity.

(2) The punishment shall be imprisonment for a felony for up to three years if public nuisance is committed:

a) in group;
b) in a manner gravely disturbing public tranquility.

(3) Banishment may also be applied as an ancillary punishment.

Fraud

§318. (1) 'Fraud' shall mean when a person uses deceit, deception, or trickery for unlawful financial gain, and thereby causes damage.

(2) The punishment shall be imprisonment for a misdemeanor for up to two years, community service work, or a fine, if the fraud results in a minor damage, or the fraud involves a petty offence value and it is committed:

a) as part of a criminal conspiracy;
b) at the scene of a public emergency;
c) by way of a business operation.

(3) (Repealed)

(4) The punishment shall be imprisonment for a felony for up to three years if:

a) the fraud results in damage of considerable value;
b) the fraud involves a minor value and it is committed in the manner defined in Paragraphs a)-c) of Subsection (2).

(5) The punishment shall be imprisonment between one to five years if:

a) the fraud results in damage of substantial value;
b) the fraud involves a considerable value and it is committed in the manner defined in Paragraphs a)-c) of Subsection (2).

(6) The punishment shall be imprisonment between two to eight years if:

a) the fraud results in damage of particularly considerable value;
b) the fraud involves a substantial value and it is committed in the manner defined in Paragraphs a)-c) of Subsection (2).

(7) The punishment shall be imprisonment between five to ten years if:

a) the fraud results in damage of particularly substantial value;
b) the fraud results in particularly considerable damage committed in the manner defined in Paragraphs a)-c) of Subsection (2).
c) as part of a criminal organization.

Paul Colton[1]

RELIGION IN CRIMINAL LAW IN IRELAND[2]

Introduction

The vicissitudes of Ireland's history, and notably of its conflicts, have a profound and inescapable religious dimension.[3] Since the Reformation, and before a new era of toleration[4] culminating in Catholic Emancipation in 1829[5] and the disestablishment of the Church of Ireland in 1871,[6] one of the aims of laws governing religion was to introduce and maintain uniformity in religious adherence and practice as an adjunct to the conquest and government of Ireland.[7] Following Irish Independence in 1922 the Constitution of the Irish Free State[8] guaranteed, and its successor, *Bunreacht na hÉireann*[9] in 1937,[10] guarantees freedom of religion.

The religious landscape of modern Ireland is a complex phenomenon but one where the people still profess religious belief and adherence.[11]

[1] Church of Ireland (Anglican/Episcopalian Bishop of Cork) and Research Associate at the Centre for Law and Religion at Cardiff University. I am grateful to Chancellor Lyndon MacCann S.C. and to my colleague at the Centre for Law and Religion at Cardiff University, Professor Mark Hill, for their advice when I was preparing this paper; and also to Dr Shane Kilcommins of the Centre from Criminal Law and Human Rights at University College, Cork for reading it and commenting on it.

[2] This paper will deal solely with the Republic of Ireland.

[3] See e.g. M. Tanner *Ireland's Holy Wars: The Struggle for a Nation's Soul 1500 -2000* (Yale University Press, New Haven, 2001). For Irish History generally see e.g. J. Beckett, *The Making of Modern Ireland, 1603-1923* (Faber, London 1966) R. Foster *Modern Ireland, 1600 – 1972* (Allen Lane, London 1988).

[4] See e.g. The Toleration Act 1689, 1 William III and Mary II, c.18, Catholic Relief Act 1778, 18 George III c. 60, Catholic Relief Act 1791, 31 George III, c. 32 and The Test Act 1673, 25 Charles II c.2.

[5] The Emancipation Act 1829, 10 Geo. IV c. 7.

[6] Irish Church Act 1869, 32 & 33 Vict, c.42.

[7] For the Reformation in Ireland see e.g. A. Ford *The Protestant Reformation in Ireland: 1590 – 1641* (Four Courts Press, Dublin 1997); S. Ellis *Ireland in the Age of the Tudors: 1447 – 1603* (Longman, London 1998); C. Lennon *Sixteenth Century Ireland* (Gill and Macmillan, Dublin 2005).

[8] Constitution of the Irish Free State (Saorstát Éireann) Act 1922 Article 8.

[9] The Constitution of Ireland.

[10] *Bunreacht na hÉireann* Article 44.

[11] See the results of the Census of Ireland 2006 www.cso.ie/census last accessed on 9th July, 2008.

In the Census of 2006, of a total Irish population of 4,239,848, all but 256,640 (who either did not state their religion or who stated that they were of 'no religion') indicated that they had a religious affiliation. This stark statistical statement takes no account, obviously, of secularisation, evaluation of intensity of levels of adherence or of sociological, theological or psychological perspectives on the place of religion in Irish society. While for many centuries there has been a small Jewish community in Ireland alongside the Christian churches (the majority Roman Catholic Church and the principal minority churches: the Church of Ireland, the Presbyterian Church and the Methodist Church), since the 1950s there has been a growing Islamic community, and now the arrival of an increasing diversity of other Christian denominations and small numbers of adherents of other faiths is perceptible since the increased immigration of the early 1990s.

The import of all this is that while historically religion has been a dynamic in the story of Ireland's tragic conflicts (which are still being dealt with today[12]) there is an emerging era in which on-going religious adherence, new religious practice and a new encounter with multiculturalism (race, language and national identity) are the formative dynamics.

It is against this historic background that religion and criminal law in Ireland are examined in line with the questions posed by the Consortium.[13]

Religion and Criminal Law[14]

Religion exists in twenty-first century Ireland in a more widely articulated and all-encompassing statutory framework than that of previous eras when specific crimes against religion were delineated. There has been a clear shift. Crimes which specifically enunciate offences against religion as an institution, and against the officials and property of religious institutions have, for the most part, been superseded by statutory offences widely articulated within the generality of the criminal law and designed to protect instead individuals who hold religious beliefs and their freedom to adhere to such beliefs.[15]

[12] See e.g. The Hard Gospel Project of the Church of Ireland: www.hardgospel.net last accessed on 9th July 2008.

[13] The European Consortium for Church and State Research meeting in Finland, October 2008.

[14] For a general introduction to criminal law in Ireland see C. Hanly *An Introduction to Irish Criminal Law* (Gill and Macmillan, Dublin 2006).

[15] It should be noted also that alongside the criminal law, civil wrongs may also be of relevance where there is an obvious overlap with the law of Torts. For the definition of a crime and classification of crimes see C. Hanly *op cit* 15-9.

For example, obstructing an ordained person on his way to take a religious service was an offence under section 36 of the Offences Against the Person Act 1861[16] but is no longer a specific offence. Instead, protection is afforded by virtue of the Non-Fatal Offences Against the Person Act 1997. The crime of sacrilege[17] was repealed by the Criminal Law (Jurisdiction) Act 1976[18] and this area of the law (offences against property) is substantially governed now by the Criminal Justice (Theft and Fraud Offences) Act 2001. Scrutiny of the Malicious Damage Act 1861[19], for example, and its replacement by new legislation (notably the Criminal Damage Act 1991) illustrates that transitions in the law such as this have resulted in a simplification of the law.[20]

In recent decades, many common law rules have been codified by legislation. [21] In addition, Ireland has been undergoing an ambitious and methodical programme of statute law revision setting, as its principal objective, the repeal of all the legislation which remains on the statute book which was enacted prior to Irish independence in 1922, leading ultimately to the codification of the Irish statute book.[22]

Church members and Crime

The obvious point which has to be made at the outset in relation to religion and crime in Ireland (and presumably any jurisdiction) is that the rule of law applies to churches and church members and they are obliged to keep the laws of the State. All churches in Ireland (and by analogy other faith communities), none of which is established, are voluntary and unincorporated associations. The formation of such "associations" is a right protected generally by the Irish Constitution,[23] which also protects

[16] 24 & 25 Vic. C.100.

[17] Larceny Act 1916 (6 & 7 Geo. V c.50) s.24.

[18] Section 21.

[19] 24 & 25 Vic. c.97.

[20] See Law Reform Commission 'Report on Malicious Damage' (LRC 26-1988)(September 1988) 9.

[21] See *Bunreacht na hÉireann*, Article 15.2.1: the exclusive power of law-making not resides with the Oireachtas (the Irish Parliament). See also House of Lords Select Committee on Religious Offences, First Report (10th April 2003) available at http://www.parliament.the-stationery-office.co.uk/pa/ld200203/ldselect/ldrelof/95/9501.htm last visited on 10th July, 2008.

[22] Statute Law Revision Act 2007. See also the website of the Attorney General of Ireland: www.attorneygeneral.ie last accessed on 1st July 2008.

[23] *Bunreacht na hÉireann*, Article 40.6.1.iii (*Bunreacht na hÉireann* – the Constitution of Ireland).

freedom of expression[24] and assembly.[25] All three rights are subject to public order and morality.[26]

Members of churches are, therefore, members of voluntary associations.[27] They are bound by the law of the land generally and, where crime is committed, church members, like any other members of society, are subject to its disciplinary and penal force.

Members of churches are also, as a matter of both civil and church law, obliged to know and adhere to the rules of their church,[28] which must be implemented in a way consonant with the requirements of constitutional/natural justice.[29] They will be taken to be acquainted with those rules.[30] Conversely, the governing authorities of an association (such as rugby clubs, [31] or a soccer league[32] – and by analogy a church) should not act *ultra vires* its own laws because they form the basis of the contractual relationship between it and the members, and the members with each other. The rules only apply to someone who is a member.[33] By resigning membership a person may, therefore, voluntarily remove him or herself from the ambit of internal church rules.

[24] *Bunreacht na hÉireann*, Article 40.6.1.i.

[25] *Bunreacht na hÉireann*, Article 40.6.1.ii.

[26] *Bunreacht na hÉireann*, Article 40.6.1.

[27] *O'Keefe v. Cullen* I.R. 7 C.L. 319; and *State (Colquhoun) v. D'Arcy* [1936] IR 641. See P. Colton 'Towards a Canonical Definition of Membership of the Church of Ireland' in [2008] Vol. 10 ECLJ 3 For unincorporated associations and clubs generally see D. Ashton and P. Reid, *Ashton and Reid on Club Law* (Jordans, Bristol 2005). See also D. McNamara, *A Legal Guide for Clubs and Associations* (First Law, Dublin 2005) and N. Cox and A. Schuster, *Sport and the Law* (First Law, Dublin 2004)

[28] *O'Dea v O'Connor* 71 ILTR, 169 and *Buckley and others v AG and Power* 84 ILTR 9.

[29] *Ahern v Molyneux* [1965] Ir. Jur. Rep., 59; *Bolger v Osborne and others and the Turf Club* [2000] 1 ILRM 250. See also *Barry and Rogers v Ginnity and others* (unreported) *Irish Times Law Report, Irish Times*, [6th September, 2005]; *Stuart v Haughley Parochial Church Council* [1936] Ch. 32; and *John v Rees* [1970] Ch 345, [1969] 2 All ER 274, [1969] 2 WLR 1294. For the same requirement in relation to other types of voluntary associations see: Athletics – *Quirke v Bord Luthchleas na hÉireann* [1998] IR 83; Weightlifters: *Baker v Jones* [1954] 3 All ER, 553. See also Article 6, European Convention on Human Rights, and European Convention on Human Rights Act 2003.

[30] *Raggett v Musgrave* (1827) 2 Car & P 555 at 252. For the internal rules of some churches in Ireland see e.g.: *Code of Canon Law* [1983] (Roman Catholic Church); *Constitution of the Church of Ireland* (2003) (Church of Ireland – Anglican/Episcopalian); and *The Code: the Book of the Constitution and Government of the Presbyterian Church in Ireland.*

[31] *Walsh v Butler* [1997] 2 ILRM 81; *Clancy v Irish Rugby Football Union* [1995] 1 ILRM, 193. See generally, N. Cox and A. Schuster, *op cit* at 62-3.

[32] *Dundalk Interim Co. Ltd. (Dundalk Football Club) v Eircom League and Kilkenny City Football Club* [2001] 1 IR, 434; See generally N. Cox and A. Schuster, *op cit*, 62-4.

[33] *Barry and Rogers v Ginnity and others* (unreported) *Irish Times Law Report, Irish Times*, [6th September, 2005].

The laws of some churches refer, in some instances, to the consequences for a member (usually an ordained person) of conviction in accordance with the criminal law of the State. For example, a member of the clergy or a bishop of the Church of Ireland shall be liable to disciplinary action if he or she is guilty of '...any crime for the time being punishable by law in any part of Ireland.'[34]

The specific issues raised by the Consortium will now be addressed.

Defamation or Outrage

In England and Wales the common law offences of blasphemy and blasphemous libel have very recently been abolished.[35] Ironically, the situation in Ireland (where the common law offences of blasphemy and blasphemous libel developed in the pre-independence era in tandem with their development in England) remains in place, even if anachronistic. However, as long as blasphemy remains an offence which is specifically articulated in *Bunreacht na hÉireann* it cannot be disregarded.[36]

The Blasphemy Act 1697[37] never applied in Ireland and there was no Irish equivalent.[38] O'Higgins points out, however, that the Irish Act of Uniformity 1568[39] '... forbade ridicule of the liturgy of the Established Church. This same Act repealed a number of early Irish Statutes against heresy, which had been revived but never put into operation during the reign of Mary.'[40]

The development in common law of the offence of blasphemy has been extensively analysed elsewhere.[41] In addition to the landmark

[34] *Constitution of the Church of Ireland* Ch. VIII s.25.

[35] Criminal Justice and Immigration Act 2008, s.79.

[36] For a full consideration of this constitutional provision see J. Casey, *Constitutional Law in Ireland* (Sweet and Maxwell, Dublin 2000) 543-74; G Hogan and G Whyte, *J.M. Kelly: The Irish Constitution* (LexisNexis, Dublin 2004) 1723-79.

[37] 9 Will. III c.32 (England).

[38] P.O'Higgins, 'Blasphemy in Irish Law' (1960) 23 MLR 151 at 155.

[39] 2 Eliz I c.2 (Ireland) Repealed by the Statute Law Revision (Pre-Union Irish Statutes) Act 1962.

[40] P.O'Higgins, *op cit* 156.

[41] C. Kenny, 'The Evolution of the Law of Blasphemy' 1 CLJ 127; P.O'Higgins, *op cit*; Law Reform Commission 'Consultation Paper on the Crime of Libel'(August 1991); Law Reform Commission 'Report on the Crime of Libel'(LRC 41-1991)(December 1991); Report of the Constitution Review Group (Dublin 1996) 291-304; N.Cox 'Sacrilege and Sensibility: The Value of Irish Blasphemy Law' (1997) 19 DULJ 87; N. Cox, *Blasphemy and the Law in Ireland* (Edwin Mellen Press, New York 2000).

English cases,[42] in Ireland the cases of Emlyn in 1703 (denying the divinity of Christ);[43] two men acquitted in 1726 (drinking a health to the devil and confusion to Almighty God);[44] John Burk in 1794 (denying the divinity of Christ and the Genesis account of creation);[45] Brother John in 1852 (burning an Authorised Version of the Bible);[46] the Reverend Vladimir Petcherine in 1855 (while burning 'evil' literature he inadvertently burned a Bible, but was found not guilty of blasphemy)[47] shaped the understanding of the common law offence. It was an offence against the established church (the Church of Ireland, which was itself disestablished in 1871[48]).

The common law evolved in its understanding of blasphemy,[49] moving from Sir Matthew Hale's strict liability ('Contumelious reproaches of God or of the religion established are punishable here... the Christian religion is part (parcel) of the law itself[50]) to a requirement that there had to be some intemperate or scurrilous language.[51] In 1917 in *Bowman v*

[42] *R v Taylor* 3 Keble 607 and 621 (1627) aka Taylor's Case (1676) 1 Vent 293, 86 ER 189 (uttered orally offensive words against religion); Woolston's Case Fitzgibbon 64, 2 Strange 834, 1 Barnardiston KB 162, 266 (1729) (coarse and offensive handling of the biblical narratives and the miracles of Christ); *R v Williams* 26 St. Tr. 653, 715 (publication of Thomas Paine's *Age of Reason*); *Shore v Wilson* 9 Cl & F 355; *R v Hetherington* (1841) 4 St Tr (N.S.) 563, 5 Jur 529 (Lord Denman took account of the tone, style and spirit of the 'blasphemy'); *Briggs v Hartley* (1850) 19 LJR Ch 416 (bequest for an essay prize in Natural Theology failed on the grounds that it was incompatible with Christianity); *R v Ramsey and Foote* (1883) 15 Cox C.C. 231 (hideously offensive caricatures of religion in a weekly paper); *Bowman v Secular Society Ltd* [1917] AC 406 (the propagation of anti-Christian doctrines was not, of itself, illegal); *R v Gott* (1922) 16 Cr.Ap.R. 87 (scurrilous ridicule of the narrative in the Four Gospels – offence, however, must be measured by the general community); *R v Lemon* [1979] AC 617 (an obscene poem and illustration allegedly vilifying the life of Christ: held that an intention to publish blasphemous matter was sufficient *mens rea* to constitute the offence of blasphemy and that it was not necessary to prove a specific intention to blaspheme); *R v Chief Magistrate, ex parte Choudhury* [1991] QB 429 (*The Satanic Verses* – the common law offence of blasphemy was confined to the Christian religions).

[43] P.O'Higgins, *op cit* 159; Law Reform Commission 'Consultation Paper on the Crime of Libel' (August 1991) p15 at par 14.

[44] P.O'Higgins, *op cit* 160.

[45] *Id.*

[46] P.O'Higgins, *op cit* 161.

[47] *R v Petcherine* (1855) 7 Cox 79.

[48] Irish Church Act 1869.

[49] See Law Reform Commission 'Consultation Paper on the Crime of Libel'(August 1991) at 80.

[50] Per Sir Matthew Hale in *R V Taylor* 3 Keble 607 and 621 (1627) aka Taylor's Case (1676) 1 Vent 293, 86 ER 189; Woolston's Case Fitzgibbon 64, 2 Strange 834, 1 Barnardiston KB 162, 266 (1729).

[51] *R v Hetherington* (1841) 4 St Tr (N.S.) 563, 5 Jur 529.

Secular Society Ltd [52] the House of Lords ruled that the mere propagation of anti-Christian doctrines was not, of itself, illegal. Lord Parker of Waddington said that '...to constitute blasphemy at common law there must be such an element of vilification, ridicule, or irreverence as would be likely to exasperate the feelings of others and so lead to a breach of the peace.'[53]

It appears that it was the common law offence of blasphemy which the architects of *Bunreacht na hÉireann* had in mind when they framed Article 40.6. 1°.[54] It provides as follows

> The State guarantees liberty for the exercise of the following rights, subject to public order and morality:
>
> i. of the citizens to express freely their convictions and opinions.
> The education of public opinion being, however, a matter of such grave import to the common good, the State shall endeavour to ensure that organs of public opinion, such as the radio, the press, the cinema, while preserving their rightful liberty of expression, including criticism of Government policy, shall not be used to undermine public order or morality or the authority of the State.
> The publication or utterance of blasphemous, seditious, or indecent matter is an offence which shall be punishable in accordance with law.

Analysing the Irish Law of blasphemy in 1960 O'Higgins referred to *Bowman* and concluded that

> .... there is considerable doubt as to the meaning of the term *"blasphemous"* as used in the Irish Constitution and in modern Irish legislation. The Constitution is open to a retrogressive interpretation which would discard the process which has been made in the legal toleration of sincere religious dissent and rational disbelief; the high-water mark of which is to be seen in *Bowman's* case. Not only may the Constitution be interpreted in a way unfavourable to the non-believer, but even to members of religions other than those which are recognised by the Constitution. Such uncertainty is undesirable.[55]

Blasphemy is referred to in a number of Irish Statutes. Under section 7 of the Censorship of Films Act 1923 the Official Censor may form the opinion that a film is unfit for general exhibition in public by reason of

[52] *Bowman v Secular Society Ltd* [1917] AC 406.
[53] *Bowman v Secular Society Ltd* [1917] AC 406.
[54] P.O'Higgins, *op cit* 150, 153. See also generally D. Keogh and A. McCarthy *The Making of the Irish Constitution 1937* (Mercier Press, Dublin, 2007).
[55] P.O'Higgins, *op cit* 166.

its being indecent, obscene or blasphemous.[56] This has been extended to include advertisements for films.[57] According to Casey, '[a]t least one film – the Monty Python *Life of Brian* – appears to have been refused a certificate as blasphemous, but otherwise this ancient offence has had no impact in modern Irish legal practice.'[58] Section 13 (1) of the Defamation Act 1961 provides that the composition, printing or publication of a blasphemous or obscene libel shall be an offence.[59] The Act, however, does not define 'blasphemous.'

The Defamation Bill 2006 which was initiated in Seanad Éireann[60] on 6th December 2006 proposed the repeal of the Defamation Act 1961 deleting, therefore, the offence of written blasphemy (with a consequent gap between the Constitution and the statutory provisions). However, on 20th May 2009, in a speech to the Select Committee on Justice, Equality Defence and Women's Rights, the Minister for Justice announced that instead of holding a referendum on whether or not the constitutional reference to blasphemy be deleted (conceding that the 'optimal approach' was to abolish it) he favoured, instead, a reform of the law.[61]

As a result at the Committee Stage an amendment was introduced and passed making provision for the offence of blasphemous libel in the following terms:

> **36.**– (1) A person who publishes or utters blasphemous matter shall be guilty of an offence and shall be liable upon conviction on indictment to a fine not exceeding €25,000.
> (2) For the purposes of this section, a person publishes or utters blasphemous matter if—
> (*a*) he or she publishes or utters matter that is grossly abusive or insulting in relation to matters held sacred by any religion, thereby causing outrage among a substantial number of the adherents of that religion, and
> (*b*) he or she intends, by the publication or utterance of the matter concerned, to cause such outrage.
> (3) It shall be a defence to proceedings for an offence under this section for the defendant to prove that a reasonable person would

[56] Censorship of Films Act 1923 to 1992.
[57] Censorship of Films (Amendment) Act 1925, s.3.
[58] J. Casey, *op cit* 573.
[59] That Act also repealed the following relevant legislation: the Criminal Libel Act 1819 (60 Geo. III & 1 Geo. I, c.8), the Law of Libel Amendment Act 1888 (51 & 52 Vict. c.64).
[60] The Irish Senate.
[61] See his speech at www.justice.ie last accessed on 24th August 2009.

find genuine literary, artistic, political, scientific, or academic value in the matter to which the offence relates.
(4) In this section "religion" does not include an organisation or cult—
(*a*) the principal object of which is the making of profit, or
(*b*) that employs oppressive psychological manipulation—
(i) of its followers, or
(ii) for the purpose of gaining new followers.

It remains to be seen whether, if tested, this provision is adjudged to be constitutional or whether prosecutions, if pursue, are successful. What is clear is that the exact nature of the offence remains vague and uncertain.

Similar vagueness and uncertainty had been identified in 1991 by the Law Reform Commission which had concluded that the offence of blasphemy was 'intended to be confined to religious beliefs in the Judaeo-Christian religion'[62] and that the offence was 'totally uncertain as to both its *actus reus* and its *mens rea*.'

Their report stated that

> We are of the view that there is no place for the offence of blasphemous libel in a society which respects freedom of speech. The strongest arguments in its favour are (i) that it causes injury to feelings, which is a rather tenuous basis on which to restrict speech, and (ii) that freedom to insult religion would threaten the stability of society by impairing the harmony between the groups, a matter which is open to question in the absence of a prosecution. Indeed, we consider the absence of prosecution to indicate that the publication of blasphemous matter is no longer a social problem.[63]

Four years later, however, in the wake of a Referendum on Divorce, John Corway, a carpenter from Dublin, maintained that a cartoon in the *Sunday Independent* insulted the feelings and religious convictions of readers generally by treating the sacrament of the Eucharist and its administration as objects of scorn and derision. The cartoon illustrated a plump and comic caricature of a priest. The priest was holding a host in his right hand and a chalice in his left hand. He appears to be offering the host to three figures on the left hand side of the cartoon. The three figures were prominent politicians; but they are turning away and appear to be waving goodbye. At the top of the cartoon are printed the words *'Hello progress*

[62] Law Reform Commission 'Report on the Crime of Libel' (LRC 41-1991) (December 1991) par. 17.
[63] *Id.*

– *bye bye Father'* (a play on one of the campaign posters in the divorce referendum campaign) followed by a question mark. Corway applied, as required by section 8 of the Defamation Act 1961, to the High Court for consent to the commencement of a criminal prosecution. The High Court rejected the application.

On appeal to the Supreme Court that decision was upheld.[64] Barrington, J said:

> In this state of the law, and in the absence of any legislative definition of the constitutional offence of blasphemy, it is impossible to say of what the offence of blasphemy consists. As the Law Reform Commission has pointed out neither the *actus reus* nor the *mens rea* is clear. The task of defining the crime is one for the Legislature, not for the Courts. In the absence of legislation and in the present uncertain state of the law the Court could not see its way to authorising the institution of a criminal prosecution for blasphemy against the Respondents.[65]

Following Corway, the common law and statutory prohibitions have been described as 'inoperable'[66] and 'neutralised'.[67]

The Constitution Review Group had, in any event, recommended in 1996 that the retention of the present constitutional offence of blasphemy is not appropriate.[68] The removal of the provision from the Constitution would require a referendum.[69] In the wake of the signing into law by the President of the Defamation Act 2006 there have been renewed calls for a referendum on the matter to be held.

Transition from Blasphemy to Incitement to Religious Hatred

In a debate in Seanad Éireann[70] on 11th March 2008, at the report and final stages of the Defamation Bill 2006, Senator David Norris raised the question of blasphemy. His remarks illustrate a transition from an understanding of blasphemy as a protection afforded to the State, the State's relationship with a particular religious outlook and indeed a protection of

[64] *Corway v Independent Newspapers Ltd* [1999] 4 IR 485; [2000] 1 ILRM 426.

[65] *Corway v Independent Newspapers Ltd* [1999] 4 IR 485; [2000] 1 ILRM 426 at 436-7.

[66] J. Casey, *op cit* 574.

[67] G Hogan, and G Whyte, *J.M. Kelly: The Irish Constitution* (LexisNexis, Dublin 2004) 1753 at 7.5.72.

[68] Report of the Constitution Review Group (Dublin 1996) 297.

[69] *Bunreacht na hÉireann*, Article 46.2.

[70] The Irish Senate or upper house.

the deity, to a contemporary emphasis on protecting the individual or groups of individuals:

> On the question of blasphemy, my view is that God, assuming he or she exists, is quite able to sustain slings and arrows of mere mortals in terms of his or her reputation. What people are usually doing when talking about blasphemy is protecting their own feelings. It is understandable that people have strong feelings, but this is covered by incitement to hatred.[71]

The then Minister for Justice, Equality and Law Reform, Brian Lenihan, T.D.,[72] (himself an eminent lawyer) appeared to share this view in the same Seanad debate when he said:

> Christianity in the general sense and, possibly, other theistic religions are protected by the law of blasphemy in our modern law. There has been no prosecution. The one attempted prosecution led to the Supreme Court consideration that we should consider modernising the law of blasphemy to protect all faiths. The difficulty in that regard is that the essence of the offence seems to consist of the hurt that is caused to the believer. This is a dangerous basis for an offence.
>
> It is far safer to have an offence based on the incitement to hatred or the immediate proximity of the statement to the causing of a breach of the peace. If we could redefine blasphemy in that way and if that were acceptable, I would be much more comfortable with the offence. I am not sure we can do that constitutionally or whether the reference in the Constitution means it is frozen in time with the meaning it carried in 1937. The all-party committee can reflect on these matters.[73]

The stirring up of hatred against a person or people on the grounds, *inter alia*, of religion is an offence under section 2 of the Prohibition of Incitement to Hatred Act 1989. There is a widely held opinion, however, that the Prohibition of Incitement to Hatred Act 1989 is ineffective.[74] Although enacted in 1989 there had been no prosecutions under the legislation by 9th November 1995.[75] In the subsequent two year period there were only eleven complaints, and charges had been brought in response to none of

[71] Seanad Debate Vol. 188 No. 22.

[72] T.D. – *Teachta Dála* (a Deputy of Dáil Éireann – the house of representatives of the *Oireachtas* – Irish Parliament).

[73] Seanad Debate Vol. 188 No. 22.

[74] See e.g. National Consultative Committee on Racism and Interculturalism 'Prohibition of Incitement to Hatred Act 1989; A Review, (August 2001) www.nccri.com last visited on 1st July 2008.

[75] Dáil Éireann Reports Vol. 458 (9th November 1995).

these.[76] A review of the legislation was announced in 2000[77] following which a number of successful prosecutions were brought under the legislation arising from racist incidents. The review has not been completed and in the light of recent statistics (about apparently racially motivated crimes) further calls for its review have been made.[78]

The Prohibition of Incitement to Hatred Act 1989 defines hatred as hatred against a group of persons in the State or elsewhere on account of their race, colour, nationality, religion, ethnic or national origins, membership of the travelling community, or sexual orientation.[79] The offences under this Act are those which may be aggravated (or attenuated) by religious motivation.

It is an offence (on the part of an individual or of a body corporate[80]) to publish or distribute written material;[81] to use words, behave or display written material (anywhere other than in a private residence, or inside a private residence so that the words, behaviour or material are heard or seen by persons outside the residence);[82] to distribute, show or play a recording of visual images or sounds, if any of these are threatening, abusive or insulting and are intended or, having regard to all the circumstances, are likely to stir up hatred.[83]

In the case of published or distributed written material, if the accused person is not shown to have intended to stir up hatred, it shall be a defence for him or her to prove that he or she was not aware of the content of the material or recording concerned and did not suspect, and had no reason to suspect, that the material or recording was threatening, abusive or insulting.[84] In the case of words, materials or behaviour in a private residence, it is a defence to show that, being in the private residence at the time, there was no reason to believe that the words, behaviour or material concerned would be heard or seen by a person outside the residence;[85] or having shown that there was no intention to stir up hatred, '…to prove that he did not intend the words, behaviour or

[76] Dáil Éireann Reports Vol.484 (10th December 1997).

[77] 'Review of Incitement to Hatred law announced' *Irish Times* 6th September 2000.

[78] 'Government urged to review Incitement to Hatred Act' *Irish Independent* 22nd June 2008.

[79] Prohibition of Incitement to Hatred Act 1989 s.1.

[80] Prohibition of Incitement to Hatred Act 1989 s.7.

[81] Prohibition of Incitement to Hatred Act 1989 s. 2 (1)(a).

[82] Prohibition of Incitement to Hatred Act 1989 s. 2 (1)(b).

[83] Prohibition of Incitement to Hatred Act 1989 s.2 (1)(c).

[84] Prohibition of Incitement to Hatred Act 1989 s.2 (2)(a).

[85] Prohibition of Incitement to Hatred Act 1989 s.2 (2)(b)(i).

material concerned to be, and was not aware that they might be, threatening, abusive or insulting.'[86]

The Act delineates further related offences (and defences) where an item involving threatening, abusive or insulting visual images or sounds is broadcast;[87] where a person prepares or is in possession of materials which are threatening or abusive or insulting and are intended or, having regard to all the circumstances, is likely to stir up hatred.[88]

Desecration of a place of worship or sacred objects

Section 24 of the Larceny Act 1916[89] delineated the offence of sacrilege. Sacrilege involved breaking and entering any place of divine worship to commit a felony or breaking out of any place of divine worship, having committed a felony. The punishment was penal servitude for life. That section was repealed by the Criminal Law (Jurisdiction) Act 1976 and the entire Act has now been repealed.[90] As has been previously noted, as a specific offence against religion, this offence no longer exists, but the crime has been subsumed within the generality of the law: in the Criminal Justice (Theft and Fraud Offences) Act 2001. That Act includes, *inter alia*, the following offences: theft,[91] making gain or causing loss by deception,[92] obtaining services by deception,[93] making off without payment,[94] unlawful use of computers,[95] false accounting,[96] burglary,[97] aggravated burglary[98] and robbery.[99]

In the Malicious Damage Act 1861[100] churches, chapels, meeting houses and other places of divine worship were specifically listed as objects of protection.[101] On 4th March 1986 three men were indicted under

[86] Prohibition of Incitement to Hatred Act 1989 s.2 (2)(b)(ii).
[87] Prohibition of Incitement to Hatred Act 1989 s.3.
[88] Prohibition of Incitement to Hatred Act 1989 s.4.
[89] 6 & 7 Geo. V c.50.
[90] Criminal Justice (Fraud and Theft) Offences Act 2001.
[91] Criminal Justice (Theft and Fraud Offences) Act 2001 s.4.
[92] Criminal Justice (Theft and Fraud Offences) Act 2001 s.6.
[93] Criminal Justice (Theft and Fraud Offences) Act 2001 s.7.
[94] Criminal Justice (Theft and Fraud Offences) Act 2001 s.8.
[95] Criminal Justice (Theft and Fraud Offences) Act 2001 s.9.
[96] Criminal Justice (Theft and Fraud Offences) Act 2001 s.10.
[97] Criminal Justice (Theft and Fraud Offences) Act 2001 s.12.
[98] Criminal Justice (Theft and Fraud Offences) Act 2001 s.13.
[99] Criminal Justice (Theft and Fraud Offences) Act 2001 s.14.
[100] 24 & 25 Vic. c.97.
[101] See Law Reform Commission 'Report on Malicious Damage' (LRC 26-1988) (September 1988) 5.

section 39 of the Act before a jury for maliciously damaging a statue of the Blessed Virgin Mary in a grotto in Ballinspittle, County Cork. The statue has become famous and a focus of veneration as the so-called moving statue.[102] However, the judge directed the jury to acquit the accused on the grounds that it had not been proven that the grotto was a place of divine worship. Crimes under that Act (*inter alia* damage to a place of worship or sacred objects) have been replaced by a general offence in respect of criminal damage to another person's property: the Criminal Damage Act 1991. That Act provides for the offences of damaging property,[103] threatening to damage property,[104] possessing anything with intent to damage property[105] and accessing computer data without authorisation.[106]

Disrupting a Religious Meeting or a Funeral and Offences against public peace in a place of worship or during a religious practice

Section 2 of the Ecclesiastical Courts Jurisdiction Act 1860[107] makes it an offence to engage in riotous, violent, or indecent behaviour in England or Ireland in any cathedral church, parish or district church or chapel… of any religious denomination… whether during the celebration of divine service or at any other time, or in any churchyard or burial ground. It is clear that the offence may be committed either in the church itself or in the churchyard or burial ground; and, moreover, that it need not only be committed during divine service but at any other time. In *Worth v Terrington* [108] Baron Parke stated that '…it is clear that an act done in a church during divine service might be highly indecent and improper, which would not be so at another time.'[109]

Under the same section of the 1860 Act it is also an offence to molest, let, disturb, vex, or trouble, or by any other unlawful means disquiet or

[102] 'Villagers gather at grotto' *Irish Times* 26th July 1985 and 'Bishop cautious on statue' *Irish Times* 31st July 1985 and 'Gang damages "moving" statue in axe attack' *Irish Times* 1st November 1985.

[103] Criminal Damage Act 1991 s.2.

[104] Criminal Damage Act 1991 s.3.

[105] Criminal Damage Act 1991 s.4.

[106] Criminal Damage Act 1991 s.5.

[107] 23 & 24 Vict. c.32. The relevant sections – sections 2 and 3 have not been repealed in Ireland (see Schedule 1 of the Statute Law Revision Act 2007). The remainder of the Act was repealed by the Statute Law Revision Act 1983.

[108] *Worth v Terrington* (1845) 13 M. & W. 781 see also *Abrahams v Cavey* [1968] 1 QB 479.

[109] *Worth v Terrington* (1845) 13 M. & W. 781 at 795.

misuse any preacher duly authorized to preach therein, or any clergyman in holy orders ministering or celebrating any sacrament, or any divine service, rite, or office, in any cathedral, church, or chapel, or in any churchyard or burial ground.[110]

Section 36 of the Offences Against the Person Act 1861[111] made it an offence by threats or force to obstruct or prevent or endeavour to obstruct or prevent '...a clergyman or other minister in or from celebrating divine service or otherwise officiating in any church, chapel, meeting house, or other place of divine worship, or in or from the performance of his duty in the lawful burial of the dead in any churchyard or other burial place...' This section has been repealed by the Non-Fatal Offences Against the Person Act 1997. The offences delineated in the 1997 Act include, for example, assault,[112] assault causing harm,[113] causing serious harm,[114] threats to kill or cause serious harm,[115] injuring or threatening to injure with a syringe,[116] coercion (intimidation, damaging the property of another, persistent following, watching and besetting, following a person with others in a disorderly manner),[117] harassment,[118] and false imprisonment.[119] In addition, under section 9 of the Criminal Justice (Public Order) Act 1994 it is an offence, without lawful authority or reasonable excuse, wilfully to prevent or interrupt the free passage of any person or vehicle in any public place (which includes cemeteries, churchyards and churches).

The Criminal Justice (Public Order) Act 1994 abolished a number of common law offences relating to public order and provided statutory offences *in lieu* of them. The Act includes cemeteries and churchyards in its definition of public places. Churches themselves are included in the definition also as '... any premises or other place to which at the material time members of the public have or are permitted to have access, whether

[110] *Cope v Barber* (1872) LT 7 CP 393 (a clergyman collecting the alms, and prevented from doing so by the churchwardens, was not protected by this section of the Ecclesiastical Courts Jurisdiction Act 1860 as he was not celebrating the divine service when collecting the alms). See also *Vallancy v Fletcher* [1897] 1 QB 265 (a clergyman can be convicted of riotous or indecent behaviour in a church or churchyard).

[111] 24 & 25 Vict. c.100.

[112] Non-Fatal Offences Against the Person Act 1997, s.2.

[113] Non-Fatal Offences Against the Person Act 1997, s.3.

[114] Non-Fatal Offences Against the Person Act 1997, s.4.

[115] Non-Fatal Offences Against the Person Act 1997, s.5.

[116] Non-Fatal Offences Against the Person Act 1997, s.6.

[117] Non-Fatal Offences Against the Person Act 1997, s.9.

[118] Non-Fatal Offences Against the Person Act 1997, s.10.

[119] Non-Fatal Offences Against the Person Act 1997, s.15.

as of right or by express or implied permission, or whether on payment or otherwise…'[120] The offences under the Act include the following when done in such a public place: intoxication;[121] offensive conduct (any unreasonable behaviour which, having regard to all the circumstances, is likely to cause serious offence or serious annoyance to any person who is, or might reasonably be expected to be, aware of such behaviour);[122] and the use of threatening, abusive or insulting words or behaviour with intent to provoke a breach of the peace (or being reckless as to whether such a breach may occur).[123] In addition, with regard to any place, the following offences are capable of being committed: entering,[124] trespass,[125] riot,[126] violent disorder,[127] and affray.[128]

On 19th June 2006 a number of Afghan refugees entered Saint Patrick's Cathedral in Dublin and went on hunger strike.[129] By their occupation the routine worship of the Cathedral could not continue in the usual place or manner. Although charges against them were ultimately dropped, they were initially charged under the Prohibition of Forcible Entry and Occupation Act 1971. It provides *inter alia* for the offences of forcible entry of land or vehicles[130] and remaining in forcible occupation of land or vehicles.[131]

Abuse of a corpse or desecration of graves

The traditional understanding in law is that there is no property in a dead body,[132] but that the executors are entitled to possession.[133] A dead body cannot, therefore, be the subject of theft.[134] However, according to

[120] Criminal Justice (Public Order) Act 1994, s.3 (d).
[121] Criminal Justice (Public Order) Act 1994, s.4.
[122] Criminal Justice (Public Order) Act 1994, s.5.
[123] Criminal Justice (Public Order) Act 1994, s.6.
[124] Criminal Justice (Public Order) Act 1994, s.11.
[125] Criminal Justice (Public Order) Act 1994, s.13.
[126] Criminal Justice (Public Order) Act 1994, s.14.
[127] Criminal Justice (Public Order) Act 1994, s.15.
[128] Criminal Justice (Public Order) Act 1994, s.16.
[129] 'Church of Ireland pleads with men to leave Cathedral' *Irish Times* 20th May, 2006; 'Peaceful end to Afghan Protest' *Irish Times* 22nd May, 2006; 'DPP drops Afghan Hunger Striker Charges' *Irish Times* 6th June, 2006.
[130] Prohibition of Forcible Entry and Occupation Act 1971, s.2.
[131] Prohibition of Forcible Entry and Occupation Act 1971, s.3.
[132] See A. Fellows *The Law of Burial* (Hadden, Best and Co, London 1940) 24; See also *R v Sharpe* (1857) Dea and Bell 160; also D. Smale *Davies' Law of Burial Cremation and Exhumation* (Shaw and Sons, Glasgow 2002) 65.
[133] *Williams v Williams* (1882) 20 Ch 659; *R v Fox* (1841) 2 QB 246.
[134] D. Smale *op cit.*

Phillimore '...the carcase that is buried belongs to no one, but when buried in consecrated ground is subject to ecclesiastical cognizance, if abused or removed; and if not buried in consecrated ground is under the protection of the temporal courts. Though, as Lord Coke says, a corpse is *nullius in bonis*; yet taking up a dead body...is an indictable offence at law, as an act highly indecent and *contra bonos mores*.'[135]

It would appear that, as in England, in Ireland, there were (and may still be) common law offences in relation to corpses such as unauthorised disinterment,[136] the sale of a body for dissection purposes,[137] refusing to deliver a body to executors on their request[138] and permitting a body to be dissected without consent.[139] Specific statutes govern inquests and exhumation.[140] It is an offence to obstruct the removal of a body where a coroner has considered it necessary to hold an inquest on, or a post-mortem examination of, the body of a deceased person.[141] In relation to a death which takes place in the State the following are among the 'qualified informants' who are obliged to register the particulars of the death within three months: a person who found the dead body, a person who took charge of a dead body or procured the disposal of it.[142]

Senseless damage to graves is, sadly, not uncommon and is frequently referred to as desecration.[143] According to Phillimore, the defacing of tombs, sepulchres or monuments (provided they were erected with the consent of the Ordinary) is a common law offence.[144] Such damage is more likely to be prosecuted under the Criminal Damage Act 1991. Specific provisions are made for the protection of national monuments which may include some churchyards and graveyards,[145]

[135] R. Phillimore *The Ecclesiastical Law of the Church of England* (Sweet and Maxwell, London 1895) Vol. I at 689. See also *Hayne's Case* 12 Co.p. 113.

[136] *R v Sharpe* (1857) Dea and Bell 160.

[137] *R v Cunnick* (1822) Dow and Ry NP 13.

[138] *R v Scott* (1842) QB 248.

[139] *R v Young* (1784) 4 Wentworth's Pleadings 219.

[140] Coroners Act 1962.

[141] Coroners Act 1962 s.46 (1).

[142] Civil Registration Act 2004 s.36(5).

[143] See e.g. 'Students blamed for smashing headstones' *Irish Times* 16th June, 2008. *Bennett v Bonaker* (1828) 2 Hag. Eccl., 25; 3 Hag. Eccl., 17; *Adlam v Colthurst* (1867) L.R. 2A and E.,30.

[144] R. Phillimore *op cit* Vol. I at 691-2; see also *Spooner v Breswter* 10 Mo. 494; *Hutchins v Denziloe and Loveland* 1 Consist 172.

[145] National Monuments Act 1930 as amended by the National Monuments (Amendment) Acts 1954 to 2004.

Freedom of Religion, Proselytising and Apostasy

Bunreacht na hÉireann guarantees certain freedoms as fundamental rights: freedom of expression, assembly and association[146] and freedom of religion.[147] This shapes the Irish legal approach to religion.

The constitutional guarantee is subject to public order and morality.[148] Under Article 44.1 the

> "... State acknowledges that the homage of public worship is due to Almighty God. It shall hold His Name in reverence, and shall respect and honour religion."[149]

While this has been interpreted as underpinning Christianity,[150] the courts have also made clear that the benefits are not confined to Christians.[151] The current constitutional position was well summarised in *Quinn's Supermarket v Attorney General* by Walsh J:

> The effect of these various guarantees is that the State acknowledges that the homage of public worship is due to Almighty God. It promises to hold his name in reverence and to respect and honour religion. At the same time it guarantees freedom of conscience, the free profession and practice of religion and equality before the law to all citizens, be they Roman Catholics, Protestants, Jews, Muslims, agnostics or atheists. But Article 44.1 goes further and places the duty on the State to respect and honour religion as such. At the same time the State is not placed in the position of an arbiter of religious truth. Its only function is to protect public order and morality.[152]

More recently, this view was quoted with approval by Barrington J in *Corway v Independent Newspapers (Ireland) Ltd.*[153]

Against this background, apostasy (the total repudiation of the Christian faith) which was, at one time, an offence '...as so openly transgresses the precepts of religion, natural or revealed'[154] is not a matter of

[146] Article 40.6.

[147] Article 44. See also European Convention on Human Rights, Article 9 and European Convention on Human Rights Act, 2003 s.2.

[148] *Bunreacht na hÉireann* Article 44.2.1.

[149] *Bunreacht na hÉireann* Article 44.1. The Constitutional Review Group, by majority decision, called in 1996 for the deletion of Article 44.1 and its replacement by the phrase "The State guarantees to respect religion."

[150] *Norris v Attorney General* [1984] IR 36.

[151] *McGee v Attorney General* [1974] IR 284 and in *Norris v Attorney General* [1984] IR 36.

[152] *Quinn's Supermarket v Attorney General* [1972] IR 1 at 23-4.

[153] *Corway v Independent Newspapers (Ireland) Ltd* [1999] 4 IR 484.

[154] HW Cripps *The Law Relating to the Church and Clergy* (Sweet, London 1863).

State law but may, in some instances be a matter of internal church law.[155] Proselytising is not a matter of State law unless it becomes so intense, relentless and insensitive that, in a possible set of circumstances, it might be construed as constituting another offence such as those enumerated previously under the Non-Fatal Offences Against the Person Act 1997 (e.g. assault,[156] coercion [intimidation, persistent following, watching and besetting, following a person with others in a disorderly manner][157] and harassment[158]) or under section 9 of the Criminal Justice (Public Order) Act 1994 (wilfully preventing or interrupting the free passage of any person or vehicle in any public place). Similarly, if any group, such as a sect or religious group, impedes the freewill of a member and detains them against his or her will, this may give rise to a charge of false imprisonment.[159]

Discrimination because of religion

Irish equality legislation makes it an offence to discriminate against someone on any one of nine grounds, including religion. Protection is afforded in relation to employment[160] and under the Equal Status Acts (buying and selling goods, provision or use of services, obtaining or disposing of accommodation and educational establishments).[161] Discrimination is treating one person less favourably than another.[162] The 'religion ground' arises where one person has a different religious belief from the other, or that one has a religious belief and the other has not.[163] In the employment context, there is an exemption, however, where it is shown that such discrimination is necessary on the part of a religious, educational or medical institution in order to preserve the religious ethos of that institution or to protect the institution from being undermined by an

[155] *Code of Canon Law* [1983] Canon 751.

[156] Non-Fatal Offences Against the Person Act 1997, s.2.

[157] Non-Fatal Offences Against the Person Act 1997, s.9.

[158] Non-Fatal Offences Against the Person Act 1997, s.10.

[159] Non-Fatal Offences Against the Person Act 1997, s.15. There are also statutory constraints on religious advertising and broadcasting: Broadcasting Authority Act, 1960 and Broadcasting Act 2001. See also *Murphy v Independent Radio and Television Commission* [1997] 2 ILRM 467; *Murphy v Independent Radio and Television Commission* [1999] 1 IR 12 and *Murphy v Ireland* 441779/98 [2003] ECHR 352.

[160] Employment Equality Acts 1998 and 2004.

[161] Equal Status Acts 2000 to 2004.

[162] Employment Equality Act 1998 s.6.

[163] Employment Equality Act 1998 s.6(2)(e).

employee.[164] An institution established to train ministers of religion does not discriminate where it admits students of only one gender or of a particular religious belief.[165]

Misuse of religious garment or false state of office

Clerical or religious attire is governed as a matter of internal church law or canon law[166] in most churches in Ireland, and in some is a matter of convention and even personal choice. There is empirical evidence of religious garments and clerical dress being used for the purpose of fun, theatre and even fancy-dress. One might envisage more sinister scenarios, however, where, for example, a person misuses clerical attire as part of a strategy in another crime, such as to commit a fraud or as part of a deception.[167] Gaining consent by deception is not consent for the purposes of a charge of theft.[168] Making a gain or causing a loss by deception is an offence,[169] as is obtaining services by deception.[170] It is not the wearing or misuse of the religious garment, however, which is the crime.[171] Similarly, where the religious garments or clerical attire have been taken by another this may amount to tort of conversion.[172]

Revelation of a secret obtained in the exercise of the ministry

Churches and church officers have significant responsibilities to protect data in accordance with Irish data protection legislation.[173] The question of pastoral or personal secrets or confidences arises most notably, however, in relation to the question of sacerdotal privilege.[174] The sacrament of penance is governed as a matter of internal Church law: for example,

[164] Employment Equality Act 1998 s.37.

[165] Equal Status Act 2000, s.7.

[166] See e.g. *Constitution of the Church of Ireland* Ch. IX s.12 (Canon 12) or *Code of Canon Law* [1983] Canons 284 and 929.

[167] 'Gardaí looking for fraudster posing as Scottish Priest' *Irish Times* 17th August 2007 and 'Sex attacker seen posing as priest' *Irish Independent* 30th July 2007.

[168] Criminal Justice (Theft and Fraud Offences) Act 2001. s.4(2).

[169] Criminal Justice (Theft and Fraud Offences) Act 2001. s.6.

[170] Criminal Justice (Theft and Fraud Offences) Act 2001. s.7.

[171] See nonetheless the ancient position of religious impostors in HW Cripps *op cit* 840

[172] See B. McMahon and W. Binchy *Law of Torts* (Tottel, Hayward's Heath, 2007) Ch.30 and J.Healy *Principles of Irish Torts* (Clarus Press, Dublin 2006) 12.63 to 12.66.

[173] Data Protection Act 1988 and Data Protection (Amendment) Act 2003.

[174] See C. Fennell *The Law of Evidence in Ireland* (Tottel, Hayward's Heath 2003) 8.65 to 8.75.

by the *Code of Canon Law* of the Roman Catholic Church in Canons 965 to 997. In Anglicanism, where auricular confession is optional and not normative, the principle of inviolability of the seal of the confession is a matter of moral imperative and convention.[175] Moreover, it has been argued in an Irish case that the seal of the confessional was respected in the courts of England before the Reformation and indeed, before the Norman Conquest.[176]

In Ireland in *Cook v Carroll* [177] Gavin Duffy, J, in a case involving a priest who had acted as spiritual adviser to an action, followed the four general principles of Wigmore[178] and held that they had been fulfilled in the case:

1. the communications must originate in a confidence that they will not be disclosed;
2. this element of confidentiality must be essential to the full and satisfactory maintenance of the relation;
3. the relation must be one which in the opinion of the community ought to be sedulously fostered;
4. the injury which would ensue to the relation by the disclosure of the communication must be greater than the benefit thereby gained for the correct disposal of litigation.[179]

Based on these principles and arguing from the special place of the Roman Catholic Church in *Bunreacht na hÉireann*,[180] he held that the priest was protected by sacerdotal privilege and that he was not in contempt of court by maintaining the seal of the confessional.

In *ER v JR*[181] Carroll, J held that communications made to a minister of religion who was acting as a marriage counsellor are privileged in that the four conditions set out in *Cook v Carroll* were present. She held,

[175] For England see e.g. N. Doe, *The Legal Framework of the Church of England* (Clarendon Press, Oxford 1996) 353-5. See also R. Bursell *Liturgy, Order and the Law* (Clarendon Press, Oxford 1996) at 227. In England, see also *R v Gilham* (1828) 1 Mood CC 186, CCR, *Broad v. Pitt* 3 C&P 518, *R v. Shaw* (1834) 6 C& P 392, *Greenlaw v. King* (1838) 1 Beav 145, and *R v. Griffin* (1853) 6 Cox CC 219.

[176] Per Gavin Duffy, J in *Cook v Carroll* [1945] IR 515 at 517.

[177] *Cook v Carroll* [1945] IR 515. See, however, *Forristal v Forristal and O'Connor* (1966) 100 ILTR 182.

[178] Wigmore *Treatise on the Anglo-American System of Evidence in Trials at Common Law* (Boston 1940) par. 2285.

[179] *Cook v Carroll* [1945] IR 515 at 520.

[180] A special status subsequently removed from the Constitution by referendum. See Fifth Amendment of the Constitution Act 1972.

[181] *ER v JR* [1981] ILRM 125.

however, (following an English case – *Pais v Pais*[182]) that the privilege was that of the spouses and not of the minister for religion and might be waived by mutual consent of the spouses.

The Law Reform Commission Report on Contempt of Court took the view that in Ireland

> [i]n the area of religious confidences, problems do not appear to have arisen in practice and it has not been suggested to us that the law is in need of any clarification. As with spousal privilege, *we do not recommend any legislation at the moment.* [183]

More recently, in *Johnson v Church of Scientology*[184] sacerdotal privilege was a key element argued in the case before the High Court. The defendants attempted to invoke sacerdotal privilege in order to avoid discovery of the plaintiff's counselling notes. The High Court rejected this claim and said that the defendant was not entitled to rely on the pre-reformation common law protecting the seal of the confessional even against waiver by the penitent. In the appeal before the Supreme Court the issue of sacerdotal privilege was not appealed and the judgment of the High Court is, therefore, instructive on this matter (notwithstanding the fact that the appeal was allowed on other grounds).

In the High Court, Geoghegan, J acknowledged that there could be situations where a privilege might arise in relation to counselling by a priest or minister, or in relation to secular counselling, any such privilege might always be waived by the person being counselled. Geoghegan, J said:

> I do accept… that there can be situations where a privilege may arise in relation to counselling by a priest or minister but any such privilege may always be waived by the person being counselled… Indeed it is difficult to see why a relationship between a parish priest and parishioner is any different than a relationship between a priest or clergyman of any kind and a person coming from anywhere being counselled by him. Furthermore,… I would be inclined to think that in modern times when all kinds of secular counselling is available, and in particular marriage counselling, there may well be a privilege which the courts would uphold in some circumstances, but it would always be capable of waiver unilaterally by the persons being counselled.

[182] *Pais v Pais* [1970] 3 DPP 830.

[183] Law Reform Commission Report on Contempt of Court (LRC 47-1994) (September 1994) at 4.21.

[184] *Johnson v Church of Scientology* [2001] IESC 25; [2001] 1 IR 682; [2001] 2 ILRM 110.

Celebration of religious marriage before civil marriage

In Ireland the formalities of marriage are governed by the Civil Registration Act 2004. Until 4th November 2007 the formalities of marriage in Ireland were regulated principally by common law and by nineteenth century statutes.[185] One of the principal recent changes is that places are no longer registered for marriage. A register – the Register of Solemnisers – is kept of those who are permitted to solemnise marriages.[186] In the case of a religious body application is made to the Registrar General for inclusion of certain of its members (clergy) on the Register of Solemnisers.[187] The law recognises as marriage that in respect of which statutory notice has been given (three months);[188] where a Marriage Registration Form has been issued by the Registrar;[189] which is solemnised by a registered solemniser (who may be either an appointed State official or a duly nominated member of the clergy) in accordance with the law;[190] in which the required declarations are made, [191] the ceremony is one recognised by the Registrar General; [192] and the marriage is registered.[193] The question of an offence being committed by celebrating a religious marriage before civil marriage does not, therefore, arise. However, there are offences arising from non-compliance with the provisions of the Civil Registration Act 2004.[194]

Female genital mutilation/cutting

Female genital mutilation is not prevalent in Ireland. In 2001 a Private Members bill – the Prohibition of Female Genital Mutilation Bill 2001 – was presented in Dáil Éireann by Deputy Liz McManus but the

[185] Marriages (Ireland) Act 1844, Marriage Law (Ireland) Amendment Act 1863, Matrimonial Causes and Marriage Law (Ireland) Amendment Act 1870, Matrimonial Causes and Marriage Law (Ireland) Amendment Act 1871, Marriage Law (Ireland) Amendment Act 1873, Marriages Act 1936, Marriages Act 1972 and the Family Law Act, 1995. For full detail of the pre -2007 formalities of marriage see A Shatter *Family Law* (4th Edition, 1997, Butterworth, Dublin) 157-77.

[186] Civil Registration Act 2004, s.53.

[187] Civil Registration Act 2004, s.54.

[188] Civil Registration Act 2004, s.46.

[189] Civil Registration Act 2004, s.48.

[190] Civil Registration Act 2004, s.51.

[191] Civil Registration Act 2004, s.51.

[192] Civil Registration Act 2004, s.51.

[193] Civil Registration Act 2004, s.49.

[194] Civil Registration Act 2004, s.69.

second reading never occurred and the Bill lapsed. Concerns have been expressed that with increasing immigration, the practice may be occurring.[195] Following a much publicised radio broadcast, the Minister for Health sought the advice of the Attorney-General and was, it appears, advised that female genital mutilation would comprise an intentional act which causes serious harm and would thus be an offence under section 4 of the Non-Fatal Offences Against the Person Act 1997. Section 4 provides that '...a person who intentionally or recklessly causes serious harm to another shall be guilty of an offence.' If the act of female genital mutilation was not found to have resulted in 'serious' harm, it would still be open to the Garda Síochána to prosecute for the similar, though less serious, offence of assaulting a person causing harm, provided for by section 3 of the 1997 Act.[196] The fear of female genital mutilation in other countries has frequently been used as an argument in applications for judicial review of decisions of the Refugee Appeals Tribunal.[197]

As an aside it is interesting to note that in 2003 the domestic circumcision with a razor blade of a male child by a medically unqualified individual resulted in the death of the four week old baby.[198] The subsequent case and acquittal of the man who performed the circumcision case raised awareness nationally of unregulated male circumcision.[199] Subsequently the Minister for Children and Youth Affairs at the Department of Health and Children established a Committee on Cultural Male Circumcision which reported in 2006 and which acknowledged the religious reasons for male circumcisions in some religions.[200] The Report acknowledged that Orthodox Jewish circumcisions are performed by trained Rabbis in Ireland: '...these circumcisions are carried out with parental consent, are deemed to be in the interest of the child, and are competently performed.'[201]

[195] 'Alert over female circumcision query' *Irish Independent* 7th March 2001.

[196] Dáil Éireann Reports Vol.630 (6th February 2007).

[197] See e.g. *A v Minister for Justice and Anor* [2007] IEHC 169; *Obende v Minister for Justice and Anor* [2006] IEHC 162; *D and Anor v Refugee Appeals Tribunal and Ors* [2008] IEHC 19; *Okeke v The Minister for Justice and Ors* [2006] IEHC 46.

[198] 'Man Charged with Illegal Circumcision' *Irish Independent* 21st November 2003.

[199] 'Jury clears Nigerian man involved in circumcision death case' *Irish Independent* 8th October 2005. See also 'Gardai investigate alleged backstreet circumcision.' *Irish Times* 19th August, 2004.

[200] http://www.dohc.ie/publications/pdf/circumcision.pdf?direct=1 last visited on 1st July 2008.

[201] *Id* at 11.

Conclusion

Ireland is a changing society where multi-culturalism and religious diversity are a new and vibrant phenomenon. The legal context of a previous (pre-1870) era, designed to bolster one religious outlook and the State which espoused that outlook, no longer pertains. In the context of an Irish constitutional framework which guarantees freedom of expression, association, assembly and religion, the religious offences of that era have, in the main, now been subsumed into modern generic laws in which also many common law offences have been codified.

It remains to be seen whether that framework meets the emerging and undoubted challenge of affording protection to individuals in an Ireland where different nationalities, other races and people of disparate religious beliefs have recently arrived to Irish communities. The perceived ineffectiveness of the Prohibition of the Incitement to Hatred Act 1989 is clearly troubling: a key concern for the future will be the outcome of the long-awaited review of that Act.

Enrico Vitali

RELIGION ET DROIT PÉNAL EN ITALIE

Protection pénale des confessions religieuses

La protection pénale des confessions religieuses est assurée en Italie par le Code Pénal et des Lois spéciales. La récente Loi 24/02/2006 n. 85 (Modifications au Code Pénal en matière de délits d'opinion) a modifié l'ancienne discipline de 1930, suite à la vague émotionnelle suscitée par la «guerre des vignettes» de 2005. Le Code (Livre II, titre IV «sur les délits contre le sentiment religieux et contre la pitié des défunts»), s'inspirait d'une considération positive du sentiment religieux comme composante du patrimoine moral de la nation italienne, pour la réalisation des fins éthiques de l'État fasciste (religion comme «instrumentum regni»). La religion catholique était donc considérée comme bien de civilisation. Sa protection était prévue par les articles 402 C.P. (outrage de la religion de l'État), 724 C.P. (juron contre Divinité, Symboles ou Personnes vénérés par la religion de l'État), 403 et C.P. (offenses à la religion de l'État par outrage aux personnes ou aux choses) et 405 C.P. (trouble ou empêchement de célébration du culte catholique). Ces dispositions donnaient lieu à une inégalité d'une part *qualitative*, parce le délit d'outrage à la religion (artt. 402 s. C.P.) et de juron (art. 724 C.P.) n'étaient pas prévus pour les autres cultes et d'autre part *quantitative*, parce que les faits visés aux art. 403, 404 et 405 C.P. étaient sujets à une peine minorée s'ils étaient dirigés contre les cultes admis (art. 406 C.P.). Il y avait une contradiction indubitable avec les principes fondamentaux de la Constitution Républicaine de 1948: principe d'égale liberté devant la loi de toutes les confessions religieuses (art. 8, 1, Const.); principe d'égalité des citoyens sans distinction de religion (art. 3 Const.); droit de libre manifestation de la pensée (art. 21 Const.); droit de liberté religieuse (art. 19 Const.). Ce fut seulement à partir des années '90 que la Cour Constitutionnelle entreprit de démolir l'échafaudage du Code en déclarant inconstitutionnelle la protection privilégiée sous le profil *qualitatif* (pour l'art. 402 C.P. Cf. Arrêt 508/2000; pour l'art. 724 C.P. Cf. Arrêt 440/1995) et sous le profil *quantitatif*, avec l'adaptation des peines prévues aux art. 403, 404 et 405 C.P. par rapport à celles, mineures, prévues à l'art. 406 C.P. (Cf. Arrêts n. 168/2005;

n. 329/1997; n. 327/2002). L'expression «outrage» et «outrager», là où la conduite n'est pas décrite mais indiquée à travers un jugement, est une formule ambiguë et indéterminée. Pour la jurisprudence le terme «outrager» évoque l'idée de raillerie, de moquerie, d'injure basse et vulgaire, de considérer lâche le bien protégé, exposer la religion au mépris. C'est un délit d'expression, par des discours, écrits, figures, etc.

La Loi de réforme a simplement restauré la discipline précédente, en effaçant toute référence à la religion de l'État/religion catholique (Cf. C. Const. n. 508/2000 et n. 1 Protocole additionnel à l'accord 18/2/1984 entre l'État Italien et le Saint-Siège, qui a déclaré que le principe selon lequel la religion catholique est la seule religion de l'État Italien n'était plus en vigueur). Le nouvel art. 403 C.P. (sur les «offenses à une confession religieuse par outrage aux personnes»), établit que «toute personne qui offense une confession religieuse en public en outrageant celui qui la professe, est puni d'une amende de € 1.000 à € 5.000» (si l'outrage est envers un ministre du culte l'amende est de € 2.000 à € 6.000). Fondamentale est la notion de «confession religieuse», expression qui a remplacé la formule «religion de l'État», qui constitue le point de référence pour le bien juridique protégé. Étant donné le manque de critères juridiques précis, la C. Const., par l'arrêt n. 195/1993, en affirmant tout d'abord qu'il ne suffit pas qu'un groupe se qualifie lui-même comme confession religieuse, a établi que la nature de confession religieuse peut résulter soit du fait d'avoir stipulé un Accord avec l'État (art. 8, 3° al., Const.), soit d'avoir obtenu une reconnaissance publique réelle d'organisme à caractère religieux par une mesure administrative, un arrêt, ou, enfin, par la commune considération (critère très incertain et indéfini). Ont été exclus de la catégorie les mouvements religieux qui n'ont pas un but extérieur et les communautés sociales à caractère mystique-philosophique ou qualifiées d'une religiosité négative (athéisme) et les associations philosophiques pures et simples. Il s'agit d'un délit qui défend tout d'abord le sentiment religieux puis la personnalité individuelle de celui qui le professe ou administre (la doctrine souhaitait le contraire).

Le nouvel art. 404 C.P. prévoit que celui qui publiquement (ou bien en privé mais à l'occasion de fonctions religieuses) «en offensant une confession religieuse, outrage par des expressions injurieuses les choses qui sont objet de culte, ou consacrées au culte, ou destinées nécessairement à l'exercice du culte» (puni d'une amende de € 1.000 à € 5.000), ou que celui qui publiquement et intentionnellement détruit, pille, barbouille ou détériore des choses objets de culte ou destinées nécessairement à l'exercice du culte (prison jusqu'à 2 ans). Le délit est plus grave si l'outrage aux choses cause une offense à la confession religieuse. La règle ne défend pas principalement le rapport particulier d'affection entre le fidèle et la chose, mais le prestige de la confession en soi, et en outre elle suit la formulation de 1930 qui défendait la religion catholique, pour laquelle le concept de choses consacrées au culte, etc., en rend problématique l'application aux autres confessions. Le nouvel art. 405 C.P. établit que «quiconque empêche (c'est-à-dire entrave efficacement) ou trouble (c'est-à-dire altère déroulement normal ou le retarde) des offices, cérémonies ou pratiques religieuses du culte d'une confession religieuse, qui ont lieu en présence d'un ministre du culte ou dans un lieu affecté au culte, ou dans un lieu public ou ouvert au public, est puni d'une peine d'emprisonnement pouvant atteindre 2 ans» (si des actes de violence aux personnes ou de menace s'y ajoutent la peine d'emprisonnement peut atteindre 3 ans). On protège la liberté de culte de ceux appartenants aux confessions religieuses, pratiquées collectivement et en public ou de toute façon à l'intérieur de lieux déterminés. Le choix du législateur italien est clair: l'expérience religieuse des associés mérite encore aujourd'hui une défense contre les expressions d'outrage, à se réaliser sans discrimination parmi les confessions religieuses et parmi les croyants des différentes confessions religieuses.

Outrage à une tombe et violation de sépulture

Le chapitre II «sur les délits contre la pitié des défunts» protège un bien immatériel par sa nature sentimentale: le culte et la vénération pour la mémoire des défunts. Il n'existe pas lien direct avec l'élément religieux. Les art. 407-413 C.P. (violation de sépulture, outrage des tombes, trouble aux enterrements, outrage à un cadavre, destruction, suppression ou soustraction de cadavre, recel de cadavre, emploi illégitime de cadavre) garantissent d'un coté les choses mortuaires et les rites funèbres et, de l'autre coté, directement les dépouilles mortelles contre des attaques symboliques (outrages) ou matériels: le délit est constitué simplement par l'accomplissement du fait, sans que sont nécessaire une enquête sur le mobile pour lequel le fait a été accompli.

Diffamation contre les communautés religieuses

À part les hypothèses d'outrage, les confessions religieuses peuvent être sujets passifs du délit de diffamation au sens de l'art. 595 C.P., qui punit de la réclusion jusqu'à un an ou avec une amende jusqu'à € 1.032 tous ceux qui, en communiquant avec plusieurs personnes, offensent la réputation d'autrui. Tandis que pour les délits d'outrage on procède d'office, en ce cas il faut que soit portée plainte par une partie. On retenait, autrefois, que le délit était constitué de l'offense à la réputation d'une personne déterminée et donc il n'existait pas si le destinataire de l'offense n'était pas clairement indentifiable. L'orientation a changé et même les associations, partis politiques, fondations ou communautés religieuses sont considérées comme pouvant être sujets passifs de diffamation, en tant que représentants d'un intérêt collectif unitaire et indivisible en relation avec les buts poursuivis, et de l'intérêt individuel des membres du groupe (ex: l'Union des Communautés Juives Italiennes et chacun des membres appartenant à la religion juive peuvent être sujets passifs du délit de diffamation contre la collectivité juive).

Répression de la discrimination religieuse

La Loi 654/75 donna exécution à la Convention internationale sur l'élimination de toute forme de discrimination raciale du 21/12/1965. Elle a ensuite été remplacée, d'abord par l'art. 1 du D.L. 122/1993, ensuite converti en Loi (205/1993), et maintenant partiellement modifiée par l'art. 13 de la Loi, 85/2006: il s'ensuit qu'est puni d'une peine de réclusion jusqu'à 1 an et 6 mois, ou d'une amende jusqu'à € 6.000, celui qui propage des idées fondées sur la supériorité ou sur la haine raciale ou ethnique, ou qui incite à commettre ou commet des actes de discrimination pour raisons raciales, ethniques, nationales ou religieuses, et d'une réclusion de 6 mois à 4 ans toute personne qui, de quelque façon que ce soit, incite à commettre ou commet violences ou actes de provocation à la violence pour raisons raciales, ethniques, nationales ou religieuses. En outre sont interdits tous mouvements organisations, associations, ou groupes ayant parmi leurs finalités l'incitation à la discrimination ou à la violence pour raisons raciales. La participation ou l'assistance à ces organisations, sont punies du simple fait de la participation ou de l'assistance. Les promoteurs ou celui qui dirige de telles organisations sont punis d'un emprisonnement de 1 à 6 ans. La Cassation pénale a décidé que l'incitation à la discrimination «tend à la nuire à l'égale dignité sociale des citoyens, à l'exclusion du principe d'égalité et à la violation des droits inviolables de l'homme», en niant chaque contraste entre l'art. 1 de la Loi 205/93 et le droit de libre manifestation de la pensée (art. 21 Const.), parce que «l'incitation a un contenu actif d'instigation à une conduite» et réalise quelque chose en plus «par rapport à une manifestation d'opinions, raisonnements ou convictions personnels».

Répression pénale des mutilations des organes génitaux féminins

La Loi n. 7/2006 comporte des dispositions concernant la prévention et la défense de pratiques de mutilation des organes génitaux féminins, perçues comme violations des droits fondamentaux de l'intégrité de la personne et de la santé des femmes et des petites filles (artt. 2, 3 et 32 Const. et IV Conférence mondiale des Nations Unies sur les femmes du 15/09/1995). L'art. 6 de la Loi déjà citée de 2006 a introduit dans notre code pénal l'art. 583-bis qui punit le délit de mutilation et le délit de lésion des organes génitaux féminins. Le 1° alinéa punit, d'une réclusion de 4 à 12 ans, tous ceux qui, en absence d'exigences thérapeutiques, causent une mutilation des organes génitaux féminins (comme «la clitoridectomie, qui consiste en l'ablation totale ou partielle du clitoris, l'excision et l'infibulation et n'importe quelle autre pratique qui cause des effets du même genre»); le 2° alinéa punit, de la réclusion de 3 à 7 ans, tous ceux qui, en absence d'exigences thérapeutiques, provoquent, afin d'affaiblir les fonctions sexuelles, des lésions aux organes génitaux féminins, différentes de celles indiquées au premier alinéa, dont dérive une maladie dans le corps ou dans l'esprit (c'est à dire tous les types d'agression aux organes génitaux féminins extérieurs, à l'exclusion d'une mutilation, totale ou partielle). L'art. 583-ter C.P. prévoit pour ceux-ci une peine accessoire spéciale.

Emploi abusif du vêtement ecclésiastique

La réglementation pénale sanctionne l'emploi abusif du vêtement ecclésiastique à art. 498 C.P. placé dans le Titre VII, relatif aux délits contre la foi publique, qui, entre autres, prévoit que «quiconque porte abusivement en public le *vêtement ecclésiastique*, est puni d'une sanction administrative pécuniaire de € 154 à € 929». L'abus se repère dans toutes les hypothèses dans lesquelles le vêtement est utilisé par celui qui – selon les règles ecclésiastiques – est dépourvu de la qualification confessionnelle nécessaire pour le porter validement. Le concept de «vêtement ecclésiastique» ne comprend pas le vêtement des religieux.

Secret des ministres du culte

Le secret des ministres de culte est protégé par l'art. 200 C. pr .pén. comme le secret professionnel. On prévoit qu'ils «ne peuvent pas être obligés de déposer à propos de ce qu'ils ont connu en raison de leur ministère, office ou profession, exception faite des cas pour lesquels ils sont obligés d'en référer à l'autorité judiciaire: a) les ministres de confessions religieuses dont les statuts ne contrastent pas avec le système juridique italien» (et pas seulement ceux des confessions religieuses avec Accord). Cette faculté est mentionnée, pour le procès civil, à l'art. 249 C. pr. civ. Il s'agit d'une protection de la fonction de ministre qui, assimilée à celle du secret professionnel, constitue une limite aux pouvoirs instructeurs du juge, auquel atteint une faculté d'abstention concédée aux ministres de culte, en raison de laquelle ils ne peuvent pas être obligés à déposer sur ce qu'ils ont connu pour des raisons liées à leur ministère. Si l'ecclésiastique viole le secret ministériel on applique l'art. 622 C.P., pour lequel quiconque, apprenant en secret un fait, en raison de son statut ou d'office, ou de sa profession ou art, le révèle, sans juste cause, ou bien l'emploie pour son propre profit ou pour celui d'autrui est puni si, de ce fait, peut dériver un dommage (Cf., C. Cass. n.8635/1996).

Le désir d'obtempérer à des préceptes religieux comme circonstance atténuante de la gravité d'un délit

Le désir d'obtempérer à des préceptes religieux dans beaucoup de cas a été considéré par la jurisprudence comme circonstance atténuante de la gravité d'un délit. Dans un cas de refus des parents de soumettre à transfusion sanguine leur fille thalassémique, refus motivé par des raisons à caractère religieux, les parents ont été condamnés pour homicide par imprudence mais les circonstances atténuantes ont été retenues en application de l'art. 62 n.1 C.P. (raisons de valeur morale particulière), en reconnaissant que les parents avaient agi afin de ne pas violer un précepte religieux.

Par contre, en aucun cas, un parent ne peut utiliser menaces et/ou moyens violents pour forcer son fils à suivre certains préceptes religieux et il a été retenu que cette espèce intègre le délit prévu et puni par l'art. 572 C.P. (mauvais traitements en famille) et non pas celui moins grave sanctionné par l'art. 571 C.P. (abus des moyens de correction).

Le cas de la Scientologie

L'Église de Scientologie en Italie, exemple typique de secte, fut objet, dès le début des années '80 du XX siècle, de dénonciations pénales et d'enquêtes diverses: on a reproché à quelques membres de l'Église les délits d'escroquerie, d'incitation à commettre un crime, d'exercice abusif de la profession médicale, d'abus de personnes irresponsables, de violations des lois qui réglementent les rapports de travail. Après une sentence du Tribunal de Milan du 2/7/1991 (dans le sens de la licité du but poursuivi par la Scientologie) et de la Cour d'Appel de Milan du 5/11/1993 (qui relevait le délit d'association pour commettre un crime), la Cour de Cassation se prononça (Arrêt 163/1995) en annulant la deuxième sentence parce que la vérification du caractère religieux de la Scientologie est *condicio sine qua non* pour l' affirmation de l'existence ou non du délit d'association pour commettre un crime, vu que, «une fois reconnu à la Scientologie le caractère de confession religieuse, il ne serait plus envisageable de transformer celle-ci en association pour commettre un crime, sauf si tous les membres de l'église avaient, d'un commun accord, changé les règles statutaires, en créant un nouveau sujet différent de celui d'origine, en constituant, de façon distincte et autonome, une association illicite». Vérification, celle-ci, à s'accomplir cas par cas.

Ringolds Balodis

LEGAL PROTECTION OF RELIGION IN THE REPUBLIC OF LATVIA

Introduction

In 1802, US President Thomas Jefferson wrote a letter to the Danbury Baptist Association,[1] which referred to the "wall of separation between church and state".[2] It was at that moment that the victory march of secularism and worldliness can be said to have begun. The United States, of course, has its specific experience with the First Amendment to the country's constitution and the interpretation of same. In this, the USA differs from the dominant approach in Europe *vis-à-vis* this "wall of separation". Still, the approach does appear in the way in which religious organisations and religious freedoms are protected by law in the member states of the European Union. In the Republic of Latvia, the "wall of separation" between state and church is established at the constitutional level,[3] but, as Horace put it long ago, nothing tends to be ideal in all aspects (the Roman philosopher was speaking about the nature of worldly affairs). Indeed, legal regulations in Latvia are far from perfect. A review of this fact will require a brief look at how criminal law has developed in Latvia.

1. The first period of independence (1918-1940)

The independent Republic of Latvia was proclaimed on November 18, 1818. On February 15, 1922, the Latvian Constitutional Assembly

[1] Baptists at that time were a religious minority in the US state of Connecticut, and they wrote to the national government to complain about the fact that their freedom of religion was not considered to be a natural right. Instead, they said, this freedom was considered nothing more than evidence of the favour of the local legislature.

[2] To wit: "Believing with you that religion is a matter which lies solely between man & his god, that he owes account to none other for his faith or his worship, that the legitimate powers of government reach actions only, and not opinions, I contemplate with sovereign reverence that act of the whole American people which declared that *their* legislature should 'make no law respecting an establishment of religion, or prohibiting the free exercise thereof', thus building a wall of separation between church and state."

[3] Section 99 of the Latvian Constitution: "Everyone has the right to freedom of opinion, conscience and religious conviction. The Church is separate from the state."

approved the country's new constitution, known as the *Satversme*. This was a triumphal moment for the Latvian people, and the Satversme represented the first development of constitutional law. This offered true evidence of political unity and the political maturity of the Latvian nation.[4] The people of the regions of Vidzeme, Kurzeme, Zemgale and Latgale had come together to form the Latvian nation, one that was able to express its own will in a political constitution and to fortify the basic foundations of their country's political philosophy at the highest level. Once the Satversme received final approval on June 9, 1922, a new law on elections was also adopted, thus opening the way for the election of a new parliamentary body – the *Saeima*.[5] The Constitutional Assembly had been a fully fledged, but extraordinary legislature. It automatically transferred its powers to the new constitutional parliament. The legislative work which had begun at the Constitutional Assembly was continued by the Saeima.

The history of democracy in Latvia was very brief, just from 1922 until 1934. In May of the latter year, Kārlis Ulmanis staged a coup and became the country's dictator. During his rule, all of the most important decisions in Latvia were made by his appointed Cabinet of Ministers. Ulmanis usurped the functions of the Saeima, and legislative power was concentrated in the hands of the government's executive branch.[6]

The punitive laws of tsarist Russia, which were adopted in 1903, remained in force in Latvia until 1933. These provided for harsh punishments against those who violated rules related to the protection of faith (Articles 73-98). A new punitive law was approved on April 24, 1933, and it stated in Section 300 that anyone who offended the religious beliefs of members of the religious society in Latvia by engaging in blasphemy or denigrating a religious organisation in any other way would be sentenced to imprisonment. There was an incident in the town of Talsi, where a bartender was punished under Section 300 for putting up a sign in his tavern which read "May God bless your entry when you are thirsty and your exit once you have paid."[7] A two-year prison sentence

[4] Balodis, R. "The Constitution of Latvia", *Rechtspolitisches Forum*, Institut für Rechtspolitik, University of Trier, No. 26., 2004.

[5] Bleiere, D., Butulis, I., Feldmanis, I., Stranga, A. and A. Zunda. Latvijas vēsture: 20. gadsimts (The History of Latvia: The 20th Century). Rīga: Jumava (2006), p. 156.

[6] *Ibid.*, p. 174.

[7] Minutes of the Saeima of the Republic of Latvia, 5th session of the 3rd Saeima, Col. 1297.

was handed down to a man who published an anti-religious brochure under the title "Evangelic Christ and His Teachings".[8]

In April 1934, the senior editor of a magazine called *Brīvdomātājs* (Free Thinker), Elza Drille, was charged with "denigrating the Holy Communion". Her "crime" was that she had published an article about the historical origins of this ancient ritual. The article did not associate the Holy Communion with the blood of Christ and, in a heretical manner, attempted to attribute it to ancient cannibalism. In February 1935, Drille spent two weeks at the Rīga Central Prison for having published the article.[9] It is clear, of course, that the blasphemous article was simply published at the wrong time. This was a period during which the authoritarian regime was preparing to take over power, and what happened to Drille was an example of how the regime sought to frighten possible dissidents. According to the Soviet-era author Zigmunds Balēvics, who was a student of the relationship between church and state, 25 people were convicted of offences related to religion in 1938.[10] A curiosity in this regard relates to a man identified only as Fricis K, who ended up receiving what seems to be a disproportionate punishment. In April 1938, during an evening worship service at the Orthodox Cathedral in Rīga, the drunken man refused to kiss a cross that was presented to him by the clergyman. He told the priest that "when the nation is dark, it kisses the hands of the bearded ones." The Rīga Regional Court punished Fricis K. with a suspended one-month sentence. The Prosecutor's Office, however, appealed the punishment. In the appeal, a deputy prosecutor argued that "criminal offences against the religious sensibilities and religious cults of members of society not only touch upon the interests of individual persons or known religious organisations, but also reduce respect toward religion itself and can weaken the foundations of national life if these criminal offences do not draw a sufficiently strict response." The court took this view into account and sent the unlucky blasphemer to prison for a five-month term.

Another anecdotal story has to do with a Russian magazine called *For You* ("Для вас"). In its 48th issue of 1939, it published a crossword puzzle in which the Political Board (the predecessor to Latvia's modern-day Security Police and Bureau to Protect the Constitution) spotted the combination of words "religious concoction" ("религиозная выдумка").

[8] Pipirs, A. Pretkristīgā propaganda un viņas veicinātāji Latvijā (Anti-Christian Propaganda and Its Promoters in Latvia). Rīga (1932), pp. 3-4.

[9] Balēvics, Z. Baznīca un Valsts buržuāziskajā Latvijā (Church and State in Bourgeois Latvia). Rīga: Latvijas Valsts Izdevniecība (1964), p. 112.

[10] *Ibid.*

The answer? "God" ("Бог"). The Political Board immediately launched a criminal investigation against the magazine. During the investigation, the magazine, with the advice of fine attorneys, showed that the incident could be attributed to "technical causes" – a problem with the typesetter. The magazine's representatives claimed that they had truly meant to offer the clue "sense of religion" ("религиозный смысл"). The police accepted this explanation and halted the case. For objective reasons, it does have to be said, however, that the Political Board dealt not only with anecdotal incidents such as this one. In the early 1920s, for instance, the board's focus of attention was on a sect in the Latvian region of Latgale which dubbed itself "Spiritual Teetotallers" ("Духовно нравственные трезвенники"). They were also known as the "bogomols" ("богомолы"), and under the smokescreen of their supposedly religious activities, they engaged in pro-Communist agitation.[11]

One can agree with something that was reported by the aforementioned Zigmunds Balēvics[12] – that Latvia's courts during the first period of independence did not support the registration of organisations that were of an anti-religious nature, and that the church at that time had a substantial influence on jurisprudence.[13]

2. The second period of independence (1990–)

On May 4, 1990, the Supreme Council of the Latvian SSR approved a declaration on the restoration of the independence of the Republic of Latvia, and this was a new element in the development of the country's constitutional law.[14] The May 4 declaration marked the beginning of the abolition of the Soviet legal system in Latvia.[15] On June 5 and 6, 1993, the 5th Latvian Parliament (the *Saeima*) was elected, and it met for its first

[11] Runce, I. "Valsts un netradicionālo konfesiju attiecības Latvijā 1920.-1934. gados" (The Relationship Between State and Non-Traditional Denominations in Latvia, 1920-1934), *Katoļu Baznīcas Vēstnesis*, No. 3 (196), 2001, 8 February.

[12] *Ibid.*, p. 30.

[13] Evidence of this can be seen in the fact that on May 30, 1930, the Rīga Regional Court refused to register the statues of the "Latvian Association of Godless People." Apparently the refusal was based mostly on the organisation's pro-Communist views. The draft statutes, which were submitted to the Political Board (the equivalent at that time of Latvia's Security Police), stated that the goal was to "bring together the mass of anti-religious working people; to struggle against the religious and mystical ideology of the church, which hinders clear thinking and hinders the development of science; to position religion and the church in an historical and scientific light; to organise working people to do spiritual and public cultural work; to promote the economic and political gains of the working people."

session on July 5 of the same year. It can be said that the election of the 5th Saeima and the subsequent establishment of a new government meant that the process of legal succession had been consistently pursued in Latvia. It is important to note that the attitude of government institutions changed from the Soviet style of repressiveness to the European style of democracy. A great deal has been achieved in the development of a liberal and democratic country. This is seen, too, in the Law on Criminal Procedure of the Republic of Latvia, which states in its very first article that the goal of the law is "the effective application of the norms of the Criminal Law and the fair regulation of criminal legal relations without unjustified intervention in the life of a person."[16] This concept also applies to limitations on religious freedom and to the protection of religion in the sense of the Criminal Law, which was adopted on June 17, 1998. Further discussion of this law can be found in the subsequent sections of this report.

2.1. *Legal protection of religious freedom in the Criminal Law of the Republic of Latvia*

2.1.1. Disrupting a religious event

Section 151 of the Criminal Law specifies sanctions for anyone who disrupts a religious event. The punishment is either community service or a fine of no more than the equivalent of 10 times the minimum monthly wage.[17] True, Section 151 speaks of "religious rituals" which have to be disrupted, and they have to be disrupted intentionally. Specifically, the punishment is to be applied to "a person who commits intentional interference with religious rituals, if the same are not in violation of the law and are not associated with a violation of personal rights." Commentary attached to the Criminal Law explains that disruption of religious rituals can involve "an unlawful closing of a house of worship; a ban on cult

[14] Latvijas tiesību vēsture (1914-2000) (History of Latvian Law (1914-2000). Rīga (2000), p. 288.

[15] Meļķīsis, E. Juridiskās metodes mācības un tiesību normas piemērošanas metodoloģijas jēdziens un nozīme / Juridiskās metodes pamati – 11 soļi tiesību normu piemērošanā (The Concept and Meaning of the Teaching of Legal Methods and the Methodologies in the Application of Legal Norms / Fundamentals of Legal Methods – 11 Steps in the Application of Legal Norms). Rīga (2003), p. 9.

[16] Kriminālprocesa likums (the Law on Criminal Procedure), *Latvijas Vēstnesis*, No. 74, 11 May 2005.

[17] In July 2008, at this writing, the minimum monthly wage in Latvia was LVL 160 (EUR 112).

ceremonies or on religious rituals such as marriages, baptisms and funerals; or violence against an individual who takes part in such a ritual or a servant of the cult."[18] The makeup of the criminal offence is formal and applies to the moment when steps are taken to disrupt a religious ritual. In any event it is believed that the subjective aspects of this offence are characterised by direct intent. As far as this section of the Criminal Law is concerned, a guilty party can interfere with religious rituals by acting against an officially registered religious organisation, its members, or individual people of faith.[19] In 2007, criminal proceedings were launched just once on the basis of Section 151 of the Criminal Law.[20] At issue was an incident in which members and employees of the Grebenschikov Old Believer congregation of Rīga were barred from entering their house of worship. The author has no further information about the development of this criminal case, although it is known that it has not yet been submitted to the courts.

2.1.2. Disrupting a funeral

There is no separate text in the Criminal Law about interference in funeral proceedings, and if such criminal offences were committed, they would probably be interpreted in the context of Section 151 of the law, which speaks to disruption of religious rituals.

2.1.3. Discrimination on the basis of religion

Section 149[1] of the Criminal Law of the Republic of Latvia specifies a fine equal to 30 times the minimum monthly wage for violations of the ban against discrimination if such an offence has been committed more than once in a single year. The section speaks of "discrimination related to race or ethnicity", and it does not specifically speak of religion. The key phrase in this section is this: "... or for the violation of discrimination prohibitions specified in other regulatory enactments." Such

[18] Krastiņš, U., Liholaja, V. and A. Niedre. Krimināllikuma zinātniski praktiskas komentārs. Nr. 2. Sevišķā daļa (Scientific and Practical Commentary on the Criminal Law. No. 2: Special Regulations). Rīga: AFS (2007), p. 313.

[19] Krastiņš, U. (ed.). Krimināltiesības. Vispārīgā un sevišķā daļa (Criminal Law: General and Special Regulations). Rīga: Tiesu namu aģentūra (1999), p. 195.

[20] A letter from the state secretary of the Interior Ministry of the Republic of Latvia, Aivars Straume, to Associate Professor Ringolds Balodis, chair of the Department of Constitutional Law of the Faculty of Law, University of Latvia, 29 May 2008.

enactments include the law on religious organisations, which states, in section 4.1, that "any direct or indirect limitation on the rights of residents, direct or indirect creation of advantages for residents, offence against religious sensibilities or fomenting of hatred vis-à-vis the attitude toward religion of residents shall be banned." This suggests that the norms of Section 149[1] of the Criminal Law apply in this regard, too. Section 149[1] speaks to a prison sentence of up to two years, mandatory community service, or a fine which is equal to no more than 50 times the minimum monthly wage if the violation against the ban on discrimination has caused substantial harm, if it has involved violence, fraud or threats, if it has been committed by a group of individuals, if it has been committed by a government official or a senior representative of a company, enterprise or organisation, or if it has been committed with the use of an automated data processing system.

2.1.4. Menaces, violence or use of force against freedom of religion or conscience

Here we are dealing with general offences such as assault, coercion, etc. The Criminal Law does not speak specifically of attacks against someone's freedom of religion or conscience, but the fact is that if an offence is sufficiently serious, such crimes can end up in court not because of their religious nature, but because they represent a general offence against an individual's private rights.

When it comes to offending a person's religious sensibilities or fomenting hostility with respect to someone's attitude vis-à-vis religion or atheism, Section 150 of the Criminal Law speaks of a prison sentence of up to two years, community service, or a fine of as much as the equivalent of 40 minimum monthly wages.[21] Here it must once again be noted that if the offence causes significant harm, involves violence, fraud or threats, is committed by a group of individuals, a government official, a senior representative of a company, enterprise or organisation, or involves automated data systems, the punishment can be a prison sentence of as much as four years. Commentary on Section 150 notes that in objective terms, this refers to activities which are manifested as a direct or indirect limitation on an individual's right, the creation of

[21] Balodis, R. Church and State in Latvia. In Ferrari, S. and W.C. Durham (eds.). *Law and Religion in Post-Communist Europe*. Leuven, Paris, Dudley, MA: Peeters Publishers (2003), p. 152.

advantages for individuals, offence against the religious sensibilities of an individual, or fomenting of hatred. These activities relate to the victim's attitude vis-à-vis religion or atheism.[22] The criminal offence that is addressed in Section 150 threatens the right of freedom of religion of an individual, because Section 99 of the Latvian Constitution declares that this is a universal right. The makeup of the criminal offence that is addressed in Section 150 is formal and applies to the moment when the activities contemplated in the section have occurred. From the subjective perspective, the offence can be committed only with direct intent, because the guilty party would have to do the aforementioned things in terms of attacking the victim's religious or atheistic beliefs. In other words, there has to be direct intent.[23]

In 2008, criminal proceedings were launched only once with respect to Section 150 of the Criminal Law (fomenting religious hatred).[24] The proceedings were eventually cancelled on the basis of Section 377.2 of the Law on Criminal Procedure – investigators did not determine that a criminal offence had been committed. The issue concerned an Internet portal, www.draugiem.lv (www.friends.lv), where someone had posted statements which were offensive to Roman Catholics.[25] In the 1990s, there were several cases related to offences against people's religious sensibilities. An organisation calling itself "Congregations of God" made statements which offended traditional religious denominations and were aimed at attracting attention.[26] One might add, too, that some of Latvia's leading researchers in the field of religion (Valdis Tēraudkalns and Solveiga Krūmiņa-Koņkova) have argued[27] that the concept of "hate

[22] Krastiņš, U., Liholaja, V. and A. Niedre. Krimināllikuma zinātniski..., *op. cit.*, pp. 311-312.

[23] Religious sensibilities can be offended by humiliating an individual, by making rude statements about the individual, by denigrating the individual's attitude vis-à-vis religion or atheism, etc. This can be done in spoken, written or another form. Fomenting of hostility refers to the dissemination of spoken or written ideas, theories or views via the mass media or otherwise so as to encourage a broader or narrower range of individuals to develop hostile attitudes vis-à-vis the representatives of another religious group or atheists. See Krastiņš, U., Liholaja, V. and A. Niedre. Krimināllikuma zinātniski..., *op. cit.*, pp. 311-312.

[24] A letter from the state secretary of the Interior Ministry of the Republic of Latvia, Aivars Straume, to Associate Professor Ringolds Balodis, chair of the Department of Constitutional Law of the Faculty of Law, University of Latvia, 29 May 2008.

[25] *Ibid.*

[26] Balodis, R. Valsts un Baznīca (State and Church). Rīga: Nordik (2000), p. 284.

[27] Krūmiņa-Koņkova, S. and V. Tēraudkalns. "Reliģiskā dažādība Latvijā" (Religious Diversity in Latvia). Rīga: Klints (2007), p. 89.

speech" should be used instead of the concept of "religious sensibilities". By this, they refer to spoken or written calls for violence, to the unjustified limitation of the rights of individuals or groups, as well as to offensive or humiliating speech which foments hatred. The experts feel that these are offences which affect not just the area of religion, but also such factors as ethnic origin, skin colour and sexual orientation.

2.1.5. Abuse of a corpse or desecration of a grave

Section 228 of the Criminal Law of the Republic of Latvia speaks of the desecration of a grave, a funeral urn, or a buried or unburied corpse. The anticipated punishment is a prison sentence of up to five years, community service, or a fine equal to 100 times the minimum monthly wage. The motivation for such criminal offences, including motivation that is based on religion, does not matter in this regard.[28] Religion is not addressed specifically in this section of the law, but it is clear that if the offence involves things such as Satanism or hooliganism (damaging crosses, for instance), then the offences will be classified in accordance with Section 228. The same is true when people desecrate gravesites with anti-Semitic symbols.

It has to be added that if desecration of a grave[29] occurs repeatedly or has been committed by a group of individuals on the basis of prior agreement, the punishment can be far more severe – eight years in prison or a fine equal to 150 times the minimum monthly wage. If the offence relates to the theft of a monument, a funeral urn, or any other object that is on or inside a grave or a funeral urn, Section 228.3 of the Criminal Law provides for a prison sentence of between 3 and 10 years, with or without confiscation of property.

[28] The exception here is greed, when someone desecrates a grave with the purpose of robbing it. Religion, however, has no specific meaning when this criminal offence is investigated. See Krastiņš, U., Liholaja, V. and A. Niedre. Krimināllikuma zinātniski..., *op. cit.*, p. 205.

[29] The Latvian Civil Law (Section 1415) defines blasphemy as "unsanctioned and indecent activities if their aim is contrary to religion, law or good morals, or are aimed at avoiding the law." The law goes on to state that these "cannot be the subject matter of a legal transaction, and any such transaction is null and void." Direct or indirect infringement of people's religious sensibilities is also prohibited in Section 4 of the Law on Religious Organisations. See Balodis, R. "Staat und Kirche in Lettland" (State and Church in Latvia). In Robbers, G. (ed.). Staat und Kirche in der Europäischen Union (State and Church in the European Union), 2nd ed.. Baden-Baden: Nomos Verlagsgesellschaft (2005), pp. 279-310.

2.2. *Other aspects of religion and legal protection of the same*

2.2.1. The confidentiality of confessions

The confidential nature of confessions and pastoral discussions is protected in special laws relating to religious denominations,[30] as well as in the Law on Civil Procedure (Section 106), the Law on Criminal Procedure (Section 121), and the Law on Administrative Procedure (Section 163). The procedural laws state that clergypersons may decline to provide evidence in administrative, criminal and civil cases about things that they have heard in confession. People who are in prison have the right to attend confession without the presence of any prison representative.[31]

In 2007, the Saeima of the Republic of Latvia adopted five of seven special laws on religious denominations. At the time of writing it is expected that the two other laws – one on the Orthodox and one on the Lutheran church – will be approved in the autumn of 2008. The legislature has covered some issues in church-related laws which should be regulated,[32] and it can be said that at this time the model in Latvia is similar to that which prevails in Italy or Spain.

2.2.2. Offences against the public peace at a place of worship or during a religious procedure – types of offences (outrage or public defamation of a public authority, incitement to civil unrest, etc.), the related material and psychological elements, and the related punishments

The Criminal Law of the Republic of Latvia speaks of the establishment or management of destructive religious groups. This is known as the "anti-sect" section of the law (section 207), and in fact it could be

[30] A law on the Latvian congregations of the Church of Seventh Day Adventists, *Latvijas Vēstnesis*, No. 93 (3669), 12 June 2007. Also a law on the Latvian Union of Baptist Congregations, *Latvijas Vēstnesis*, No. 86 (3662), 30 May 2007. Also a law on the Jewish congregation in Rīga, *Latvijas Vēstnesis*, No. 98 (3674), 20 June 1998. Also a law on the Latvian Unified Methodist Church, *Latvijas Vēstnesis*, No. 91 (3667), 6 July 2007. Also a law on the Latvian Pomora Church of Old Believers, *Latvijas Vēstnesis*, No. 89 (3674), 20 June 2007.

[31] Cabinet of Ministers regulations on the internal procedures of places of incarceration, *Latvijas Vēstnesis*, No. 32 (2607), 27 February 2002.

[32] Unresolved issues at the time of writing include taxation, organisations of public benefit, religious holidays, etc. See Balodis, R. Baznīcu tiesības (The Rights of Churches). Rīga: Religious Freedom Association (2002), p. 699.

applied against any organisation which engages in religious activities.[33] This is true irrespective of whether the organisation has been registered as a religious organisation, as well as of whether it is a traditional or non-traditional organisation.

Section 227 is entitled "Causing Danger to Public Safety, Order and the Health of Individuals While Performing Religious Activities". Offences related to Section 227 can lead to imprisonment for up to five years, community service, or a fine of no more than the equivalent of 100 times the minimum monthly wage. In commentary about the Criminal Law, Professor Valentīna Liholaja from the University of Latvia Faculty of Law notes[34] that the criminal offence that is addressed in Section 227 involves activities which lead to the organisation of a group which harms public safety and order, the health of individuals, or the legally protected rights and interests of individuals through religious instruction, evangelisation or rituals. It also applies to running such a group or taking part in these types of activities.

Professor Liholaja also writes that the organisation and management of activities which are referred to in Section 227 means bringing people into such groups (sects), creating the circumstances that are needed for such groups to operate (facilities, equipment, objects for rituals, various kinds of information materials), dividing duties among participants in the group, proclaiming the relevant religious instructions, or engaging in religious rituals. Criminal liability is also faced by people who take part in such activities.[35]

When it comes to harming the health of individuals, Professor Liholaja writes[36] that this involves physical processes vis-à-vis the victim in the context of which the victim is beaten or tortured, he or she feels physical pain, suffers physical harm at various levels of seriousness, or faces psychological pressures which create mental or spiritual traumas. The commentary also says that when there are offences against the legally protected rights and interests of individuals,[37] this can involve a ban

[33] Religious activities include worship services, worship ceremonies, rituals, meditation, and missionary activities (evangelisation). See Likumdošanas aktu terminu vārdnīca (Dictionary of Legislative Terms). Rīga: Senders (1999), p. 359.

[34] Krastiņš, U., Liholaja, V. and A. Niedre. Krimināllikuma zinātniski..., *op. cit.*, pp. 201-203.

[35] Krastiņš, U. (ed.). Krimināltiesības..., *op. cit.*, p. 259.

[36] Krastiņš, U., Liholaja, V. and A. Niedre. Krimināllikuma zinātniski..., *op. cit.*, pp. 201-203.

[37] *Ibid.*

against working, studying or attending theatrical performances, encouragement to halt public activities, voting in elections, engaging in military service, etc.

3. Additional notes about the situation in Latvia

Latvia's Criminal Law does not provide for any punishment related to the celebration of a religious marriage before a civil marriage. Latvia's laws say nothing about proselytising. Female genital mutilation is not defined as a crime as such. If such an offence were committed, it would be prosecuted on the basis of other norms in the Criminal Law which seek to protect the individual.

The Criminal Law and the Administrative Law do not speak specifically of offences that are aggravated by religious motivation. The Criminal Law does not speak specifically of blasphemy, but punishment for such activities can be based on other, aforementioned sections of the law. If animals are sacrificed as part of religious rituals, the punishment can be based on Section 230 of the Criminal Law (Cruel Treatment of Animals). Commentary on the Criminal Law focuses on Section 4 of the law on protecting animals, which speaks to mistreatment of animals in terms of organising fights among animals, involving animals therein, crippling or torturing animals, etc., but commentators also note that the rules would apply to the killing of animals as part of a religious ritual.[38]

Conclusion

In order to determine the situation which actually exists in regard to the issues referred to in this paper, the author, in the spring of 2008, surveyed those Latvian government institutions which are responsible for issues related to Section 227 (Causing Danger to Public Safety, Order and the Health of Individuals While Performing Religious Activities), Section 150 (Incitement of Religious Hatred), and Section 151 (Interference With Religious Rituals) of the Criminal Law. According to data from the information system of Latvia's judiciary,[39] no one had been convicted of any

[38] *Ibid.*, p. 209.

[39] A letter from the deputy state secretary of the Justice Ministry of the Republic of Latvia for judicial issues, Inese Kalniņa, to Associate Professor Ringolds Balodis, chair of the Department of Constitutional Law of the Faculty of Law, University of Latvia, 23 April 2008.

of the crimes referred to in the aforementioned sections of the Criminal Law as of April 21, 2008. Indeed, no such case had been heard by the courts.

According to Latvia's Interior Ministry,[40] as of May 2008, none of the criminal proceedings launched on the basis of Sections 124, 137, 149.1, 226, 227, 228 and 230 of the Criminal law related to offences against people's attitudes vis-à-vis religion.

The Prosecutor General's Office of the Republic of Latvia has provided no information about any clergymen who have refused to testify in court in accordance with the rights which are afforded to them in Section 121 of the Criminal Law.[41] Similarly, neither the Interior Ministry nor the National Police know of any incident in which a clergyman has refused to testify on the basis of the confidentiality of a confession.[42]

[40] A letter from the state secretary of the Interior Ministry of the Republic of Latvia, Aivars Straume, to Associate Professor Ringolds Balodis, chair of the Department of Constitutional Law of the Faculty of Law, University of Latvia, 29 May 2008.

[41] A letter from Rudīte Āboliņa, a senior prosecutor in the Operations Analysis and Management Department of the Prosecutor-General's Office of the Republic of Latvia to Associate Professor Ringolds Balodis, chair of the Department of Constitutional Law of the Faculty of Law, University of Latvia

[42] A letter from the state secretary of the Interior Ministry of the Republic of Latvia, Aivars Straume, to Associate Professor Ringolds Balodis, chair of the Department of Constitutional Law of the Faculty of Law, University of Latvia, 29 May 2008.

Andrius Sprindziunas

Mykolas Romeris University

RELIGION AND CRIMINAL LAW IN LITHUANIA

Introduction

In historical retrospect, since 1529, when the First Statute of Lithuania[1] was confirmed, Lithuanian law can be seen to be oriented toward becoming a secular legal system. The First Statute of Lithuania formally gave equal rights to Orthodox and Catholic Christian nobles and formulated no legal sanctions on the grounds of religion and beliefs. Some restrictions, related to heterodoxy, were later established during the long period of the tzarist Russian administration from 1795 to 1918, until an independent Republic of Lithuania was established.

It is meaningful to mention that, during the period of Soviet occupation in Lithuania, criminal law was over-emphasized and, as a juridical vehicle, it was used as the main instrument of social control. As in all territories of the Soviet Union, in Lithuania criminal law was used to exert general pressure on the people and to inflict a multitude of offences against dissentients and religious communities. Legal and illegal psychological pressure, defamation, threats and violence were used to decrease religious practices, to close religious institutes and to persecute active clergymen, despite formal guarantees, in the Soviet Constitution, of freedom of conscience and of the right to practise religion.

It must be noted that the Soviet criminal code has had a long-term influence on the content of the criminal code of the independent state of Lithuania. A typical example is the former Article 144 of the Criminal Code of the Republic of Lithuania (CC) called "An encroachment against personality and rights of people under the veil of religious ceremonies";[2] it reads as follows: "Organising a group, under the veil of performance of religious ceremonies, whose actions are related to the harm of the health of people or encroachment against the personality or rights of

[1] Valikonyte S., Lazutka S., Gudavicius E. Pirmasis Lietuvos Statutas (1529 M.). Vilnius, 2001.

[2] The Criminal Code of the Republic of Lithuania, Chapter IV-144. Vilnius, 1997.

people… as well as leading such a group, shall be punished by imprisonment for a period of up to 5 years". Considering that Soviet demagogy believed religion to be a total deceit of the working class it is obvious that this article could be applied to incriminate active clergymen of any religious community. Article No.144 CC prevailed for several years after 1990 when an independent Republic of Lithuania was re-established and new editions of the Criminal Code instituted, although since 1990 no one was prosecuted under that particular article.

Currently the Criminal Code of the Republic of Lithuania contains one chapter with explicit references to religion and freedom of conscience; it is Chapter XXV "Crimes and misdemeanours against equal rights and freedom of conscience", and has articles on discrimination, incitement and disturbance of religious ceremonies or celebrations, and at least two chapters with implicit references, Chapter XX, "Crimes against liberty of the person", which has an article on restricting a person's freedom of action and Chapter XXII, "Criminal acts and misdemeanours against a person's honour and dignity", which has articles on libel and insult.

1. Defamation and outrage reflecting on the content of religion

The Criminal Code of the Republic of Lithuania,[3] until now, does not differentiate precisely between offences against the content of religious beliefs and the dignity of religious persons, or of religious communities, in the apparent circumstances of defamation or outrage. Article 170, CC reads as follows:

> "1. Any person who, by the use of oral, written, or communicated through the mass media, public statements, ridicules, expresses contempt towards, incites hatred against or encourages discrimination against a group of people or against an individual person on account of their belonging to a specific national, racial, ethnic, religious or other group, shall be punished by a fine, or restriction of liberty, or imprisonment for a period of up to 2 years.
> 2. Any person who publicly incites violence or the use of deadly physical force against a group of people or an individual person on account of their belonging to a specific national, racial, ethnic, religious or other group, or who pays for or provides other financial aid for such acts, shall be punished by a fine or restriction of liberty, or imprisonment for a period of up to 3 years.
> 3. Enterprises shall also be criminally liable for the acts specified in paragraphs 1 and 2 of this Article".

[3] The Criminal Code of the Republic of Lithuania. Actual edition. Vilnius, 2008.

The protected good here is that of the equality of people. The prohibition against ridiculing, expressing contempt towards, inciting hatred or violence towards people, etc. here expresses attitudes of Article 25.4 of the Constitution of the Republic of Lithuania, stating that "Freedom to express convictions and to impart information shall be incompatible with criminal action – incitement of national, racial, religious, or social hatred, violence and discrimination, with slander and misinformation". Regarding this, one can identify some extra protected goods like societal safety, human life, health, and human dignity.

Comments on the Criminal Code address the objective (*actus reus*) and subjective (*mens rea*) elements of the crime. In the case of Article 170 CC the objective elements could be ridiculing some group or a person who belongs to some group, scorn, incitement of hatred and discrimination. These acts are formally treated as crimes if they were performed by public statements in oral, written or mass media forms. So, such statements could be considered as public only if they are addressed to the whole of society (undefined circle of people), but not to a particular addressee. The act should be directed against a group of persons or a single person because of sex, sexual orientation, race, nationality, language, origin, social status, religion, or convictions. The act would be considered as formally committed, after the public statements of these kinds have reached their addressee – society.

The commentaries on the Criminal Law by Lithuanian lawyers prompt us to consider the context of public statements weighting up the circumstances, purposes and form of those public statements, with special precaution to be exercised concerning humorous statements.

The basic subjective elements of such acts are responsibility and intentionality on the part of the actor, such as understanding what type of crime is being committed and willingness to act that way. Only persons no younger than 16 year of age and enterprises can be subject to proceedings under Article 170 CC.

The 2nd part of Article 170 CC sets out even more dangerous criminal acts, like public incitement to use violence or deadly physical force against a group of people or an individual person because of their belonging to a specific group and financial support of such-like acts. Incitement to use violence or deadly physical force can be understood as direct or indirect encouragement to use physical or psychological violence: murder, maiming, sexual compulsion, expatriation, isolation, destruction or damage to property (in this case treated as a kind of psychological violence).

These acts are criminal whether or not threats are included. If acts of violence were actually committed, the perpetrator should be liable for murder, injury, complicity in funding the crime, causing material damage, breach of the public peace, etc. Although the perpetrators of the violent acts are considered responsible for what they have done, it is clear they might also be liable for hooliganism under Articles 129,135,138 CC and, perhaps, with the crime of genocide (Art. 99 CC).

Proof of intention is required in order to prosecute under part 2 of Article 170 CC.

It is important to note that the formal content of blasphemy is not defined in Lithuanian law. Manifestations of blasphemy, defamation or outrage could be constituted by ridiculing, inciting hatred or violence, or as a crime against personal dignity, public peace or justice. In such cases Article 214-12 of the Code of Misdemeanours of the Administrative Law of the Republic of Lithuania imposes punishments for incitement of national, racial and religious conflict in the media. It provides: "Production or possession with the purpose of distribution, as well as distribution or public demonstration of printed material, video, audio or other products, which propagate national, racial or religious conflict, shall be punished by a fine from 1000 to 5000 Litas and confiscation of the products still in the process of production, storing, being demonstrated and distributed, as well as confiscation of the main means of production, or without confiscation of the means of production. The same acts, performed by a person, who was previously punished by administrative penalty for transgression as described in the first part of this article, shall be punished by a fine from 5000 to 10000 Litas and confiscation of the production as well as confiscation of the main means of production and demonstration of those products, or without confiscation of the above-mentioned means."

An example of legal consideration of incitement of religious discord and church desecration could be the case of the Internet website www.satan.lt (launched in 2000, Lithuania), with regard to the contents of the website and often-even-more-offensive commentaries by the visitors to the website. In 2002 the authors of the website were warned by state Security Department of the Republic of Lithuania about possible provocation of religious discord in their website, but no legal proceedings were initiated. It was concluded that the content of the website www.satan.lt is rather more atheistic than satanic or targeting other religions.

A more recent suit was instituted with respect to the plans of the "MTV Networks Baltic" "MTV Lietuva" channel plans to show a controversial film, "Popetown", on Christmas day. Despite protests, the film started to be broadcast in the winter of 2006. Later the TV company was found guilty and fined for showing "Popetown" without special provision to prevent minors from suffering negative media influence. The film was also blamed for being blasphemous and for inciting discrimination on grounds of religion. Recently, the Administrative Court of Vilnius District confirmed the relevance of an earlier decision of the Lithuanian Radio and Television Commission to punish the company "MTV Lietuva" with the maximum fine available under the Law for the protection of minors from the harmful influence of the media.

2. Defamation and outrage against a church or religious community

The Constitution of the Republic of Lithuania and the Law of Religious Communities and Associations of the Republic of Lithuania guarantee that all registered religious groups and associations, including philosophical associations, will be treated equally according to the law. But the law of religious communities and associations[4] includes a list of 9 traditional religions in the Republic of Lithuania, namely: Roman Catholic, Eastern Rite Catholic, Russian Orthodox, Old Believers, Lutherans, Reformed, Jewish, Sunni Muslim and Karaite. Moreover, the Seimas (Lithuanian parliament) gave the status of religion "recognized by the State" to several other religious groups, and all of these religious groups, consequently, were better protected by the State. Some religious associations have special agreements with the state; for example, with respect to Roman Catholics, there is an agreement between the Holy See and the Republic of Lithuania concerning juridical aspects of the relationship between the Catholic Church and the State. This agreement provides: "The Republic of Lithuania shall recognise the freedom of the Catholic Church to carry out its pastoral, apostolic and charitable mission. The Catholic Church shall pursue its social, educational and cultural activities in accordance with Canon Law and the procedure prescribed by the laws of the Republic of Lithuania. The Republic of Lithuania shall also recognise the freedom of the Catholic Church and its communities to perform publicly religious rites, develop its structure, educate and offer pastoral assistance to the faithful, as well as acknowledge the total competence of the Catholic Church in its sphere."[5]

[4] The Law of Religious Communities and Associations of the Republic of Lithuania. Valstybes zinios, No. 89-1985. Vilnius, 1995.

[5] Agreement between the Holy See and the Republic of Lithuania concerning juridical aspects of the relations between the Catholic Church and the State. Art. 4. Vilnius, 2000.

3. Desecration of a place of worship

The Criminal Code of the Republic of Lithuania does not speak about crimes of desecration, but the above-mentioned agreement between the Catholic Church and the State reads: "The Republic of Lithuania shall guarantee respect for the sacred character of churches and chapels, as well as buildings, territories and religious places of worship directly related thereto, and shall defend them at the request of the competent authority of the Catholic Church". So, actually, places of worship of the religious groups recognised by the state are protected better than the rest. Here it is important to note that the 9 traditional religions are held also as recognised by the state. In criminal practice, any acts of vandalism, such as desecration of churches or cemeteries, are treated in a manner proportionate to the material harm inflicted on them. Vandalism against sacred objects is usually an aggravating factor.

4. Disrupting a religious meeting

Article 171 CC, "Disturbance of Religious Ceremonies or Celebrations of Religious Groups" reads: "Any person who, through violent acts, noise-making, or similar acts disrupts a service or other rites of a church or religious community recognised by the state, or a celebration of a religious group, commits a misdemeanour, and shall be punished by community service or a fine, or restriction of liberty, or detention." The protected good in this case is freedom of conscience.

Article 43 of the Constitution of Lithuania (CRL)[6] provides: "The State shall recognise the churches and religious organisations that are traditional in Lithuania, whereas other churches and religious organisations shall be recognised provided that they have support in society and their teaching and practices are not in conflict with the law and public morals… Churches and religious organisations shall be free to proclaim their teaching, perform their practices, and have houses of prayer, charity establishments, and schools for the training of clergy". The Constitutional Court of the Republic of Lithuania, referring to Article 26-1 CRL, explained that freedom of thought, conscience and religion must be considered as one of the most fundamental human rights and shall not be restricted. This right is a guarantee for people of different outlooks to live peacefully in an open, legitimate and consistent civic society. Freedom

[6] Constitution of the Republic of Lithuania. Vilnius, 1992.

of thought, conscience and religion was recognised as a key value of democracy and also an important prerequisite for the implementation of other constitutional rights and freedoms.

The *actus reus* of Article 171 CC may be articulated as disruption of a religious meeting or other ceremonies of a religious community or association recognised by the State.

State recognition means that the State supports the spiritual, cultural and social heritage of the particular religious communities. Religious meetings and ceremonies of those communities are allowed in their churches and temples, at private houses and apartments, and in the chapels at cemeteries and crematoria. On the request of believers, religious meetings and ceremonies might also be organised in hospitals, boarding-houses, and prisons. The time and other details of those meetings or ceremonies should be organised in agreement with the administrators of the particular institution. The administration of military bodies may allow the organisation of religious ceremonies according to their statutes. If students and their parents request religious meetings and ceremonies of religious communities recognised by the State, these may also be organised in public institutions of education, provided such ceremonies do not contradict the lay status of the institution and freedom of choice to participate/not. Religious ceremonies may also be organised in other public places if they do not breach the public peace nor cause risk to the health of people, morals, human rights and freedoms.

Disruption may also involve negative consequences and the causal connection between the act and its consequences. According to the law the material elements of the act of disruption could be using four-letter words, aggressiveness, menace, sneering, vandalising. A consequence of the act of disruption could be discontinuity of the ceremony, disappointment of the participants because of temporary break in the ceremony, the need to call the police, etc.

The case envisaged in Article 171 CC may also represent violation of public order according to Article 284 CC. One can note that punishment for disruption of religious events may be less severe if read in the light of Article 171. Let us assume that in the case of disruption, if negative consequences also ensue, Article 284-1 CC[7] could be applied together with Article 171 CC.

[7] "Any person who, by aggressive acts, threats, degrading treatment or acts of vandalism, demonstrates disrespect to neighbouring people or the environment and disrupts public peace and order in a public place, shall be punished by community service, or a fine, or a restriction of liberty, or detention, or imprisonment up to 2 years": Art.284-1 CC.

The subjective elements of disruption are the responsibility of the guilty person and his or her intention to disrupt a religious meeting or ceremony. The commentaries on the Criminal Code emphasize the importance to clarify whether the offender perceived the act of disruption as an act against a religious meeting or ceremony. If the action is stimulated by some personal or selfish motivation, the act should not be treated as directed against freedom of conscience.

If the offender specifically aimed to disrupt the religious ceremonies of a religious group or community not recognised by the State, he or she shall not be liable for deliberate actions under Article 171 CC but rather under Article 284 CC part 1 or 2.

It was likely that the Article would be used in a recent case of a woman who caused disorder during a Catholic Mass at which priests used Latin rather than the Lithuanian language. Formally the case fell under the ambit of Article 171 CC, but because the disturbance was minimal, the judge decided to apply Article 174 of the Code of Misdemeanours of the Administrative Law of the Republic of Lithuania, prescribing a fine for violation of public order.

5. Menaces, violence or force used against another's freedom of religion or conscience

Article 170 and Article 171 CC dealing with the punitive protection of violation of the principle of equality of the people and freedom of conscience were covered above in 1 and 2.

6. Discrimination on grounds of religion

Article 169 CC, "Discrimination of the basis of nationality, race, sex, origin, religion or belonging to other groups", reads as follows: "Any person who commits acts aimed at a certain group of people or a member thereof on account of that group's nationality, race, sex, sexual orientation, origin or religion with a view to interfering with their right to participate as equals in political, economical, social, cultural or labour activity or to restrict the human rights or freedoms of such group of people or any its members, shall be punished by community service or a fine, or detention, or imprisonment for a term of up to 3 years".

The protected good here is equality. The article matches Article 29 CRL which reads: "All persons shall be equal before the law, the courts, and other State institutions and officials. The rights of the human being may not be restricted, nor may he be granted any privileges on the ground of gender, race, nationality, language, origin, social status, belief, convictions, or views".

The principle of equal treatment is a commonly recognized norm according to the Universal Declaration of Human Rights, Articles 1 and 2, and also in the Convention for the Protection of Human Rights and Fundamental Freedoms, Article 14, which suppose enjoyment of the set of rights and freedoms without discrimination on any ground such as sex, race, colour, language, religion, political or other opinion, national or social origin, etc.

In Lithuanian legal practice, most of the current complaints of discrimination on the grounds of religion and beliefs are received by the Equal Opportunities Ombudsman (EOO). The EOO office monitors implementation of the Law of the Republic of Lithuania on Equal Opportunities,[8] and reports an increasing annual number of complaints about violations of principles of equal opportunities in the field of religion and beliefs, mostly from the side of non-traditional and thus non-State-recognised religious groups.

It is important to note also that recent sociological investigations reveal highly negative attitudes amongst Lithuanian people towards basic civic rights of members of religious minorities as well as towards deeply religious persons in general. Members of the traditional Christian communities and members of individual world-view groups were understood as those the best treated by the respondents of the sociological inquiry.

7. Disrupting a funeral

Article 313-1 CC reads as follows: "Any person who, seeking to express contempt for the deceased, disturbs the peace at a funeral, commits a misdemeanour, and shall be punished by community service or a fine or restriction of liberty, or detention". Here the material element of the crime is disturbance of the peace at the funeral, and its psychological element is the intention of the offender to express contempt for the deceased.

8. Abuse of a corpse or desecration of a grave

Article 311 CC provides: "1. Any person who takes a corpse or a part of it against the will of the executor of the burial or who abuses a human

[8] Law of the Republic of Lithuania on Equal Opportunities. Vilnius, 2003.

corpse, shall be punished by community service or restriction of liberty or detention, or imprisonment for a term of up to 1 year. 2. Any person who illegally opens a grave and desecrates the remains of the deceased or takes articles from inside the grave, shall be punished by detention or imprisonment for a term of up to 2 years". Also Article 312 CC reads: "Any person who destroys a grave, damages a tombstone or otherwise defiles a grave in some other way, shall be punished by community service or restriction of liberty or detention, or imprisonment for a term of up to 1 year".

9. Proselytizing

There are no references to this in the CC.

10. Apostasy

There are no references to this in the CC.

11. Misuse of religious garments or false state of office

There are no references to this in the CC.

12. Revelation of secrets

There are no references in the Criminal Code of the Republic of Lithuania to the issue of secrets obtained in the exercise of religious ministry. However, Article 8 of the Agreement between the Holy See and the Republic of Lithuania, concerning juridical aspects of the relations between the Catholic Church and the State, reads as follows: "1. The Republic of Lithuania shall guarantee the inviolability of the secrecy inherent in sacramental confession, even when a priest is called to give witness or intervene in judicial proceedings. 2. Upon the instigation of criminal procedures against a member of the clergy, the relevant legal institutions, in consideration of their pastoral responsibility for the faithful, shall inform the competent ecclesiastical authority thereof, provided it does not negatively affect the investigation process".

13. Celebration of religious marriage before civil marriage

There are no references about this issue in the Criminal Code of the Republic of Lithuania. Religious communities and associations recognised by the State may conclude an agreement with the State to achieve legal recognition of religious marriage. For instance, Article 13 of the Agreement between the Holy See and the Republic of Lithuania states: "1. A canonical marriage will have civil effects pursuant to the legal acts of the Republic of Lithuania from the moment of its religious celebration provided there are no impediments to the requirements of the laws of the Republic of Lithuania. 2. The time and manner of recording a canonical marriage in the civil register shall be established by the competent authority of the Republic of Lithuania, in co-ordination with the Conference of Lithuanian Bishops".

14. Offences against public peace in a place of worship

See above in sections 1, 2, and 3.

15. Female genital mutilation

There are no references to this in the CC.

16 and 17. Aggravation or attenuation by religious motivation

There are no explicit references to this, but one may notice that according to the Criminal Code of the Republic of Lithuania the offender may be punished more or less depending on the character of their intentionality to act. In some cases, religious motivation may stimulate lesser punishment, for instance, Article 171 v.s. Article 284 CC. But in the perspective of the Law of the Republic of Lithuania on Equal Opportunities, religious motivation may be treated as the critical subjective element in the crime of discrimination.

18. The sectarian milieu

There are no special regulations on or legal definition of a sectarian community in Lithuanian law.

Conclusions

Lithuanian penal law, as it relates to religion, protects freedom of conscience, the equality of people, human dignity, public peace, and the memory of deceased persons. The religious communities and associations recognised by the State, including the nine traditional religions of the Republic of Lithuania, are well protected by the Criminal Code and other laws of the Republic of Lithuania. To-date, the European Court of Human Rights has received no complaints in this field and there are no suits against the Republic of Lithuania on religious matters.

Alexis Pauly (†) et François Moyse

RELIGION ET DROIT PÉNAL – LUXEMBOURG

Le droit pénal fut beaucoup utilisé au Luxembourg au 19e siècle et au début du 20e siècle, au moment des tensions qui existaient entre les camps catholiques et libéraux. Les tribunaux eurent à rendre de nombreuses décisions relatives à la diffamation envers la religion catholique ou au contraire pour freiner les ardeurs religieuses à l'égard un État qui serait trop libéral.

Ces tensions sont l'affaire du passé et avec l'évolution vers une société beaucoup plus laïque, le droit pénal n'est guère plus invoqué en justice actuellement en la matière. Le Luxembourg s'est vu influencé par l'évolution du droit international privé au fil du temps.

I. Protection pénale de la religion

1. *La diffamation et l'injure à l'égard du contenu de la religion*

L'infraction de diffamation et d'injures à l'égard du contenu d'une religion n'existe pas en droit luxembourgeois.

Religieusement, c'est la profanation du Saint-Sacrement qui constitue le blasphème.

En revanche, l'incitation à la discrimination, à la haine ou à la violence à l'égard d'une personne ou d'un groupe de personnes (communauté) en raison de leur religion est spécifiquement visée à l'article 457-1 du code pénal luxembourgeois.

La peine prévue est de huit jours à deux ans et d'une amende de 251 euros à 25 000 euros ou de l'une de ces peines seulement.

La protection pénale s'étend également aux opinions philosophiques ce qui pourrait englober des associations anthroposophiques. Les convictions n'étant que protégées par la loi antidiscriminatoire civile et ne figurant pas dans le code pénal, semblent ne pas être visées.

La protection doit s'appliquer à toutes les religions. Celles reconnues officiellement ne posent pas de problème. Cependant, des mouvements sectaires pourraient ne pas être reconnus comme religion protégée par ces dispositions.

Il faut établir le dol de la part de la personne poursuivie, ou une volonté de nuire ou une méchanceté.[1]

2. *La diffamation et les injures contre l'Église ou une communauté religieuse*

A) L'infraction de diffamation et d'injures contre une Église ou une communauté religieuse n'existe pas en tant que telle en droit luxembourgeois.

Seul l'outrage à un ministre du culte dans l'exercice de son ministère est réprimé d'une peine de 8 jours à 3 mois de prison et une amende de 251 à 5000 euros, par l'article 145 du code pénal, l'outrage consistant en faits, paroles, gestes, menaces, écrits ou dessins.

Selon la jurisprudence, le mot outrage, contrairement à celui d'injure, a un sens général et comprend tout ce qui d'une manière quelconque peut blesser ou offenser une personne.[2]

Cependant, la diffamation et les injures sont réprimées aux termes des articles 443 et 448 du code pénal et celles adressées à une communauté religieuse seront donc poursuivies sur base de ces articles.

a) Les éléments constitutifs de l'infraction de diffamation sont:

1) l'articulation d'un fait précis
2) l'imputation de ce fait à une personne déterminée
3) le fait doit être de nature à porter atteinte à l'honneur de cette personne ou à l'exposer au mépris public
4) la publicité de l'imputation
5) l'intention méchante
6) l'imputation d'un acte de la vie privée ou professionnelle qui ne constitue pas une infraction et dont il est impossible ou interdit de faire la preuve.

b) Les éléments constitutifs de l'injure sont:

1) l'absence d'articulation d'un fait précis
2) une intention méchante

[1] L'ancien article 12 de la loi sur la presse du 20 juillet 1869 portait des peines contre ceux qui, par des attaques directes et méchantes, insérées dans les journaux ou dans des placards exposés ou distribués, avaient outragé ou tourné en dérision un culte établi, disposition abolie par la loi du 8 juin 2004 sur la liberté d'expression dans les médias.

[2] Cour, 5 février 1979, Pasicrisie 24, p. 230.

Il résulte des éléments constitutifs des infractions de diffamation et d'injures, que celles-ci ne sont réprimées pénalement que lorsqu'elles visent une personne précise.

Cependant, la jurisprudence reconnait la diffamation ou l'injure à l'égard des membres d'une communauté religieuse, lorsque ces infractions, bien que ne visant pas une personne précise, sont cependant présentées de telle façon qu'elles puissent rejaillir sur tous les membres de la communauté religieuse.[3]

B) L'incitation à la discrimination, à la haine ou à la violence à l'égard d'une personne ou d'un groupe de personnes en raison de leur appartenance à une Église ou à une communauté religieuse est spécialement incriminée aux termes de l'article 457-1 du code pénal luxembourgeois et est punie de la même peine que celle visée sous le point 1).

La protection pénale s'étend également aux opinions philosophiques.[4] La franc-maçonnerie n'est pas reconnue explicitement dans les textes luxembourgeois.

3. *La profanation d'un lieu ou objet sacré d'une religion*

A) La profanation d'un lieu n'est pas expréssement visée, mais l'article 526 du code pénal incrimine la destruction ou la dégradation des monuments, statues, tableaux d'art quelconques, placés dans les églises, temples ou autres édifices publics.

L'infraction n'existe que quand il y a destruction, abattement, mutilation ou dégradation d'objets qui se trouvent dans une église ou autre lieu de culte public. L'infraction est punie d'une peine d'emprisonnement de huit jours à un an et d'une amende de 251 à 5 000 euros.

B) L'article 144 du code pénal réprime également l'outrage aux objets d'un culte, soit dans les lieux destinés ou servant habituellement à son exercice, soit dans au cours de cérémonies publiques de ce culte.

L'outrage se réalise soit par des faits, des paroles, des gestes, des menaces, des écrits ou des dessins et la peine prévue est l'emprisonnement de quinze jours à six mois et une amende identique à celle prévue sous A).

[3] Cour, 30 janvier 1904, Pas. 6, p. 429; Cour, 23 mars 1912, Pas. 8, p. 364.
[4] Voir point 1.

4. *L'empêchement ou la perturbation d'une pratique religieuse*

L'empêchement et la perturbation de la pratique religieuse sont réprimés aux termes respectivement des articles 142 et 143 du code pénal.

A) Les éléments de l'infraction de l'article 142 du code pénal sont des violences ou menaces.

Ces violences ou menacent doivent contraindre ou empêcher une ou plusieurs personnes à exercer un culte, y assister, célébrer certaines fêtes religieuses, observer certains jours de repos.

L'infraction est punie d'une peine d'emprisonnement de huit jours à deux mois et d'une amende de 251 à 2 000 euros.

B) Les éléments constitutifs de l'infraction de l'article 143 du code pénal sont:

- des troubles ou des désordres
- qui empêchent, retardent, ou interrompent
- l'exercice d'un culte
- qui se pratique dans un lieu destiné ou servant habituellement au culte ou dans les cérémonies publiques de ce culte.

L'infraction est punie d'une peine d'emprisonnement de huit jours à trois mois et d'une amende de 251 à 2 000 euros.

Les associations philosophiques ne sont pas visées spécifiquement. Cependant, leur protection est garantie par les principes généraux de droit pénal.

5. *Les violences, les menaces et les voies de fait contre la liberté religieuse ou de conscience de l'individu*

Les violences, les menaces et les voies de fait contre la liberté religieuse ou de conscience de l'individu sont punies par l'article 142 du Code pénal, comme mentionné au point 4.

6. *La discrimination en raison de la religion*

La discrimination en raison de la religion est punie aux termes des articles 454 et 455 du code pénal[5].

[5] La loi du 29 novembre 2006 concernant l'interdiction des discriminations vise également les convictions, mais ce terme n'est pas repris dans le code pénal, qui ne réprime donc pas les atteintes aux convictions.

Les éléments constitutifs de l'infraction sont:

a) Une distinction opérée entre les personnes physiques, les personnes morales, les groupes ou les communautés de personnes en raison de leur appartenance à une religion déterminée.

b) Cette distinction doit avoir pour but:

- soit de refuser aux personnes appartenant à une religion la disposition ou la jouissance d'un bien ou d'un service;
- soit de subordonner la fourniture d'un bien ou d'un service à l'appartenance à une religion déterminée;
- soit d'indiquer dans une publicité l'intention de refuser un bien ou un service ou de pratiquer une discrimination lors de la fourniture d'un bien ou d'un service en raison de l'appartenance à une religion déterminée;
- soit d'entraver l'exercice normal d'une activité économique quelconque en raison de l'appartenance à une religion déterminée;
- soit de refuser d'embaucher, de sanctionner ou de licencier une personne en raison de l'appartenance à une religion déterminée;
- soit de subordonner l'accès au travail, à tous les types de formation professionnelle, ainsi qu'à certaines conditions de travail, l'affiliation et l'engagement dans une organisation de travailleurs ou d'employeurs à une condition religieuse.

Une peine aggravée existe si l'auteur est une personne dépositaire de l'autorité publique ou chargée d'une mission de service public, en cas de refus du bénéfice d'un droit accordé par la loi et d'une entrave à l'exercice normal d'une activité économique quelconque.

La discrimination à raison de l'appartenance à une religion déterminée est punie d'une peine d'emprisonnement de huit jours à deux ans et/ou d'une amende de 251 à 25 000 euros.

Le dol spécial est requis pour punir cette infraction.

7. *La perturbation des cérémonies funèbres*

L'infraction de perturbation des cérémonies funèbres n'existe pas en tant que telle dans la législation luxembourgeoise.

Cependant, toute perturbation à l'encontre des cérémonies funèbres, peut être sanctionnée sur base de l'article 143 du code pénal qui réprime les troubles ou des désordres qui empêchent, retardent ou interrompent l'exercice d'un culte qui se pratique dans un lieu destiné ou servant habituellement au culte ou dans les cérémonies publiques de ce culte.

8. *La profanation de cadavre ou de sépulture*

La profanation de cadavre et de sépulture est réprimée aux termes de l'article 453 du code pénal.

A) La profanation de cadavre (article 453 alinéa 1)
L'infraction existe s'il y a une atteinte à l'intégrité d'un cadavre et ce par n'importe quel moyen. Elle est punie d'une peine d'un mois à deux ans de prison et d'une amende de 251 à 2 000 euros.

B) La profanation de sépulture (article 453 alinéa 2)
Les éléments constitutifs sont:

- une violation ou une profanation
- celle-ci doit porter sur des tombeaux, sépultures ou de monuments édifiés à la mémoire des morts;
- elle peut se faire par n'importe quel moyen.

La peine prévue pour cette infraction est également un mois à deux ans de prison et une amende de 251 à 25 000 euros. La peine est portée à trois ans d'emprisonnement et à 37 500 euros d'amende lorsque la profanation de sépulture est également accompagnée d'atteinte à l'intégrité du cadavre.

9. *Le prosélytisme*

L'infraction de prosélytisme n'existe pas en droit luxembourgeois.

10. *L'apostasie*

Cette infraction n'existe pas en droit luxembourgeois.

11 *L'usage incorrect des habits religieux ou de service*

Selon l'article 228 du code pénal, *«toute personne qui aura porté publiquement un costume, un uniforme, une décoration, un ruban ou autres insignes d'un ordre qui ne lui appartient pas, sera punie d'une amende de 500 à 10 000 euros».*

Selon la jurisprudence, *«le costume de ville du ministre d'un culte, soumis à une discipline intérieure dans laquelle l'État n'intervient pas, mais qu'il reconnaît est protégé par la loi…»*.

Il n'est pas nécessaire que le costume usurpé soit identique à celui de la personne autorisée à le porter, mais il suffit qu'il y ait entre eux une ressemblance telle que la méprise soit possible.

Pour être punissable, le fait matériel du port du costume doit avoir été commis dans une intention frauduleuse, c'est-à-dire avec l'intention de persuader de l'existence de la qualité à laquelle il est attaché, sans cependant qu'il soit nécessaire que celui qui porte indûment un costume ait eu l'intention de s'immiscer dans les fonctions dont le costume est l'insigne.[6]

II. Infractions des ministres du culte

L'article 19 de la Constitution garantit la liberté des cultes, celle de leur exercice public, ainsi que la liberté de manifester ses opinions religieuses, sauf la répression des délits commis à l'occasion de l'usage de ces libertés.

12. *Les révélations de secret obtenu dans l'exercice du ministère du culte religieux*

La violation du secret obtenu dans l'exercice du ministère du culte religieux est réprimée aux termes de l'article 458 du code pénal qui dispose que « *les médecins…et toutes autres personnes dépositaires, par état ou par profession, des secrets qu'on leur confie, qui, hors le cas où ils sont appelés à rendre témoignage en justice et celui où la loi les oblige à faire connaître ces secrets, les auront révélés, seront punis d'un emprisonnement de huit jours à six mois et d'une amende de 500 à 5000 euros.»*.

Il résulte de cet article qu'un ministre de culte se rend coupable de violation du secret professionnel que lorsqu'il révèle les confidences qui lui sont faites par une ou des personnes ayant eu recours à son ministère.

Les devoirs de dénoncer n'est prévu qu'en cas de témoignage en justice ou dans les cas prévus par la loi. On peut penser notamment au danger de mort qui entraînerait une infraction de non-assistance à personne en danger.

[6] Trib. corr. Diekirch, 21 décembre 1962, Pas. 19, 148.

Il est cependant reconnu qu'un ministre du culte ne peut pas être forcé à témoigner en justice, du moins en matière civile. Ainsi, les tribunaux ont reconnu qu'on ne pouvait forcer un prêtre à prêter un serment litis-décisoire dans une affaire de testament, au risque de violer son secret professionnel.[7]

La jurisprudence a admis dans une affaire pénale que *«les personnes astreintes au secret professionnel peuvent, lorsqu'elles sont citées comme témoin, déposer en justice, mais ne peuvent être forcées de le faire»*.[8] De même, la doctrine semble reconnaître le droit de se taire aux confidents nécessaires.[9]

13. *La célébration d'un mariage religieux antérieur au mariage civil*

L'article 21 de la Constitution prévoit que le mariage civil devra toujours précéder la bénédiction nuptiale. L'éventuelle abrogation de cet article est actuellement discutée.

Tout ministre d'un culte qui célèbre le mariage religieux avant le mariage civil est puni d'une amende de 500 à 5 000 euros aux termes de l'article 267 alinéa 1 du code pénal. La récidive est passible d'une peine de prison de huit jours à trois mois (alinéa 2).

14. *L'atteinte à la paix publique dans un lieu de culte ou à l'occasion de l'exercice du culte*

L'atteinte à la paix publique dans un lieu de culte ou à l'occasion de l'exercice du culte est punie aux termes de l'article 268 du code pénal.

En effet, les ministre des cultes, qui dans un des discours prononcés ou par des écrits lus, dans l'exercice de leur ministère, et en assemblée publique, ou par un écrit contenant des instructions pastorales, en quelque forme que ce soit, auront attaqué directement le Gouvernement, une loi, un arrêté royal ou tout autre acte de l'autorité publique, seront punis d'un emprisonnement de huit jours à trois mois et d'une amende de 251 à 5 000 euros.

De même, le ministre du culte auteur de l'instruction pastorale, du discours ou de l'écrit qui contient une provocation directe à la désobéissance aux lois ou aux actes de l'autorité publique, ou qui tend à soulever

[7] Cour, 8 janvier 1885, Pas. 2,323.
[8] CSJ, cass.crim., 21 mars 1957, P. 17, p. 43.
[9] Alain Steichen, Le secret bancaire face aux autorités nationales et étrangères. p. 7.

ou à mobiliser une partie des citoyens contre les autres, est puni d'un emprisonnement de trois mois à deux ans.

Si l'instruction pastorale, le discours ou l'écrit sont suivis de désobéissance, le ministre du culte est en plus puni d'une amende de 500 à 10 000 euros.

Une célèbre affaire avait abouti au 19e siècle à un arrêt qui stipulait que *«se rend coupable d'attaque, dirigée en chaire contre une loi, le ministre du culte qui, en chaire, qualifie le mariage civil de concubinage, et ajoute des commentaires grossiers et obscènes, de nature à illustrer son appréciation sur cette institution civile»*.[10]

III. Infractions liées à des actes de culte ou à des rites

15. *La mutilation génitale féminine*

La mutilation génitale féminine ne constitue pas une infraction particulière. Elle est considérée par la jurisprudence comme une circonstance aggravante de l'infraction de coups et blessures réprimée aux termes de l'article 398 du code pénal.

C'est dans ce sens que la Cour supérieure de Luxembourg s'est prononcée dans son arrêt du 13 juillet 1956.[11]

En effet, elle a déclaré dans ledit arrêt que: *«En ce qui concerne spécialement le délit de coups et blessures volontaires, la circonstance d'une mutilation grave ou celle de la perte de l'usage absolu d'un organe ne crée pas un délit nouveau, mais seulement un délit aggravé, alors que ces circonstances se rattachent d'une façon intime au fait principal»*.

Les éléments constitutifs sont:

a) un élément intentionnel, à savoir la volonté d'attenter à une personne déterminée
b) un élément matériel, à savoir les blessures causées à une personne et des coups portés à cette personne
c) ces coups et blessures doivent avoir entraîné une mutilation, c'est-à-dire une perte d'organe du corps utile à la vie.

L'infraction de coups et blessures est punie d'une peine d'emprisonnement de huit jours à six mois et d'une amende de 251 à 1 000 euros. La préméditation augmente la peine de prison à une échelle d'un mois à un an et une amende doublée.

[10] Cour, 31 mai 1879, p. 1, 641.
[11] Pasicrisie 16, p. 536.

La mutilation génitale, en tant que circonstance aggravante de l'infraction de coups et blessures entrainera une augmentation de la durée maximale de la peine d'emprisonnement ainsi que le montant de l'amende.

16. *Les infractions ayant pour mobile ou comme cause d'aggravation une motivation religieuse*

Selon l'article 457-2 du code pénal, la profanation de cadavre ou de sépulture emporte une peine plus sévère si elle a été commise à raison de l'appartenance ou de la non-appartenance, vraie ou supposée à…une religion déterminée.

Il existe aussi des infractions pour lesquelles la qualité de ministre du culte constitue une circonstance aggravante.

Il s'agit de l'attentat à la pudeur et du viol, si l'infraction a été commise par des ministres d'un culte qui ont abusé de leur position pour le commettre (article 377), ainsi que pour les infractions de prostitution, exploitation et traite des êtres humains (article 380).

17. *Les infractions à l'égard desquelles la motivation religieuse est une excuse atténuante*

Il n'existe pas de telles infractions au Luxembourg.

18. *Les infractions pénales ayant pour cadre les sectes*

Il n'existe pas en droit luxembourgeois d'infractions se rapportant exclusivement aux sectes.

Sophie van Bijsterveld

RELIGION AND CRIMINAL LAW IN THE NETHERLANDS

1. Introduction

Dutch criminal law contains a variety of explicit references to religion. These relate to utterances, gatherings, and religious rituals. Although the subject of discussion from time to time, they are for the most part taken for granted – that is, until recently. Incidental discussions usually related to specific instances, but as these instances tended to be rather isolated, the discussions died down quickly. The specific provisions were also challenged from time to time from a more principled point of view, but criticism never gained much support.

In the last few years, however, the situation has changed. Freedom of expression, especially, whether based on religion or with regard to religion, is a topic of profound debate in academia, society and politics. These debates concern both the legal provisions as well as the application of these provisions in concrete situations. Issues related to these topics are capable of stirring up great interest and emotion throughout the country. Eyecatching examples are the controversial statements of the assassinated politician Pim Fortuyn on Islam in the run-up to the parliamentary elections of 2002; the production and launch of the anti-Islam film 'Fitna' by the Dutch Parliamentarian Geert Wilders in 2008, which kept the nation divided and politicians 'hostaged' for over half a year; and notably since the beginning of the new century a host of utterances of radical Islamic imams which gained broad publicity. International developments, such as the outbursts of violence following the publication and international spread of the 'Danish cartoons' on the prophet Mohammed in 2006 also had their effects on debates in the Netherlands. The issue is not yet settled and debates on the topic will certainly continue.

This contribution provides an overview of the explicit references to religion in Dutch criminal law. It will deal in turn with controversial statements (Section 2), gatherings (Section 3), religious rituals (Section 4), and offences linked to religion (Section 5). Then, a few observations are made on acts related to religion that do not constitute an offence (Section 6). These are followed by a brief conclusion (Section 7).

2. Controversial statements[1]

For our purpose, controversial statements include statements *against* a (person or group of persons on the ground of their) religion or *on the basis* of a religion. Over the last few years, some of these provisions have been extended in terms of the grounds of defamation as well as the circumstances in which the defamation takes place and with respect to the maximum penalty.

Defamation: Dutch criminal law penalises as 'serious offences against public order' defamatory statements about a group of persons on the grounds of *inter alia* their religion or personal beliefs (Article 137 c). The same Article also penalises defamatory statements on other grounds: race, hetero- or homosexual orientation, and physical, psychological, or mental handicap. This includes statements made on the basis of religious conviction (notably relevant with respect to homosexual orientation). The requirement is that the statements must be made 'publicly' and 'intentionally'; they include statements made orally, in writing, or by image.

Similarly, incitement of hatred of or discrimination against persons or violence against their person or property is penalised as a serious offence against public order (137d). Article 137e of the Criminal Code penalises making an offensive statement 'for any other reason than that of giving factual information', where a person 'knows or should reasonably suspect this is the case' or 'incites hatred of or discrimination against people or violence against their person or property'. The grounds are those mentioned above. The distribution of an object or having it in stock for that purpose is covered as well.

In the case of a second offence, the Article allows the possibility of disqualification from a profession if the offence was commited in the practice of that profession and less than five years have elapsed since the previous conviction (Article 137e). Financial or other support for discriminatory activities on the grounds mentioned above is also penalised (Article 137f).

As a lesser offence related to public order, Article 429 of the Criminal Code penalises discrimination against persons, on the grounds mentioned in Article 137e, in the exercise of an office or profession or in carrying on a business.

[1] The Criminal Code Articles referred to are formulated in quite a detailed manner, as can be expected for such Articles. In the brief reference we make to these Articles it is unavoidable that some of the nuances are lost.

Blasphemy, ridicule of church ministers and religious objects: Specific provisions exist with respect to blasphemy, ridicule of church ministers, and religious objects.

Making public statements offensive to religious feelings through 'scornful blasphemy', orally, in writing, or by image is penalised as a serious offence against public order by Article 147 of the Criminal Code. Likewise, ridiculing a church minister in the lawful exercise of his office is penalised. The same is true for ridiculing objects dedicated to worship, at the place and time of lawful worship (both of which offences are also found in Article 147).

Article 147a penalises, among other things, the dissemination of writings or an image that contains statements offensive to religious feelings through 'scornful blasphemy' or having it in stock for that purpose provided that the person knows or has serious reasons to suspect that such statements are contained in the material.

As a lesser offence related to public order, Article 429 of the Criminal Code, penalises exhibiting writings or images with such content in a way that is visible from a public road.

3. Gatherings

Obstructing or disturbing a religious meeting: Both are liable to criminal procecution. This also relates to the non-religious counterparts, as well as to funeral or cremation ceremonies. Article 145 of the Criminal Code penalises the obstruction by force or threat of force of religious and non-religious worship as well as funeral or cremation ceremonies. The maximum penalty is higher than the penalty set for obstructing an 'ordinary' meeting. Article 146 penalises the disturbance of such gatherings by deliberately creating disorder or noise. The addition of the non-religious dimension in these provisions dates from 1988.

Entering a place of worship by public officials in the exercise of their functions: The Criminal Procedures Act provides (in Article 123) that places of worship may not be entered by police officers during worship unless the person they are pursuing is caught in the act.

In the General Act on Entering Places there is a similar provision for those public officials who have a legal authority to enter places. Article 12 states that except in cases of a person being caught in the act, the entering of places designated for worship or non-religious reflection is not allowed during religious worship or gathering for non-religious reflection.

4. Religious rituals: offences by church ministers

Only one criminal offence exists which specifically relates to church ministers. This concerns the solemnisation of a wedding. Marriage is clearly defined by the Civil Code. The Civil Code states that it regards marriage only in its civil aspects (Article 1:68). Religious ceremonies with regard to marriage are not legally binding and cannot take place prior to the performance of a legally valid marriage. A church minister who performs a religious wedding ceremony without having verified the existence of a legally binding marriage is liable to prosecution under criminal law (Article 449 Criminal Code).

5. Offences linked to acts of worship, to rites, or religion

Many offences may have links to religion, either because they might address practices related to a religion (such as female genital mutilation) or because they are fuelled by a religious dimension (assaults, coercion) or even commited because of the religion of the person (desecration of gravestones or burial sites).

Another category of offences linked to religion is offences committed out of conscientious objection (such as refusal of a driver of a car to cooperate with a blood test).

These offences are treated as ordinary offences. The religious dimension may play a role in the determination of the criminal sentence. It goes without saying that with offences that are almost by definition linked to religion, such as female genital mutilation, this is not the case.

6. No criminal offences

Finally, a few comments are offered on acts that do not constitute a criminal offence. One of these is proselytising. No reference whatsoever is made to this. Nor is apostasy a criminal offence. On the contrary, freedom of religion also entails the freedom not to have any religion, to change religion, or to abolish one's religion. This right has gained new topicality in relation to Islam.

With respect to ministers of religion, no specific criminal provisions exist with regard to (breach of) secrets obtained in the exercise of their ministry. Neither do any specific criminal provisions exist with respect to wearing religious garments which give a false impression that the person is a cleric.

There are no specific provisions with respect to religious sects. Sects do not represent a legal category in the Netherlands.

7. Concluding remarks

As was mentioned in the introduction, the provisions of the Criminal Code on defamation are quite a sensitive issue in politics, society, and academia. The debate on the extent and limits of freedom of expression concerns both the formulation of the Criminal Code (the principles) as well as the interpretation and application of these provisions by the criminal courts in concrete cases. The scope of this contribution does not lend itself to an analysis of this debate.

However, two brief observations can be made. It seems that generally speaking, the dominant public opinion favours more liberty to express controversial non-religious statements that are critical towards religion than to express controversial religious statements.

A second observation is that the debate tends to focus on criminal law and the application of the Criminal Code. In reality, the legal instruments to channel controversial statements are much more diverse. The Civil Code, for instance, fulfils a role in this respect, as does, perhaps unexpectedly, the General Equal Treatment Act. Non-legal instruments may even be as important.

Michał Rynkowski

RELIGION AND CRIMINAL LAW: POLAND

1. Introduction – short historical overview

Poland has been proud of its history, one relatively free of religious persecution. In 1573, just one year after the infamous night of St. Bartholomew in France,[1] the gathering of Polish gentry known as the Warsaw Confederation adopted an act declaring freedom of religion and equal rights for people of different denominations. The freedom guaranteed was broader than that of the German Augsburg Peace (1555), where only the ruling duke had the right to choose the religion of his people. The 1573 act lasted for many years and was changed only gradually after 1658. The "3 May Constitution", from 1791, stated clearly in Article I that any person changing their faith from the Holy Roman Catholic Religion to any other religion shall be subject to punishment for apostasy. This penalty referred only to those who wanted to leave the Catholic Church; freedom of religion in general was guaranteed. The 1791 Constitution was one of the last legal acts before the partition of Poland; the acts issued after 1918 (during the so-called II Republic) did not refer to apostasy.

After Poland was reunited in 1918, the first penal code was adopted in 1932. Chapter XXVI was entitled "Crimes against religious feelings" (Art. 172-174). The following were penalised: blasphemy against God (which was the last time blasphemy was penalised, with up to 5 years' imprisonment), public insult of a religious community, their dogmas, faith, as well as an intentional disturbance or interruption of a ceremony of a legally recognized church or religious community. The commentators of this era (Makarewicz, 1938) underlined that the subject of the protection was not the belief or faith of an individual, but rather public peace and the protection of religion as an important social factor. The despoilment of a corpse was penalised in a separate Article (Art. 168).

After World War II, the communist government passed an infamous decree "on the protection of freedom of conscience and religion"

[1] J. Bardach, Historia państwa i prawa polskiego, Warszawa, p. 209-213.

(5 August 1949). The penal code adopted in 1969 repeated more or less the provisions of this decree: it constitutes a good example of the difference between the official legislation and the actual situation. The whole of Chapter XXVIII was devoted to religious issues and it listed nine specific crimes (more than there are nowadays), *inter alia*:

- limitation of the freedom of a citizen (Art. 192)
- insult due to either a person's lack of religious affiliation or his/her religious affiliation (in this order, first lack of affiliation, then affiliation, Art. 193 §1)
- abuse of freedom of conscience and religion (Art. 194)
- abuse of a person's religious beliefs (Art. 195)
- interruption of a religious ceremony or defamation of a corpse (Art. 197 §1)
- despoilment of a corpse (Art. 197 §2)
- offence to a person's religious feelings (Art. 198)

The crimes relating to freedom of religion have almost the same numbers in different succeeding codes (Arts. 192-198, currently Arts. 194-196).

The Constitution of 1997 provides in Article 25 for the principle of equality between churches and religious communities and in Article 53 guarantees the protection of freedom of conscience and religion. The provisions of the Constitution are developed in a number of statutes, including the statute on the guarantees of freedom of conscience and religion from 1989,[2] in the penal code from 1997,[3] in the Concordat from 1993 and in the statutes referring to the relations between the state and a given church or religious community (there are 15 such statutes). With regard to definitions, Polish criminal law uses general categories: *przestępstwo* (crime), which can be either *zbrodnia* (felony, no less than 3 years' imprisonment) or *występek* (misdemeanor). The majority of crimes discussed below are misdemeanours.

2. Defamation, outrage and incitement to hatred

Article 196 CC reads: "[Any person] who offends religious feelings of other persons by public defamation of an object of religious devotion or place used for carrying out religious rites, shall be punished with a fine,

[2] Consolidated text in Official Journal (Dziennik Ustaw, hereinafter as Dz.U), 2000, No. 26, item 319)

[3] Dz. U. 1997, No. 88, item 555.

limitation of freedom or withdrawal of freedom [which is the official Polish term for imprisonment – MR] for up to 2 years". The provision itself seems to be clear, and so the Constitutional Court has referred to it only once, in its judgment from 1995 concerning the notion of "Christian values", used in the statute on broadcasting. In this case,[4] the Court underlined that "Religious feelings, due to their character, are the subject of special protection. These are directly connected with freedom of conscience and religion, which is 'a constitutional value'". As the Court also mentioned the word "conscience", it may be assumed that protection goes beyond simply religious feelings.

According to the commentaries, defamation may be oral (speech, remarks), written (flyers, books), graphic (posters, commercial), or by gesture (parody). Public character and intentional acts constitute important elements of the offence. The act of defamation must be carried out publicly or its results shall be known to the public, and can refer to items or goods, which are of particular importance to the denomination in question: a cross, pictures of saints, etc. The value protected is God or a god, but not the object itself (idolatry).[5] Criticisms of a religious community or of the statements and opinions of religious leaders are not punishable.[6]

To-date two cases have been brought before the courts: one concerned a poster of the movie "Scandalist Larry Flint" and the other, by Dorota Nieznalska, showing the male organs on the cross. In the first, on 23 September 2004, the Court of Second Instance decided to discontinue the case. The second one was far more complicated: the Court in Gdańsk first sentenced the artist to six months' limitation of freedom, but the judgment was overruled in April 2004 at second instance, which demanded the re-run of the entire proceedings; they restarted in November 2007.

According to Article 7 of the statute on freedom of conscience and religion from 1989, the citizens of other states and stateless persons have the same rights as Polish citizens.

Incitement to hatred, "based on national, ethnic, racial or religious differences or due to lack of religiosity", is also punishable – by fine,

[4] K 17/93, OTK 1994, cz. I, it. 11, p. 90.

[5] A. Wąsek, Przestępstwa przeciwko przekonaniom religijnym de lege lata i de lege ferenda, Państwo i Prawo 1995/7, p. 33.

[6] B. Kunicka-Michalska, J. Wojciechowska, Przestępstwa przeciwko wolności, wolności sumienia i wyznania, wolności seksualnej, obyczajności oraz czci i nietykalności cielesnej, Warszawa 2000, p. 86.

limitation of freedom, or withdrawal of freedom, for up to two years (Art. 256, CC). The next Article (Art. 257, CC) penalises public insults to a group of persons or an individual, due to their national, ethnic, racial, religious affiliation or due to the lack of such affiliation – but in this case, the CC provides for imprisonment, but not a fine or limitation of freedom, which is proof that this crime is considered to be more serious. The same punishment is foreseen for a person who violates the physical integrity of another person (Art. 257, CC). The value protected is primarily that of the dignity and integrity of the person, and secondarily that of public order. The insult must be actual and not subjective.[7] These crimes are prosecuted *ex officio*, which means that there is no need for the individual to bring the case to the court; the action is taken by the prosecutor.

3. Discrimination

Article 194 CC states: "[Any person] who limits a person in his/her rights because of his/her religious affiliation or because of the lack of such an affiliation, shall be punished with a fine, limitation of freedom or withdrawal of freedom for up to two years".

This article is nothing other than a prohibition on discrimination: everybody is protected, both an individual and a group. The object of protection is not a god or a religion, but the religious (or non-religious) feelings of "anyone", not only citizens of the Republic (which complies with international law). The offence may be caused by an act or an omission. The commentators agree[8] that intention must be proved, on the basis of the wording "because of the religious affiliation...."

The penal code does not specify the object of protection: whether it is affiliation to the church or religious community with a clear legal position in Poland, or any religious affiliation. Despite the lack of commentaries on this subject it could be assumed – taking account of the idea behind this provision – that Art. 194 aims to protect every kind of religious feelings and affiliation. Therefore, discrimination based on membership in a church or religious community which has no clear legal position in Poland is also forbidden. The discrimination shall be prosecuted *ex officio*.

[7] Pływaczewski, w: A. Wąsek, Kodeks karny. Duże komentarze Becka. Część szczegółowa. A. Wąsek (ed.), Warszawa 2006, vol. 2, p. 420.

[8] A number of them quoted in: Kodeks karny. Duże komentarze Becka. Część szczegółowa. A. Wąsek (ed.), Warszawa 2006, p. 773.

The crime described in Article 194 may also be aggravated in several ways, in which case the penalty is higher:

- if it is connected with assault or threat (Art. 119 CC), or
- if it causes public outrage or violates the integrity of the person (Art. 257 CC), or
- if it is committed by an official of a public authority (Art. 231 CC).

As in many other European states, the display of crucifixes in a public place is also an issue in Poland. An inhabitant of Łódź watching a TV-broadcast of a session of the city council saw a cross hanging in the council chamber. He claimed that it was against his conscience and asked in a formal letter for the removal of the cross from the chamber. After the city council refused to do so, the matter was addressed to the court and finally to the Chief Administrative Court (NSA). The NSA confirmed in its judgment[9] that freedom of conscience or religion was not violated and that no form of discrimination had taken place. The debate which followed this judgment showed very different points of view.

L. Wiśniewski[10] appreciated the judgment, agreeing that the person's freedom had not been limited in any way; thus there was no discrimination in any form. The city council hanging a cross in the council chamber was acting in its capacity as administrator of the building (*dominium*) but not as legislator (thus it was not exercising its *imperium*). L.Wiśniewski agreed with the court that a cross is much more than a religious symbol of one denomination, because it also conveys very broad and positive messages.

On the other hand, M. Pietrzak[11] argued that the principle of the rule of law allows the citizens to act in all ways which are not prohibited by law, whereas in comparison public authorities may act only when they were permitted by law to do so.

4. The disturbance of religious acts and funerals; the despoilment of corpses

Article 195 CC penalises the "disturbance of the performance of a public religious act of a church or religious community having a regulated situation in Poland". It is clear that this provision covers a very broad

[9] ACa 612/98, OSP 1999, N. 10, pos. 177; OSA 1999/6, it. 26/21.
[10] L. Wiśniewski, Glosa w: Przegląd Sejmowy 2000, No. 3, p. 105-108.
[11] M. Pietrzak, Glosa w: Przegląd Sejmowy 2000, No. 3, p. 108-110.

spectrum of activities, but (different from Article 194) it relates exclusively to denominations having a regulated situation. However, Polish law is very liberal in this respect and almost all communities willing to register as religious entities may do so.[12]

Commentators underline that if there is a disturbance not of public services in the church but only of individuals praying privately in the church, then the crime is one under Article 196 (see above). The meetings, gatherings and other manifestations of associations (including philosophical associations, though they are not expressly mentioned) are protected by Article 260 CC, which foresees a fine, limitation of freedom of withdrawal of freedom for those guilty of disturbance.

Any person who maliciously disturbs a funeral, or other mourning ceremony or rites, shall be punished under Article 195 §1. The ceremony does not have to be a religious one, and it may be performed in public or in private.[13] The good protected is the honour of a deceased person and the religious feelings of the participants; the provision states clearly that only "malicious" disruption is punishable.

Any person who defames a corpse or any of its parts or "the place of inhumation", shall be punished by fine, limitation of freedom or withdrawal of freedom for up to 2 years. Despoilment of a corpse or sepulchre is penalized more severely, with up to 8 years' imprisonment. Both crimes are found in Article 262 CC and they do not have to be committed in public,[14] as a human corpse is legally protected from the moment of death.

5. The seal of confession

Secrets disclosed in confession are protected in the code of penal procedure (*kodeks postępowania karnego* from 1997, CCP) and in the code of civil procedure (*kodeks postępowania cywilnego* from 1964, CCivilP). At first glance it is possible to see that this question is of greater importance in the criminal procedure, where it is broadly discussed.

According to paragraph 2 of Article 178 of the CCP, it is forbidden to hear a priest as a witness concerning facts which he was told while listening to a confession. This ban is absolute, and can not be relaxed, neither by the priest himself,[15] nor by anybody else. Any such evidence is null

[12] M. Rynkowski, Religious entities as legal persons, in: L. Friedner (ed.), Churches and other religious organisations as legal persons, Leuven 2007, p. 177-182.

[13] J. Wojciechowska, w: Przestępstwa przeciwko, op. cit., p. 80.

[14] Pływaczewski, op. cit., p. 443.

[15] Decision of the Appeal Court in Kraków, 1.1.1995, II Akz 237/95, KZS 1995/6/36.

and void, and cannot be used in the trial.[16] However, there is no punishment for a priest who would reveal such secrets. Nevertheless, a couple of remarks must be added by way of commentary:

- this ban applies only to the situation when the priest is to be heard as a witness – thus, it is not applicable when the priest is accused or is a suspect;
- the ban refers only to the matters entrusted to the priest while listening to the confession; he can be a witness to all other matters falling outside the confession;[17]
- a "priest" is understood to be a priest of the Catholic Church or a believer of another church or religious community who has a special role in that community, as when appointed for the regular performance of celebrations (as defined by a resolution issued by seven judges of the Supreme Court (I KZP 1/91, OSNKW 1992, 7-8/46);
- the rules of course refer only to those churches and religious communities which practise an individual confession of sins.[18]

Thus, the secrets of a confession are protected along with those entrusted to an attorney (No. 1 Art. 178). These two categories of secret are regarded as of higher value than a "state secret" or "service or professional secret" laid down in Articles 179 and 180 respectively. The bans on disclosure of the latter can be lifted in order to give the person concerned the opportunity to speak in court.[19]

Article 261 §2 of the code of civil procedure mentions briefly that a priest **may** [emboldened by MR] as a witness refuse to give a testimony concerning facts he was told while listening to the confession.[20] Presumably, some of the remarks listed above apply here, but they are not discussed in the commentaries to civil procedure code.

6. Responsibilities of clergy and celebration of religious marriage before civil marriage

In 1998, after ratification of the Concordat and resultant changes in the Family Code, it has become possible to celebrate a religious marriage

[16] J. Bratoszewski et al., vol. I, p.479.

[17] J. Grajewski, Kodeks postępowania karnego, Kraków 2006, p. 487.

[18] A. Kryże, Niedzielski, Petryna, Wirzman, Kodeks postępowania karnego. Praktyczny komentarz z orzecznictwem, art. 178.

[19] A. Kryże, op. cit., p. 326-331.

[20] A. Jakubecki (ed.), Kodeks postępowania cywilnego, Kraków 2005, p. 361-362.

which has effects in civil law. The parties are obliged to address first the local Civil Registration Office in order to obtain a certificate that under state law there is no hindrance to enter the marriage. The priest is not allowed to solemnize the marriage if this document is not presented to him.[21] The commentaries discuss hypothetically (no such case has been known thus far) what would happen if the priest solemnizes such marriages lacking such certification. According to K. Gromek, the final decision is for the head of the Civil Registration Office: if he/she confirms after the event that there have been no objections, the marriage shall be regarded as valid.[22]

Another problem is connected with the fact that the priest is obliged to notify the marriage to the local Civil Registration Office within five days of its solemnization. What happens if he fails to do so? The deadline of five days is absolute. Thus, if the court does not find or does not agree with a reason which could justify a delay, the head of the Civil Registration Office must refuse registration, and such a marriage would be null and void. This does not refer to a delay caused by *vis major*.

As a consequence of the priest's failure, the priest is liable for the damage caused.[23] He shares this responsibility with the parish, being a legal entity. There is no doubt in the literature that if the marriage was performed by a priest outside the parish (who was asked by the parties to celebrate the marriage), the local incumbent is nevertheless responsible for the registration and liable in this respect, if he has allowed the "guest priest" to perform the ceremony. Finally, a practical question should be asked – if the priest is liable, to what extent and for what kind of damage? In the contemporary world, the fact of living together without marriage is no longer perceived as negative, and the same applies to children born outside marriage. One could argue that damage could be caused by the fact that the (unsuccessful) husband and wife cannot submit their joint tax declaration (*lucrum cessans*), or due to the impossibility of being *ex lege* an heir of each other.

Persons who concluded a religious marriage, without the intention of registering it in the Civil Registration Office, in a church or religious community which is not authorised by the state law to celebrate marriage

[21] R. Sobański, Zaświadczenie urzędu cywilnego a przesłanki małżeństwa „konkordatowego", in: Państwo i Prawo, 2003/5.

[22] K. Gromek, Kodeks rodzinny i opiekuńczy, Warszawa 2006, p. 57.

[23] Remarks concerning the liability of the priest are based on the extensive article by T. Smyczyński, Odpowiedzialność odszkodowawcza duchownego z powodu naruszenia prawa przy zawieraniu małżeństwa, RPEiS 2002, Nr. 2, p. 165.

with civil effect, or in any church or religious community before 1998, are not deemed to be married. Nevertheless, the priest who married such persons is not subject to any punishment.

An official announcement of the Ministry from 21.02.2008 lists all the persons (or, more precisely, all the functions and posts) in different churches and religious communities who are authorised by state law to perform such a marriage.[24]

7. General matters

There are no provisions on proselytism, unless it involves an assault. Female genital mutilation could be treated as serious harm to the body (thus punished with imprisonment for up to 5 years, Art. 157 §1), but there is no specific provision in this respect. There are no particular criminal provisions concerning sects.

The statute of 1989 (see above) states explicitly that priests may wear their religious clothes; the abuse of such rights and its consequences are not foreseen by the criminal law.

According to Article 107 of the penal code regulating execution of sentences (*kodeks karny wykonawczy* 1997), prisoners sentenced for acts motivated by politics or religion do not share cells with other prisoners, may keep their own clothes and shoes, and they do not have to work. This provision does not relate to persons who used violence while committing such a crime.

So far there have been only two almost identical relevant cases before the European Court of Human Rights. The popular weekly "Wprost" published on its cover page the image of a "Black Madonna" from Częstochowa with a gas mask. The readers asked the Commission to take action, as they felt insulted and discriminated against (cases 33490/96, 34055/96 and 35579/97). In these two cases the Commission agreed with the publisher that adding a gas mask was supposed to attract the attention of readers to environmental issues, in particular air pollution in the region of Częstochowa, and found these applications inadmissible.

8. Conclusions

It seems that both Polish legislation and Poles themselves are moderate when it comes to the question of religion and the criminal law. The legal

[24] Monitor Polski, 2008, No. 18, it. 191.

framework is there (though less elaborate than it was in the communist era), but there are neither extensive commentaries nor numerous cases in this field. This is not a question of negligence by Polish courts, as only two cases of this kind have gone to Strasbourg, and both were considered to be inadmissible.

José de Sousa e Brito

RELIGION AND CRIMINAL LAW IN PORTUGAL

The history of religious offences in Portuguese criminal law[1] is characterised by the conjunction of two factors: first, the general history of criminal law, marked by two Codes – the Penal Code of 1852, which underwent various revisions,[2] until in 1983 it was entirely replaced by the Penal Code of 1982, itself substantially revised in 1995; and, secondly, constitutional evolution, marked in State-religion relations by the change in 1910 from State religion in the monarchy to separation in the republic. The separation of State and religion caused a new system of criminal offences equally related to all religions, having the scope of protecting the liberty of conscience and religion and not the State religion. Within the period of separation, the evolution followed once more constitutional history: a period of extreme laicism created offences protecting its specific form of separation, which were partially abolished in the following period of the concordats of 1940 and 2004.

I. The protection of religion in the criminal law

Defamation or outrage reflecting upon the content of religion

Outrage reflecting upon any dogma, act or object of the cult of the Catholic religion, if made in public or by means of any publication, was punishable by the Penal Code of 1852 (Article 130).[3] This crime was abolished by the Decree of 15 February 1911 (Article 4).

[1] See José Joaquim Almeida Lopes, "Os crimes contra a liberdade Religiosa no direito penal português", *Liberdade religiosa. Realidade e perspectivas*, Lisboa, Universsidade Católica Portuguesa, 1998, 175-237.

[2] After its republication in 1886, which included the 1867 and 1884 revisions, it was called the Penal Code of 1886.

[3] See Levy Maria Jordão, *Commentário ao Código Pena l portuguez*, II, Lisboa, 1853, 8 e F. A. F. da Silva Ferrão, *Theoria do Direito Penal*, IV, Lisboa, 1856, 1. Some court decisions on this article are reported by Luís Osório, *Notas ao Código Penal português*, 2nd ed., II, Lisboa, 1924, 10.

Defamation or outrage of a person or a group of persons by reference to religion

In 1998 a new Article 240 on "racial or religious discrimination" was added to the Penal Code; Article 240.2 provides: "a person who in a public meeting, by writing proposed for publication or by any means of social communication … defames or outrages a person, or a group of persons, on grounds of her, or their, race, colour, ethnic or national origin, religion, sex or sexual orientation, namely through denial of war crimes or of crimes against peace and humanity, intending to incite to racial or religious discrimination or to encourage it, shall be punished with imprisonment from 6 months to 5 years".

This article followed the adoption of the Council of the European Union of the Joint Action of 15 July 1996 concerning measures to combat racism and xenophobia (96/443/JHA), according to which each Member State shall eventually take steps to see that the following types of behaviour are punishable as a criminal offence:

> "(a) public incitement to discrimination, violence or racial hatred in respect of a group of persons or a member of such a group defined by reference to colour, race, religion or national or ethnic origin; …
> (c) public denial of the crimes defined in Article 6 of the Charter of the International Military Tribunal appended to the London Agreement of 8 April 1945 insofar as it includes behaviour which is contemptuous of, or degrading to, a group of persons defined by reference to colour, race, religion or national or ethnic origin;…"

The crime of defamation or outrage by reference to religion protects the right to equality, especially to equal respect and honour as a person. In addition, it protects the honour of the person or persons involved. Its objective elements are an act of defamation or of outrage, and the circumstances of a public meeting or writing proposed for publication or the use of a means of social communication. Its psychological element is intention or reckless knowledge of the defamation or of the outrage with knowledge or reckless knowledge of one of the said circumstances and the specific intention of inciting to religious discrimination or of encouraging it. The penalty exceeds by far the penalty for crimes of defamation or of outrage under the same circumstances, which must not exceed 2 years of imprisonment or a fine of no less than 120 days (Article 183, no. 2 of the Penal Code).

Outrage on grounds of religious belief

According to Article 251 of the Penal Code "a person who in public offends another person or mocks her on grounds of her belief or religious function, in a way likely to disturb public peace, shall be punished with imprisonment up to 1 year or a fine up to 120 days". This version of the article was introduced in 1995, by eliminating the circumstance "in a mean, vile or gross way" which appeared in the 1982 version and by introducing the circumstance "in a way likely to disturb public peace". Therefore, the crime protects both "religious sentiments" as indicated in the title of the chapter in which it is included ("Concerning crimes against religious feelings and the respect due to the dead") – behind religious sentiments lies religious liberty as the legal good protected – and public peace.[4] The new version may be considered a more precise description of the same offence, making clear that offence to the religious sentiments of the public was punishable only when done in a way likely to disturb public peace, which is usually the case when it is "mean, vile or gross".

The original version of Articles 251 and 252 in the 1982 Code was clearly inspired by Article 261 of the Swiss Penal Code, which has the heading: "crimes and offences against public peace". The objective element is the outrage or offence to another person on grounds of her religious belief or function performed publicly and in a way likely to disturb public peace. "Religious belief" includes any belief relating to religion such as atheism and the beliefs of philosophical associations (*Weltanschaungsvereine*) such as Freemasonry or anthroposophist associations. This interpretation remains within the possible meaning of the expression ("crença religiosa") and is clearly derived from the Constitution (Article 41) and the Religious Liberty Act (Law no.16/2001, Article 8).[5] The offence must be made known to the public but need not actually disturb the peace. It is sufficient that such an offence is in general likely to disturb public peace. The psychological element is intention or reckless knowledge.

Desecration of a place of worship or of sacred objects

Another form of the crime of outrage on grounds of religious belief (No. 2 of Article 251 of the Penal Code) consists in "desecrating a place or object of worship or religious veneration in a way likely to disturb public peace". This is again the description of the objective element. "Object

[4] See J. M. Damião da Cunha in Jorge de Figueiredo Dias (ed.), *Comentário Conimbricense do Código Penal. Parte Especial*, II, Coimbra, Coimbra Editora, 1999, 637.

[5] So Damião da Cunha, *ibidem*, 639.

of worship" is a material object used in the cult, where cult or worship ("culto") includes rituals of philosophical associations. General likelihood to disturb the public peace is sufficient: it is a crime of "abstract danger".[6] The psychological element is intention or reckless knowledge.

Hindering, disturbance of or outrage to religious worship

According to Article 252 of the Penal Code: "A person: a) Who through violence or menace of serious evil hinders or disturbs the legal exercise of religious worship; b) Who vilifies in public any act of religious worship or mocks it; shall be punished with imprisonment up to 1 year and a fine up to 120 days."

"Religious worship" includes collective and individual, public and private forms of worship, in the broad sense outlined above, since the aim is to protect religious liberty. "Legal exercise" imposes limits derived from human rights or from the law (see Article 8, g) of the Religious Liberty Act). The psychological element is intention or reckless knowledge.

It is difficult to explain why the penalty for Article 252 a) is lighter than that for coercion (Article 154: "1. A person who through violence or menace of serious evil coerces another person to an act or an omission or to be exposed to an activity shall be punished with imprisonment up to 3 years or with a fine. 2. The attempt is punishable."). The way out of the difficulty is indicated by the fact that the 1995 reform of the Penal Code eliminated Article 221 of the 1982 Penal Code concerning religious coercion because the general crime of coercion in Article 154 should also apply to religious coercion.[7] As soon as particular acts of particular persons are directly hindered through violence or menace of serious evil, the crime of coercion should apply. This is also suggested by the different wording in a) ("religious worship") and b) ("acts of religious worship"). Therefore, Article 252 a) applies only to general or indirect forms of violence (blocking access to a place of worship, for example) or of menace ("anyone who comes risks death") and to disturbance. The crime of coercion protects all expressions of religious liberty against violence or menace of serious evil.

Where the coercion is qualified by circumstances – such as menace with a crime punishable by imprisonment for more than 3 years, or it is

[6] Damião da Cunha, *ibidem*, 642 speaks of "concrete danger", but this is not entailed by "appropriate".

[7] *Código Penal. Actas e Projecto da Comissão de Revisão,* Lisboa, Rei dos Livros, 1993, 294.

committed against a defenceless person because of age, deficiency, illness or pregnancy, or against public officials in charge or cult ministers acting as such, or by an official through serious abuse of his authority or causing the victim to commit or attempt suicide – allowing a penalty from 1 to 5 years (Article 155), only the qualified crime is applicable.

Religious discrimination

Following the adoption of the Council of the European Union of the Joint Action of 15 July 1996, on measures to combat racism and xenophobia (96/443/JHA), Article 240 created three other crimes besides the one on defamation or outrage already dealt with:

> "1. A person:
> a) Who founds or constitutes an organization or develops activities of organized propaganda that incite to racial or religious discrimination, hate or violence against a person, or a group of persons, on grounds of her, or their, race, colour, ethnic or national origin, religion, sex or sexual orientation, or encourage them;
> b) Who participates in the organization or the activities referred to in a) or gives them assistance, including finance;
> shall be punished with imprisonment from 1 to 8 years.
>
> 2. A person who in a public meeting, by writing proposed for publication or by any means of social communication:
> a) Provokes acts of violence against a person, or group of persons, on grounds of her, or their, race, colour, ethnic or national origin, religion, sex or sexual orientation;...
> c) Menaces a person, or a group of persons, on grounds of her, or their, race, colour, ethnic or national origin, religion, sex or sexual orientation;
> intending to incite to racial or religious discrimination or to encourage it, shall be punished with imprisonment from 6 months to 5 years".

The psychological element in each of these crimes is intention or knowledge or reckless knowledge of the objective elements and in the crime of provocation of acts of violence the specific intention of inciting to religious discrimination or of encouraging it.

Hindering or disturbing a funeral ceremony

The Penal Code has separate protection for religious liberty and the respect due to the dead ("crimes against the respect due to the dead"). The elements of and the penalty for the crime of hindering or disturbing a funeral ceremony (Article 253) correspond to hindering or disturbing the legal exercise of religious worship. Namely: "A person who through violence or menace of serious evil hinders or disturbs a funeral procession or ceremony shall be punished with imprisonment up to a year or with a fine up to 120 days". It is clear that whenever there is a religious funeral both norms concur and only one (Article 253) is applicable. When coercion is involved, we have the same problems discussed above. If the disturbance amounts to a riot (Article 302) both crimes are committed.

Desecration of a corpse or grave

Article 254 of the Penal Code reads:

> "1. A person who:
> a) Without authorization of the right-holder abducts, destroys or hides a corpse or a part of it, or ashes of a deceased person;
> b) Desecrates a corpse or a part of it, or ashes of a deceased person, through acts offensive of the respect due to the dead; or
> c) Desecrates a place where a deceased person rests or a monument erected there in his memory, through acts offensive of the respect due to the dead;
> shall be punished with imprisonment up to 2 years or a fine up to 240 days.
>
> 2. An attempt is punishable."

Once more, what is protected is respect due to the dead independently of any religion. Therefore, this crime and the former one do not belong to religious criminal law proper. Similar to these is the offence against the memory of a deceased person (Article 185 of the Penal Code), which protects the honour of a person for 50 years after death.

Proselytising

Proselytising for a different religion or for a sect reproved by the Catholic Church was a crime under Article 130 no. 3 of the Penal Code of 1852, until abolished by Article 4 of the Decree of 15 February 1911.

Apostasy

The crime of apostasy was punishable in accordance with Article 135 of the Penal Code of 1852 until abolished by Article 4 of the Decree of 15 February 1911.

Misuse of religious garment or false state of office

Article 15 of the Decree of 20 April 1911 altered Article 134 of the Penal Code of 1852 by establishing that "a person who pretending to have the quality of a minister of a religion exercises publicly any of the acts of the same religion which may only be exercised by its ministers duly authorised to do so, shall be condemned to the penalty of article 236 §2 of the Penal Code". Article 15 was not expressly abrogated in 1982 by the Decree-Law No. 400/82 of 23 September, as were Articles 11, 12 and 13 of the same Decree, but Articles 134 and 236 were abrogated with the whole Penal Code and therefore Article 15 was abrogated along with it.[8]

II. Criminal offences committed by ministers of religion

Revelation of a secret obtained in the exercise of ministry

In the Penal Code of 1852 the disclosure of a sacramental secret by a minister of the Catholic Church was punishable as a form of abuse of religious functions (Article 136 §1). The Law no. 4/71 created a new crime of violation of religious secrecy applicable to any religion or confession (Article XX). This article was abrogated by the Decree-Law No. 400/82 (article 6 no. 2). The Penal Code of 1982 includes among the crimes against privacy the violation of professional secrecy: "A person who, without consent, reveals another person's secret, whose knowledge she obtained because of her state, office, work, profession or art, shall be punished with imprisonment up to 1 year or a fine up to 240 days". The right to privacy is the good legally protected here. Ministers of religion are covered by the references to "state" (the ecclesiastical state of the ministers of a church) or "office". Other persons who obtain knowledge of a secret through the exercise of religious functions are also possible agents.[9] The psychological element is intention, knowledge or reckless knowledge. Whether the duty of confidentiality prevails over the duty to denounce an offence depends on the circumstances. In principle, the duty of confidentiality prevails after the offence but not before it, if it is possible to avoid it.[10] However, the Concordat of 2004 states: "ecclesiastics can not be asked by magistrates or other authorities about facts and things of which they obtained knowledge because of their ministry" (Article 5,

[8] Differently, Almeida Lopes (note 1 above), 199.

[9] For a restriction to ministers of religion, see Manuel da Costa Andrade in *Comentário Conimbricense* (note 4 above), I, 787.

[10] So Costa Andrade, *ibidem*, 793.

identical with Article XII of the Concordat of 1940). Article 16 no. 2 of the Religious Liberty Act (Law no. 16/2001 of 22 June) establishes the same for ministers of any religion.

Religious marriages before civil marriages or without prior civil publication

These were criminal offences under the Penal Code of 1852, as a form of abuse of religious functions (Article 136 §2), until such Code was abrogated by the Decree-Law No. 400/82 (Article 6 no. 1).

Offences against public peace in a place of worship or during a religious practice

Such an offence existed in the Penal Code of 1852 (Article 137, with a new redaction by Article 48 of the Decree of 20 April 1911). It was abolished by the Decree-Law No. 400/82 (Article 6 no. 1).

III. Criminal offences related to worship and ritual

Female genital mutilation/cutting

In the 2007 revision of the Penal Code (Law No. 59/2007 of 4 September), Article 144 b), about grave offences to physical integrity, was altered to include the circumstance to "deprive or affect in a serious way the capacity of another person to sexual fruition". In the Law Proposal of the Government (Law Proposal 98/X) the addition was justified on the basis that "it would forbid such practices as female genital mutilation". No reference was made to the Resolution of the European Parliament on female genital mutilation (2001/2035); this called on the Member States to "regard any form of female genital mutilation as a specific crime, irrespective of whether or not the woman concerned has given any form of consent, and to punish anybody who helps, encourages, advises or procures support for anybody to carry out any of these acts on the body of a woman or girl". Nor was reference made to the Council of Europe Resolution of 12 April 1999 on female genital mutilation, nor to the Resolution 1247 of the Parliamentary Assembly of the Council of Europe (2001) on female genital mutilation. However, it is reasonable to suppose that these resolutions contributed in some way to the inclusion of the subject in the agenda of the proposed revision of the Penal Code. The psychological element is intention, knowledge or reckless knowledge. The offence is punishable with imprisonment from 2 to 10 years.

IV. Religious motivation as aggravation or attenuation

Religiously aggravated offences

The circumstance of "being determined by religious hate" is "susceptible to revealing a special censurability or perversity" in the agent of some criminal offences. Whether or not it does reveal such a disposition depends on the circumstances of each case. But only in a positive case is the offence qualified or legally aggravated. Such offences are: qualified homicide, punishable with imprisonment from 12 to 25 years (Article 132 of the Penal Code) instead of imprisonment from 8 to 10 years (Article 131: homicide); qualified offence to physical integrity relative to simple offence to physical integrity, punishable with imprisonment up to 4 years (Article 145 no. 1 a); see Article 145 no. 2) instead of imprisonment up to 3 years or fine (Article 143); qualified offence to physical integrity relative to grave offence to physical integrity, punishable with imprisonment from 3 to 12 years (Article 145 no. 1 b); see Article 145 no. 2) instead of imprisonment from 2 to 10 years (Article 144).

The various criminal offences of racial, religious or sexual discrimination, through defamation, injury or menace, represent qualifications to the latter crimes. So is defamation, or injury, under Article 240 no. 2 b), punishable with imprisonment from 6 months to 5 years instead of imprisonment up to 2 years or a fine for not less than 120 days (Article 183). Menace in Article 240 no. 2 c) is punishable with imprisonment from 6 months to 5 years, and up to 3 years in case of coercion (Article 154).

The offence of criminal damage is qualified when the damaged property "is linked to religious worship or the veneration of the memory of the dead or is in a place of worship or in a cemetery" (Article 213 no. 1 e)), being then punishable with imprisonment up to 5 years or a fine up to 600 days instead of imprisonment up to 3 years or a fine (Article 212).

V. Criminal law and sects

There are no criminal offences related to sects.

Andi Bogdan

RELIGION AND CRIMINAL LAW IN ROMANIA

Penal protection of religion

In Romania, the separation of state and religion culminated in the period of communism, which was characterised by severe limitations on religious freedom through interference with the internal organisation of religious communities and extensive controls over religious life. In this context, the communist Penal Code contained very few explicit provisions for the protection of religion and religious communities, such as hindering the freedom of religious denominations (Art. 318) and the profanation of tombs (including monuments, funeral urns and corpses: Art. 319).

After the fall of communism certain amendments were made to the Penal Code, with new legislation on discrimination and the prohibition of fascist, racist or xenophobic organizations. Moreover, there is a new law on freedom of religion and on the general status of religious denominations. It was enacted in order to align Romanian legislation to international instruments for the protection of religious freedom and to balance freedom of expression and respect for religious beliefs.

1. Given its communist past, with very little concern and respect for religion, Romania did not inherit any criminal provisions explicitly prohibiting blasphemy. However, the new law on religious freedom and on denominations in Romania (Law no. 489/2006) forbids (Art. 13 para. 2) all forms of slander against religions, as well as public actions offensive to religious symbols; but this legislation provides no sanctions in the event of breach of these prohibitions. The provision on religious symbols was introduced during parliamentary debates on the law when in its draft form; the draft law proposed by the government and submitted to the Venice Commission – see Opinion 354/2005, adopted at the 64th plenary session of October 2005 – did not include it. It seems that its inclusion was influenced by the European debates on the Prophet Mohammed caricatures (following an express request of the Muslim

religious denomination, supported by the commissions of the Parliament).[1]

However, an analysis of the Penal Code currently in force – which is inherited from the communist regime – reveals that certain general crimes could provide a mechanism for restricting blasphemous material (insult, libel, desecration of tombs, offence to good morals, disturbance of public order, and distribution of obscene materials).

Insult and libel are both treated in Romania as crimes against human dignity. Yet, their description in the law makes no reference to religion. Insult is an affront to the honour and reputation of a person through words, gestures or any other means or through exposure to outrage; it is punishable with a fine (Art. 205 of the Penal Code). Libel is the action of affirming or accusing a person in public of a determined act which, if true, would expose that person to a penal, administrative or disciplinary sanction or public contempt; it is punishable with a fine (Art. 206 of the Penal Code). Both insult and libel require intention, direct and indirect, on the part of the accused. Due to pressure from non-governmental organizations and several reports condemning their possibility of restricting free speech and allowing excessive sanctions, insult and libel were abolished in 2006 (by Law no. 278/2006). However, as a result of decision no. 62/2007 of the Constitutional Court, which declared the law abolishing insult and libel unconstitutional, both offences continue to be in force.

The offence to good morals is the act of a person who commits, in public, acts or gestures, propagates words or expressions or engages in any other manifestation that is an affront to good morals or produces public scandal or disturbs public peace and order in any other way (Art. 321 of the Penal Code). Proof of direct and indirect intention is required. Neither the concept of "good morals" nor "public peace" is clearly defined, which gives too much room for interpretation, since our idea of good morals and public peace varies from time to time, from one community to another etc. Thus, the ways of acting against good morals and those of producing public scandal are extremely varied, leading to unpredictability in the law and uncertainty with respect to its interpretation.

[1] Reply from Romania, Study no. 406/2006 of the European Commission for Democracy through Law (Venice Commission), Annex II to the preliminary report on national legislation in Europe, concerning blasphemy, religious insults and inciting religious hatred. Collection of replies to the questionnaire on domestic law concerning blasphemy, religious insults and inciting religious hatred by Albania, Austria, Belgium, Denmark, France, Ireland, the Netherlands, Poland, Romania, Turkey, United Kingdom: Strasbourg, 23 March 2007, p. 67.

The distribution of obscene materials is the act of selling or distributing as well as of making or possessing for distribution objects, drawings, writings or other materials of an obscene character (Art. 325 of the Penal Code). Because the protected good is that of pudicity and the sense of decency related to the intimacies of sexual life, which is again not clearly defined and varies in terms of time and place, there is a real possibility that the provision might be misused or employed for other purposes.

Although none of the above offences contains an explicit reference to religion, they could easily be applied to cases involving religious matters and organisations.

As for offences with an explicit reference to religion, in 2006 the offence of nationalist-chauvinist propaganda (nationalist-chauvinist propaganda, stirring up hatred based on race or nationality) was amended and changed to incitement to discrimination (Art. I point 66 of Law no. 278/2006). Therefore, according to Article 317 of the Penal Code, incitement to hatred based on race, nationality, ethnicity, language, religion, sex, sexual orientation, political affiliation, beliefs, fortune, social origin, age, disability, non-contagious chronic disease or HIV infection shall be punished with 3 to 6 months imprisonment or a fine. The legislator may be understood to have intended to widen the area of protection against incitement to hatred because of race and nationality to a more general incitement to discrimination on several explicitly listed grounds, including religion. The protected good is the equality of all citizens without distinction on prescribed grounds which could disturb the relationships between different citizens and limit diversity. Incitement to discrimination means stirring up and encouraging hatred against certain categories of citizens which may be committed in any way or by any means. From the point of view of its mental element, this offence requires intention, in its either direct or indirect form.

Furthermore, the Emergency Government Ordinance no. 31/2002 was enacted to prevent and combat incitement to hatred on grounds of race or religion. It deals with the prohibition of fascist, racist or xenophobic organizations and symbols and the promotion of the cult of persons guilty of committing crimes against peace and humanity. The ordinance criminalises the establishment of or affiliation to fascist, racist or xenophobic organizations (Art. 3; punishable with 3 to 15 years imprisonment). It also criminalises the act of making, selling, distributing and possessing for the purpose of distribution of fascist, racist or xenophobic symbols, the public use of these symbols (Art. 4; punishable with 3 months to 3 years imprisonment), the promotion of the cult of persons guilty of committing crimes against peace and humanity or the promotion – through propaganda by any means – of fascist, racist or xenophobic ideologies (Art. 5; punishable with 3 months to 3 years imprisonment) and the public denial of the Holocaust or its effects (Art. 6; punishable with 6 months to 5 years imprisonment and suspension of certain rights). Emergency Ordinance no. 31/2002 defines fascist, racist or xenophobic organizations as groups "promoting fascist, racist or xenophobic ideas, concepts or doctrines, such as hatred and violence based on ethnic, racial or religious motives....".

2. Defamation or outrage against a church or a religious community as such is not a crime according to Romanian criminal law. However, certain acts could satisfy the constitutive elements of one of the crimes outlined above and be liable to punishment as such.

3. Similarly, the desecration of a place of worship or of sacred objects of any religion is not a crime as such. However, such acts could amount to the general crime of destruction of other persons' goods (Art. 217 of the Penal Code), punishable with one month to 3 years imprisonment or by way of fine. This crime does not only exist when goods are actually destroyed, but also when they are degraded or measures for their conservation or safeguarding are hindered or prevented. Should such acts be directed against goods of special artistic, scientific, historical, archival or other similar value, the punishment is one year to 10 years imprisonment (aggravated form).

Furthermore, Article 360 of the Penal Code provides for the punishment of the destruction, plundering or appropriation of valuable cultural items. The destruction in any way, without military necessity, of monuments, museums, great libraries, archives of historical or scientific value, works of art, manuscripts, valuable books, scientific collections or important collections of books, archives or reproductions of these goods or generally any cultural values of peoples shall be punished with 5 to 20 years imprisonment.

4. Hindering or disrupting a religious meeting *per se* is not a crime according to Romanian law. Yet, Article 318 paragraph (1) of the Penal Code provides for the more general crime of hindering freedom of religion, which consists of hindering or disturbing the freedom of exercising any religious cult organized and functioning according to law; it is punishable with 1 to 6 months imprisonment or fine. Hindering freedom of religion consists of any direct or indirect activity that renders impossible

the exercise of a certain cult, while disturbing freedom of religion is any activity that obstructs the normal exercise of a cult. Both forms may be committed by means of direct or indirect intention. This crime may also have a material object if for example certain acts of hindering or disrupting are directed against objects that serve for the exercise of a religious cult.

5. According to Romanian law, menaces, violence or the application of force against another person's freedom of religion or conscience are punished through the general offences of assault and battery, wounding and causing grievous bodily harm, threat, unlawful deprivation of freedom etc. Also, Article 318 para. (2) of the Penal Code provides that the act of obliging a person, using constraint, to participate in religious services of a cult or to perform a religious act related to the exercise of a cult amounts to hindering freedom of religion by acting against one's will and conscience. Constraint may be physical or moral and may be committed with direct and indirect intention.

6. Discrimination because of religion as such is not a crime according to Romanian law. Discrimination is regulated by Government Ordinance no. 137/2000 which outlaws all forms of discrimination. Discrimination on any ground, including religion, is an administrative offence (if it does not, however, amount to a crime under criminal law). A special body, the National Council for Combating Discrimination, has been created for the investigation, establishment and enforcement of the offences set out in the legislation.

There is, however, a more specific crime in the Penal Code which refers to discrimination based on prescribed grounds, including religion, committed by public officials. Article 247 deals with abuse of office through limiting certain rights. This crime represents the limiting by a public official of the use or exercise of a person's rights or the creation of a situation of inferiority on the grounds of race, nationality, ethnicity, language, religion etc. for this person; it is punished with 6 months to 5 years imprisonment. Liability may arise by way of commission or omission, with both direct and indirect intention. The law also provides for a particular motive: an impulse or tension that renders the official liable to differentiate between people based on their race, nationality, religion etc.

7. Disrupting a funeral as such is not a crime according to Romanian law. Yet, similar acts could amount to other crimes such as hindering the freedom of religious denominations or the offence against good morals and disturbing public peace.

8. According to Article 318 para. (1) of the Penal Code, the desecration by any means of a tomb, a monument or funeral urn or a corpse is a crime, punishable by 3 months to 3 years imprisonment. Desecration represents the destruction or act of showing disrespect for a tomb, monument etc. Usually, it is a violent action that results in the destruction, degradation, spoiling of a tomb, monument etc or in the destruction, mutilation, or changing the position of a corpse. However, it may also be carried out without violence, by acts which show the same lack of respect, such as drawing obscenities, writing injurious words etc. on the tomb or monument. This crime may be committed with direct and indirect intention. Desecration may also constitute the objective element of another crime, such as destruction or an offence against good morals. Such cases amount to a plurality of crimes (multiple crimes) which may be punished more severely.

9. and 10. Neither proselytising nor apostasy are crimes according to Romanian law and have long since been abolished.

11. Law no. 489/2006 on religious freedom and the general regime of denominations introduced in Article 23 paragraph (4) a provision stating that the exercise of the office of priest or any other office that presumes the exercise of a priest's competencies without authorisation or express approval from religious structures (which may or may not have legal personality) shall be punishable according to criminal law.

Article 281 of the Penal Code sets out the crime of the unlawful exercise of a profession, which consists of the unlawful exercise of a profession or any other activity that shall be authorized according to law. The crime also covers the exercise of these activities under unlawful conditions if a special law provides that committing such acts is forbidden according to criminal law (punishable with one month to 1 year imprisonment or fine). It may be committed only with intention (direct or indirect).

Therefore, the exercise of the office of priest or of a priest's competencies without authority amounts to unlawful exercise of a profession.

Offences by ministers of religion

12. According to Article 23 para. (3) of Law no. 489/2006 on religious freedom and the general regime of denominations the clerical and assimilated staff of recognised cults may not be obliged to reveal acts entrusted to them or those they have become aware of in the exercise of their office. Disclosure of a secret obtained in the exercise of ministry is

implicitly prohibited by the general provisions on the disclosure of professional secrets set out in Article 196 of the Penal Code; it is punishable with 3 months to 2 years imprisonment. Therefore, confessional and other professional secrets are equally protected in Romanian law. Disclosure of professional secrets may only be committed by persons who exercise a profession or office by virtue of which they are entrusted with or become aware of data related to someone else's personal life. In order to be a crime, the disclosure of professional secrets must be unlawful. There are situations when the disclosure of such data is not unlawful. Thus, disclosure is not unlawful when the data refer to the commission of certain crimes – exhaustively listed in Article 170 of the Penal Code – which must be denounced according to law (the obligation to denounce certain serious crimes against the state, against persons and patrimony etc.) or if disclosure is approved by the person they refer to. This crime may be committed with both direct and indirect intention, while culpable revelation is not sanctioned by law.

13. The celebration of religious marriage before civil marriage is not a crime in Romania. The only sanction for celebrating a religious marriage before a civil marriage is the lack of validity/non-existence of this marriage from the perspective of state authorities.

14. A breach of the public peace in a place of worship or during a religious service as such is not a crime in Romania. However, similar acts committed by ministers of religion could amount to other crimes, previously mentioned, or even to public incitement and those crimes provided by Article 324 of the Penal Code ("The act of inciting the public through words, in writing or by any other means to disrespect for laws or to commit acts that amount to crimes shall be punished with 3 months to 3 years imprisonment…"). If public incitement is committed by a person who performs an important state activity or other important public activity, the punishment shall be 1 year to 5 years imprisonment. The law does not define "an important state activity or other important public activity". Thus, it is for the courts to decide in each individual case whether a person performs important state or public activities. The literature emphasises that these activities may only be considered important when they take place at the level of the direction/management of a body or organization and imply high responsibility. Highest-ranking cult leaders would fall into this category, if we also take into consideration that in Romania recognised religious cults are public utility entities whose leaders have offices analogous to public functions.

Offences linked to acts of worship or to rites

Acts of worship or rites are not crimes *sui generis* according to Romanian law. Female genital mutilation or other similar acts are forms of grievous bodily harm in its aggravated form (Art.182 para. 3 of the Penal Code), i.e. having one of the following consequences: loss of a sense or organ, organ failure, a permanent physical or psychological infirmity, mutilation etc. and committed with the purpose of producing these consequences; it may be punished with 3 years to 12 years imprisonment.

Religious motivation as a cause of aggravation or of attenuation of the offence

Article 75 para. (1) c^1 of the Penal Code provides that if crimes are committed on grounds of race, nationality, ethnicity, language, religion, gender, sexual orientation, opinion, political affiliation, convictions, fortune, social origin, age, disability, non-contagious chronic illness or HIV infection, these represent an aggravating circumstances. Therefore, religious motivation – among other grounds exhaustively listed in the law – is a general aggravating circumstance for any crime provided by law. There is no similar provision with respect to attenuating circumstances.

Criminal law and sects

No special crimes are provided in Romanian law for conduct considered typical of some sectarian religious movements. Yet, certain crimes such as the act of forcing a person, using constraint, to participate in religious services of a cult or to perform a religious act related to the exercise of a cult, threats or offences against good morals or disturbing public peace could be used in relation to religious movements considered sectarian.

Matúš Nemec

Comenius University of Bratislava
Faculty of Law
Department of Legal History

RELIGION AND CRIMINAL LAW IN THE SLOVAK REPUBLIC

A. Religion and Criminal Law until 1949

Blasphemy and sacrilege had been public criminal offences in the collection of medieval Hungarian customary law – *Opus Tripartitum* – from the 16th century. The relevant part of the medieval Hungarian criminal law, which had been valid in the area covered by the contemporary Slovak republic, contained the following crimes against religion: witchcraft – this crime was established by King St. Stephen in the 11th century, but King Coloman abolished the punishment of witches, retaining, however, punishment of this crime in cities by means of burning at the stake; the disturbance of religious ceremonies; the non-celebration of religious (church) holidays; and blasphemy. These crimes had been punished by beating or the cutting of hair.[1]

In the first Czecho-Slovak republic (1918-1939), and until 1949, blasphemy (also called disturbing religion) had been a crime. According to §122 of the Criminal Code, blasphemy meant disparagement, disrespect, derision or disdain with regard to religion – for example, if a person had *blasphemously* denied the divinity of Jesus Christ or *blasphemously* denied that God is almighty.[2]

Paragraph 303 of the Criminal Code – the so-called "pulpit paragraph" from 1919 – penalized anyone who publicly (at a public place, in books, articles, or pictures) derided the doctrine, practices or institutions of a legally-recognized church or religious association, or anyone who offended their ordained ministers at a service of worship or who behaved during public worship in such an unbecoming way as to make other

[1] Beňa, Jozef – Gábriš, Tomáš: History of law in Slovakia I. (until 1918). Bratislava: Vydavatel'ské oddelenie PF UK, 2008, p. 110.

[2] Cf. Bednář, František: Sbírka zákonu ve věcech náboženských a církevních. Praha: Husova evangelická fakulta, 1929, p. 366.

people appalled. It could also cover ridicule of a Holy cross, as an object of universal honour, or the use of offensive language about the papacy.[3] This offence had been punished by one to six months in prison.

These acts also constituted an ecclesiastical offence but the difference between this and the crime was the mental element – the criminal offence required direct intention to disturb the exercise of religion (penal judgment from December 21, 1923).

This same law penalized any ordained person or minister of any church (legally recognized or not), who at a religious event (a procession or in the context of religious education) spoke about state or political affairs or criticized state laws or government orders, urged people to vote (or not) for any political party, read the publications of any particular political persuasion or movements, or interfered with electioneering.

Under §174 of the Criminal Code, theft of something valuable (over 50 crowns) from a place of worship, was a criminal offence because the serious social danger of this act.

B. Religion and Criminal Law from 1949 to 1990

In the socialist state, of which Slovakia had been a part, radical changes took place to the legal system. The law protected freedom of religion only formally and special criminal offences from the former democratic period were abolished. In 1950 the crime of "Violation of the Family Code" was introduced in §207 of the Criminal Code.

The new Criminal Code of 1961 (law n. 140/1961) made it possible to punish a clergyman with a sentence of up to one year in prison if he violated §7 of the Family Code.[4] The clergyman committed this criminal offence when he celebrated a religious marriage rite before marriage had been contracted in accordance with the civil (state) law. The Family Code of 1963 (law n. 94/1963) in §10 required an obligatory civil marriage rite with very rigorous words: "*Religious wedding rites are not permitted before marriage is contracted*". This criminal offence was abolished after the political changes in December 1989 (law n. 159/1989).

Control over churches and religious associations in other matters was also of central importance to the State. The system of control was established in 1948 and was confirmed by the law n. 217/1949 establishing

[3] BEDNÁŘ, F: Sbírka zákonů ve věcech náboženských a církevních, pp. 370-371.

[4] §7 of Family code: "*Religious wedding rites are permitted, but only after marriage was contracted*".

the *State Office for Church Matters*. This Office had extensive administrative competences – first of all, it granted approval to the highest-ranking religious dignitaries to carry out their spiritual work, and at a lower level for other religious persons to engage in public pastoral care.

The Administrative Criminal Law, from 1950,[5] prohibited persons from threatening or disturbing state control of church property; this was punished with a sentence of up to three months in prison or a 20,000 crown fine (it was an administrative offence for delinquency). This vague provision, which contradicted well-known legal principles of criminal law, made it possible to punish whatever the state institutions regarded as threatening or disturbing state control over the churches. An equivalent offence was contained in the Criminal Code from 1950 (law n. 86/1950). According to §173 of this code, anyone who had carried out spiritual work in the church without state approval, or worked in an ecclesiastical position to which he had not been appointed, could be punished by a sentence of up to three years' imprisonment. The penalty was higher if anyone appointed another person to an ecclesiastical position without state approval.

The most important provision of the Criminal Code 1950 was §123 which was entitled *Exploitation of religious functions*. This defined in §28 the limits of the exercise of religious freedom (on the basis of the law protecting the people's democratic republic – law no. 231/1948). It was designed to prevent exploitation of religious freedom against state integrity and the people's democracy and to prevent clergy from exerting political influence. This regulation (§123) had been a part of the first chapter of the Criminal Code regulating crimes considered most injurious to the public. The Criminal Code of 1961 (law. No. 140/1961) established this criminal offence similarly in §101.

After 1956, criminal offences concerning religion were modified a little in the form of §178 of the Criminal Code entitled *Counteraction of state control over the churches and religious associations*. This penalized intentional counteraction or obstruction of the exercise of state control over the churches, particularly violations of the Law on Economical Assistance of Churches and Religious Associations. The body of the offence (its subject matter) was operative until the end of 1989 as §178 of Criminal Code. In 1970 several people were punished under this paragraph.

The elements of this criminal offence were met (reputedly) by making a public appeal to build new churches without state permission. The minister of justice at that time had asked the Supreme Court of the Slovak

[5] Law n. 88/1950, §101: The protection of order in ecclesiastical matters.

Republic to interpret §178 of the Criminal Code. The Supreme Court gave its interpretation: the violation of §178 could be committed by anyone (not only religious persons) and that liability would arise for breach of §178 and any other public statutes, internal instructions and directions even if these had not been published in the statute-book and were therefore not universally legally binding. Ignorance of these internal instructions had been judged in accordance with the degree of dangerousness of a particular act to the system.[6]

There were many trials of clergy, often important church dignitaries, under various provisions of the Law on the Protection of the Peoples-Democratic State (law n. 231/1948), especially for alleged high treason (§78 of this law). These trials were symptomatic more of the underlying repressive anti-church political character of the state than of its system of ecclesiastical law.

C. Religion and Criminal Law in the Slovak Republic (since 1993)

1. *Introduction*

The Criminal Code in the Slovak Republic now contains only one criminal offence explicitly relating to religion, and protecting the freedom of religion of natural persons: the offence of *restraint of religious freedom*, established in §193 of the Criminal Code (law n. 300/2005). Next come criminal offences which do not expressly mention religion but one of their elements concerns motives resulting from negative attitudes towards religion and belief. These are punished with a more severe penalty when the offender commits the crime because of the religious belief of the victim – extortion (§189, sect. 2(c)), murder (§145, sect. 2(d)), and bodily harm (§155, sect. 2(c)).[7]

2. *Restraint of religious freedom (§193 of the Criminal Code)*

Objective elements of the offence

a) The following constitute the external elements of the offence: coercion of another person to take part in a religious act; unlawful restraint

[6] Cf. *Opinion of the Penal Board of Supreme Court of Slovak Republic from May 23rd, 1971*. In: HRDINA, Antonín (ed.): Texty ke studiu konfesního práva III. Československo. Praha: Karolinum, 2006, pp. 276-277.

[7] Cf. HRDINA, A: Náboženská svoboda v právu České republiky. Praha: Eurolex Bohemia, 2004, p. 243.

of another person to take part in a religious act; unlawful restraint of another person to exercise religious freedom. Restraint means (and this is typical for the crimes of this chapter of the Criminal Code) using immediate physical or psychological violence, menace of violence or menace of other great harm. §193, sect. 2 represents the more serious form (or "qualified body") of the offence and requires: seriousness in the mode of acting, or commission with a special motive (anti-religious fanaticism) or commission in public.[8]

b) Religious act: a religious act is any kind of act or ceremony related to the profession of faith of any church or religious association, e.g. the mass, other worship, celebration of the sacraments, or religious teaching.

c) Restraint to take part in a religious act: restraint must be unlawful; in spite of the fact that taking part in a religious act is a right arising from individual religious freedom as a basic human right (which is established in Article 24, sect. 1 of the Constitution), the exercise of this right (under Art. 24, sect. 4 of the Constitution) can be limited by law if it is necessary in democratic society in order to protect public order, health and morality or rights and liberties of others. Such limitation, if published, legalizes the restraining acts, since a norm of public law can be interpreted only strictly.

d) Other restraints on the exercise of religious freedom: these might include violence leading to destruction of objects used for the performance of a religious act.

Subjective elements of this criminal offence

This criminal offence always requires an intentional action.

Penalty

The punishment is imprisonment for up to two years; with regard to the qualified body of the offence, imprisonment for up to six years.

3. *Other penal provisions concerning religion*

(a) The protection of confessional secrecy

There are provisions under §340 sect. 3 of the Criminal Code on the non-reporting of a crime and §341 sect. 4 on the non-circumvention of a crime.

[8] Cf. IVOR, Jaroslav: Trestné právo hmotné 2 – osobitná časť. Bratislava: Iura Edition 2006, p. 102.

In these cases, clergy of the recognized churches are exempt from criminal responsibility for actions which would contravene the inviolability of the secrecy of confession.[9] This is guaranteed by the treaty between the Holy See and the Slovak Republic (2000)[10] and the agreement between registered churches and religious associations and the Republic (2002).[11]

According to §340 sect. 3 of the Criminal Code, any person who commits a crime under sect. 1 is not liable if reporting a crime would have infringed the secrecy of confession or the confidentiality of information revealed orally or in writing to a person commissioned for pastoral ministry. Nor is §341 sect. 1 violated when circumvention of a crime would infringe the secrecy of confession.

The category of protected interests includes a witness who refuses to testify if this infringes the secrecy of confession or confidential information revealed orally or in writing to a person commissioned to exercise pastoral ministry in a church registered by the state (§130 of the Code of Criminal Procedure – law number 301/2005).

(b) Protection of personal freedom and life of perpetrators on the grounds of religious affiliation

The Criminal Code protects a foreigner – who commits a crime – against expulsion if because of his expulsion his personal freedom or life would be threatened *inter alia* on grounds of his religious affiliation (§65 sect. 2 (b) of the Criminal Code).

Similarly, a person, who might be subjected to persecution in the country requesting his expulsion, *inter alia* on the grounds of his religion, is procedurally protected through a decision of the Minister of Justice (§510 (b) of the Code of Criminal Procedure).

Both these regulations derive from Article 12 sect. 2 of the Constitution of the Slovak Republic which guarantees protection of basic human

[9] The canon law punishes a direct infringement of a confession secret by the highest penalty – excommunication (porov. kán. 1388, §1 CIC 1983 a kán. 1456, §1 CCEO).

[10] Article 8 Základnej zmluvy medzi Svätou stolicou a SR:

1. *Confidentiality of the confessional is inviolable. The inviolability of the secret confessional comprises the right to refuse to make a deposition before the organs of the state of the Republic of Slovakia.*
2. *The Republic of Slovakia also guarantees the inviolability of secret information, made orally or in writing under the condition of confidentiality to a person entrusted with pastoral care.*

[11] The text of the Art. 8 of this Treaty is identical to the text of the abovementioned Treaty.

rights to all inhabitants without regard to (amongst other things) belief and religion.

(c) Protection against crimes motivated by religious hatred (§418 – genocide; §423 – defamation of race, nation and belief)

This category includes crimes for which one of the motives can be religious hatred. As a result, the peaceful existence of a religious group, the life of its members (who enjoy protection against physical violence), biological reproduction of the religious group, its identity (which is protected against the violent proselytism of children from another religious group) and a respectable life are values protected by law. The criminal law imposes as a penalty imprisonment for 15 to 20 years.

The Criminal Code also protects a religious group against defamation of its religious belief. In this context, the European Court of Human Rights,[12] in 2006, decided that the conviction of Mr. Martin Klein by courts of the Slovak Republic in 2000-2001 for a crime of defamation against nation, race and belief (under the then §198 of the Criminal Code) in proceedings instituted by two private interest groups, was a breach of Article 10 of the European Convention of Human Rights. It declared that Mr. Klein's statements in the magazine *Domino Effect* (March 3, 1997) did not excessively affect the rights of believers to express their religious belief or defame their religious belief; thus, his conviction was excessive.[13] The European Court of Human Rights in this case did not decide on the merits whether Article 9 of the Convention had been breached, that is, whether Mr. Klein's statements could be viewed as an infringement of the right of religious belief through e.g. defamation of religious feelings.

(d) Other information (work in prisons, sects)

Agencies involved (under §4 of the Criminal Code) in the enforcement of the criminal law, if they consider it appropriate and useful, may cooperate with interest groups of citizens, which can include churches and

[12] European Court of Human Rights: Klein versus Slovak Republic, Application no. 72208/01 from October, 31st, 2006.

[13] One of the statements of Mr. Klein was about archbishop Sokol: *"I do not understand at all why decent Catholics do not leave the organisation which is headed by such an ogre."* Porov. HERCZEG, J.: Trestné činy z nenávisti. Praha: ASPI, Wolters Kluver, 2007, str. 56-57.

religious associations recognized by the state. This cooperation is being played out through agreements between individual churches and relevant institutions with regard to providing spiritual and pastoral care for persons in prisons in the manner contemplated by the law number 308/1991 on freedom of religious belief and status of churches and religious associations (Art. 9). Condemned persons have a right to have spiritual and religious literature of their own choice.

The criminal law of the Slovak Republic does not deal with sects. The law does not use this term. Only the Institute for Relations between State and Churches of the Ministry of Culture of the Slovak Republic uses a sociological definition of this term. The Home Office of the Slovak Republic published in 2001 internal ordinance no. 2 about measures against extremism. Article 2 of this ordinance defines "sect" as: "a destructive religious group, established on the base of fanatical confession, ultimately on the basis of the deceitfulness of its founder, which depraves the development of the younger generation or violates the laws, and ultimately through their ideology and thoughts threatens lives, health or property and violates other generally legally binding statutes".

Preventing the influence of sects and sectarian tendencies is realized through a system of registration. In making a request for registration, personal information must be provided as well as information about the basic characteristics of the church or religious association seeking registration, its doctrine and mission.

Agustín Motilla
Universidad Carlos III de Madrid

RELIGION IN SPANISH CRIMINAL LAW

1. *Introduction*

After the 1978 Spanish Constitution came into force, legislators saw the need to reform the Penal Law in order to adapt it to those principles and values protected by the Constitution. As a provisional measure, it was decided to reform partially the Code then in force, which dated back to 1944, through Organic Law 8/1983 of June 25. Included under the new part "Offences against fundamental human rights and public liberties", was a section "Offences against freedom of conscience". In 1995, and after various failed attempts, a new Penal Code was enacted, approved by Organic Law 10/1995 of November 23. The 3rd section of chapter II of title II includes a part on "criminal offences against freedom of conscience, religious sentiments, and respect for the deceased". A large part of the offences included existed in other historical periods. For this reason, our presentation on Penal Law in religious matters will cite past judicial decisions in an attempt to clarify and pinpoint just what such specified actions are, while highlighting the changes introduced by the current Code and the interpretation of the types of offences in keeping with constitutional values and principles.

I. Penal protection of religion

2. *Defamation or outrage reflecting upon the content of religion or against a church or religious community*

The offence of blasphemy does not exist in Spanish Penal Law currently in force. The said offence disappeared from the Penal Code in 1988.[1] Blasphemy had been defined by our jurisprudence as "uttering injurious words against God, the Virgin Mary or the Saints".[2] The exclusive

[1] Organic Law 5/1988, June 5, of the Penal Code reform.
[2] See, along these lines, the Circular of the High Court of January 31, 1945 and the Ruling of said Court of June 24, 1954.

protection of persons or dogma of the Catholic Religion, and difficulties over its application to other religious minorities, were the reasons motivating the legislature to decide on its suppression. In any case, the legal value which it protected can be considered to fall under the offence of defamation or outrage of the religious dogmas which will be dealt with in the following section.

The offence of defamation and outrage protects the religious teachings and beliefs of all religions without distinction. This is contemplated in Article 525 of the Penal Code which punishes those who engage in public defamation, through word, documents or other written texts, of the dogmas, beliefs, rites or ceremonies of religions, or who publicly harass those who profess or practise such religion, and thus offend the sensibilities of the members of those religious groups. The legal object protected is that of the religious sensibilities of the members of the religions. As for the elements of the offence, we can point to the following.

The objective element diverges in two ways: defamation or prolonged verbal harassment with the purpose of publicly insulting, or gross and insulting statements issued "in a public way, the dogma, rites, or ceremonies, that is, the true fundamentals, rules of worship and the external acts of religious practices".[3] The subjective or psychological element required is the wilful or malicious intention to offend religious sensibilities. In the words of the High Court, "regarding the element of guilt, not only the behaviour and the wilful intent of the action incriminate as an offence, but a specific aim to slander, as a deliberate synonym of offend".[4] This thereby eliminates the application of the offence to reasonable and measured criticism. "*Animus injurandi* is excluded – which the Ruling of January 19, 1982 upheld – when *animus criticandi* exists, which is recognized by a serious, scientific, and profound theological study in which some of the truths held, which are the basis of the Catholic faith, are denied; but is not detected in mere antireligious rebuffs, scoffing or the mockery of basic dogmas".[5]

A controversial aspect of the offence of derision presented by doctrine before the coming into force of the current text of Article 525.1 of the Code is the requirement or lack thereof of the acts being made public. A case which stirred controversy over the public nature of an act was the prosecution of the director of a theatre group, which, in a closed locale,

[3] High Court Ruling of February 14, 1984.
[4] Ibidem.
[5] See, along the same lines, High Court Ruling of November 26, 1990.

had performed a play called "*Teledeum*" parodying liturgical elements of the Catholic Church, the Mass and the sacrament of Confession. The Provincial Court, in spite of affirming both the objective and subjective elements of the offence, absolved the play's director, upon not perceiving the public nature of the acts of derision, as the play was performed in private, with access restricted by payment of the price of a ticket. The High Court, in its Ruling of November 26, 1990, affirmed, and citing previous decisions,[6] that in the offence of defamation "publicizing, spreading or disclosing are not constitutive elements, but rather, defamation has to be exteriorized in some way". Concluding in the case presented, the Court continued: "in addition to the acts taking place in a public place, such as a theatre, it cannot, however, be denied that there was public relevance". The new drafting of the offence in Article 525 will leave no room for doubt that the act being of a public nature is a necessary requirement in all cases.

As to the means of commission, paragraph 1 of Article 525 continues, together with the traditional words and documents of our Law, to cover "any type of document", thereby receiving a long jurisprudence which determined the content of certain drawings and cartoons to constitute defamation or outrage. A case in point is one which portrayed a priest in a confessional saying to a penitent: "That will be 345.70 pesetas and a donation";[7] or the exhibition in a private dwelling, but one frequently visited and visible to a diverse public, of a drawing of a parodied temple on a toilet door and of the Virgin Mary being sexually assaulted;[8] or the publication in a university gazette of obscene drawings of monks and nuns, or ones of the Holy Trinity[9].

The most significant innovation in the drafting of the offence of defamation and outrage is the extension of the same to non-religious convictions. According to paragraph 2 of Article 525, "the same punishment – a fine of eight to twelve months – will be incurred by those who engage in public defamation, by word or document, of those who do not profess any religion or creed". Despite the fact that this paragraph is to guarantee the application of the offence without discrimination in terms of beliefs – and with that, we highlight its complete agreement with the Constitution

[6] The High Court Rulings of October 13, 1980 and February 19, 1982 are expressly cited.

[7] The High Court Ruling of October 11, 1973.

[8] The High Court Ruling of July 1, 1975.

[9] The High Court Ruling of February 19, 1982.

in the legislative option to protect religious and non-religious convictions through this offence[10] – it is true that the more intense sensitivity of religious beliefs to gratuitous offences, as the courts' experience demonstrates, leads one to believe that the offence will be applied only in relation to religious beliefs.

Related to the protection of religious sensibilities and social peace against uncontrolled attacks driven by hate or violence against some religions are the offences included in the Spanish Penal Code. Article 510 of the Penal Code establishes punishment entailing a prison sentence of one to three years and a fine of six to twelve months for those who provoke discrimination, hate or violence against groups for reasons, among others, of the religion professed, or those who spread slanderous information about them. Article 515 also takes into account illicit associations, carrying a punishment for those who instigate, lead and cooperate as well as those members who foment discrimination, hate, and violence because of the religious beliefs of persons or groups.

3. *Desecration of a place of worship or sacred objects of any religion*

Article 524 of the Penal Code punishes with a prison term of six months to a year or a fine of twelve to twenty-four months, those who "in a temple, a place of worship or during religious ceremonies carry out acts of profanation offending legally protected religious sentiments". The criminalization of such acts also aims to protect the religious sensibilities of individuals.

As to the elements of the offence, the objective elements, the acts of profanation, have been interpreted by the jurisprudence[11] in the literal sense of the verb "to profane", which is, to treat a sacred object without the respect due to it, to apply profane uses or make indignant use of it, in

[10] The constitutionality of the offence of defamation or outrage of religious convictions was analyzed in the Decree of the Constitutional Court 18/1986, of February 21. In the appeal an individual requested that the Court annul the same – in the draft of 1983 – because it went against religious freedom and the lay nature of the State in paragraphs 1 and 2 of Article 16 of the Constitution. In its 2nd legal foundation, the Constitutional Court affirmed that "it is unimaginable how a precept which aims to guarantee respect for religious convictions of all citizens can affect the right to religious freedom and the religion of each individual...The lay nature of the State does not imply that the religious beliefs and sentiments of society cannot be the object of its protection. Article 16.3 itself of the Spanish Constitution affirms... that public powers also take into account the religious beliefs of Spanish society... It explains that in comparative European law the incriminations of similar acts, be the rule and that the legal texts have, in general, a concept similar to the precept."

[11] In this sense, see High Court Rulings of December 11, 1950, December 10, 1982 and March 25, 1993.

addition to, as stated by the High Court Ruling of July 15, 1982, "being committed with intent to offend religious sensibilities". The said offence, which the Court itself considers to be demonstrable in diverse acts of disrespect for the sacred objects of the Catholic Church, was described in *de facto* cases of judicial rulings such as, "taking the host out of one's mouth after receiving communion by throwing it, or spitting it out just after receiving communion",[12] "taking it out of one's mouth and exhibiting it to those present in a show of defamation",[13] "opening the tabernacle and taking the host",[14] "opening the tabernacle, taking the chalice and eating part of the host and putting the rest in a pocket",[15] or "drinking wine from the chalice, dumping the host on the floor, burning it with matches, and leaving the empty bottle inside the tabernacle and various coins in the chalice".[16]

The subjective element requires wilful intention to offend religious sensibilities in a temple or place of worship. In the case considered in the High Court Ruling of March 25, 1993, a television presenter and director were accused of this offence in a show about the latest artistic trends that broadcasted a music video in which a coffin appeared, upon which, instead of a crucifix, was a human figure on a cross with the head of an animal. The Court absolved the accused of the crime of profanation, holding that, amongst other reasons, *animus injurandi* was lacking, and the specific wilful aim of the programme was not to offend, but rather to show the latest modern music.

In addition, with the aim of safeguarding places of worship sacred to their believers, Article 613 of the Penal Code punishes with imprisonment from four to six years, those who during wartime destroy or order the destruction of places of worship.

4. *Hindering or disrupting a religious meeting*

Article 523 of the Penal Code punishes those who "with violence, threats, tumult or acts, impede, interrupt or disturb the acts, functions, ceremonies or demonstrations of the religions inscribed in the public registry of the Ministry of Justice or the Interior", with a punishment of "six years to six months imprisonment, if the act is committed in a place of worship, or a fine of four to ten months if it occurs in any other place".

[12] Court Ruling of December 22, 1913.
[13] Court Ruling of December 31, 1896.
[14] Court Ruling of February 27, 1929.
[15] Court Ruling of July 15, 1982.
[16] Court Ruling of December 10, 1982.

As can be seen upon the reading the norm, protection of religious worship and ceremony is restricted, by literal adherence to the precepts of the Penal Code, to those who participate in religions inscribed in the Registries of the Ministry of Justice or the Ministry of the Interior – the Registry of Associations. The fact that the acts carried out by religions which are not so inscribed are outside penal protection, as well as those carried out by non-religious philosophical associations, suggests that the legal objects protected are acts of worship of recognized religions, and not, as it should be, the right of any person to carry out acts of worship, the individual right recognized in Article 2.1.b. of the Organic Law 7/1980, of July 5, of Religious Freedom.

The material element of the offence is conduct impeding, interrupting or disturbing acts of worship, or religious demonstrations, conduct carried out with violence, threats or commotion. No special psychological element is required, with the offence being committed with the intended realization of the aforementioned violent acts. The action of interrupting a funeral, which is considered to be an act of worship, is included in Article 2.1.b of the Organic Law of Religious Freedom, within the acts, functions and ceremonies of religions protected from violent interruptions or disturbances, contemplated in Article 523 of the Penal Code.

5. *Menaces, violence or force against another's freedom of religion or conscience*

Article 522 is specifically aimed at punishing acts against religious freedom or the consciences of persons. The offence has two different modalities, sharing the means of commission – using violence, intimidation, force, or any other illegitimate pressure – and the punishment – a fine of four to ten months.

In the first modality, the material element is impeding "a member or members of a religion, from practising acts pertaining to the beliefs which they profess, or attending the same". A judge was accused of this offence because he had ordered a blood transfusion for a woman belonging to the Jehovah's Witnesses in order to safeguard her health, following the advice of a medical team treating her, after she had suffered from several hemorrhages from having given birth. Despite the transfusions, the woman died. The husband, also a Jehovah's Witness, filed a criminal complaint against the judge for the offence of acts against religious freedom. The Constitutional Court, in Decree 369/1984, June 20, justified the decision of the judge: "there existed a legitimate authorization under articles 3 and 5 of the Organic Law of religious freedom for the judicial action, since the right to religious freedom guaranteed by article 16.1 of the Spanish Constitution is limited by the health of individuals, and the Magistrate-Judge acted in favour of that limitation by authorising the blood transfusions, and that said behaviour did not itself include the element of specific injustice of a criminal type".

The second modality is constituted by the acts of forcing "another or others to practise or conform to worship or rites, or to carry out telltale acts of professing or not a religion or to change the beliefs which they profess". In general terms, the conduct described could be included within the framework of so-called illicit proselytizing, qualified, we must reiterate, by employing a means of commission meant to restrict the free will of individuals: violence, intimidation, use of force or any other illegitimate pressure.

The use of such means also extends to associations which promote the alteration or control of personalities, which, and in accordance with Article 515.3 of the Penal Code, renders such groups when convicted to be considered illicit associations. We will deal with this offence, closely related to the activities attributed to so-called sects, in the section dealing with the application of Penal Law to sects.

6. *Discrimination based on religion*

The Spanish Penal Code punishes two forms of behaviour, having as a common denominator the infringement of equality, on grounds of, among other reasons, the religious beliefs of persons: discrimination in public and private employment (Article 314) and the denial, on the part of a public service or a professional, of work requested by an individual or association which has a right to such work (Articles. 511 and 512). In both cases, the offender is aware of the religious condition of the individual or association and denies employment or work because of such beliefs.

The punishment for the offence of discrimination varies depending upon who commits it: if it is carried out in the area of conceding public or private employment, the offender will be punished with a prison term of six months to two years or a fine of twelve to fourteen months; in the case of a civil servant who denies work, the stiffer punishment will be applied with the additional punishment of being barred from employment or public office for a period of four years. The same punishment will be applied to a professional who commits an act of discrimination, with the difference that the period of the bar from office is from one to four years.

7. *Abuse of a corpse or desecration of a sepulchre*

According to Article 526 of the Penal Code, "one who fails to show due respect to the memory of the deceased, violates gravesites or tombs, profanes a cadaver or its ashes, or wilfully outrages, destroys, alters or damages funeral urns, pantheons, gravestones, or tombs, will be punished with imprisonment for twelve to twenty four weekends and fined from three to six months".

The legal object protected is not strictly speaking religious sentiments, but rather, as the rule states, due respect for the memory of the deceased (itself deeply rooted in society) which is extended to all types of beliefs, religious or otherwise. Prior to the coming into force of Article 526, the High Court (analysing in its Ruling of November 26, 1984 the wilful misconduct of those prosecuted for the offence of violating graves and profaning cadavers according the equivalent regulation in the previous penal code) had referred to "wilfully and consciously disturbing the eternal rest and peace of the dead, as well as the due respect of their memory and the sentiments of their friends and loved ones".

In this provision, various forms of behaviour are punished: desecration of sepulchres, abuse of a corpse or its ashes, and the destruction of urns, mausoleums, and tombstones. All of these cases require proof of specific wilful conduct to show disrespect for the deceased or for the grief or bereavement of family members.

If the offence was committed with the religion of the buried person in mind – for example in attacks on Jewish cemeteries perpetrated by anti-Semitic groups – the generic aggravating circumstance will be applied under Article 22.4 of the Penal Code, with the criminal action having been motivated by the religious beliefs of the victims.

8. *Offences against the Catholic religion: apostasy*

Religious offences – which include public apostasy of the Catholic religion – were punishable by the Courts of the Inquisition, ecclesiastical courts which were supported by civil authority. In 1820, the Courts of Spanish Inquisition were abolished. But three years later, with the reestablishment of absolutism under King Ferdinand VII, the offences of religion continued to be judged by the so-called Juntas of Faith, or special courts. These were established in each diocese under the authority of the archbishop and bishop, and with the collaboration of the State in carrying out the punishment. The Juntas of Faith finally disappeared, and with them so did apostasy and other offences related to the non-Catholic religious beliefs of persons, in 1835. No legal text from the 19th or 20th century defines apostasy of the Catholic faith as a criminal offence.

II. Offences by ministers of religion

9. *Revelation of a secret obtained in the exercise of ministry*

The legal objects of intimacy and privacy are protected under Article 199 of the Penal Code punishing those who reveal secrets to third parties – a provision which could be applicable to secrets obtained by ministers in the exercise of their ministry – with a prison sentence of one to three years, and a fine of six to twelve months.

From another angle, safeguarding information discovered in the exercise of religious attendance or worship is reflected in the penal regulation of ministerial secrets. The Law of September 14, 1882 of *Enjuiciamiento Criminal* (Criminal Trial Proceedings) imposes the obligation to report offences (Article 263) and to testify as a witness (Articles 417.1 and 707) with respect to deeds revealed in the course of ministry. The regulation of these exemptions is similar to those applied to other occupations which are subject to professional secrecy, such as those of a doctor, lawyer, or journalist.

10. *Offences related to the celebration of religious matrimony*

The Spanish legal system attributes civil effects to religious matrimony – to-date, marriages performed in the Catholic, Evangelical, Muslim, or Jewish rites have civil effects. The legal framework, while not requiring the celebration of civil matrimony, but rather allowing a plurality of forms of marriage with civil effects, does not penalize the minister of previously contracted religious marriages. The offence contemplated in Article 219 of the Penal Code, on the other hand, would apply in matrimonial matters to ministers of the Catholic, Evangelical, Jewish, and Muslim faiths: "He who authorizes a marriage in which there is some cause for nullity or there exists a claim for such, will be punished with a prison term of six months to two years, and will be banned from office for two to six years in the case of a public employee or public figure". In the previous Code, enacted in 1944 and thus in force during the era of the Catholic State, Article 478 punished "the ecclesiastical minister or the judge who authorized a marriage prohibited by law or for which there was some impediment from which there is no dispensation". The most frequent case was allowing the marriage ceremony of baptized persons previously united by civil matrimony, which for the Catholic Church does not constitute a legitimate union. The jurisprudence of the High Court was reluctant to condemn either the parties who had been united in a canonical marriage after a civil ceremony when they had trusted the advice and the opinion of the hierarchy of the Church[17], or to find the priest guilty who had given his consent to the religious union. In the latter case, the High Court Ruling of February 24, 1962 absolved a cleric because, "in order for the actions... punishable by law, to be considered offences, they must be carried out wilfully and with malicious intent ... with the awareness that the act is punishable and that he is guilty of committing such an act". The reluctance of our jurisprudence during the era of the Catholic State, to condemn priests in the performance of null marriages, should apply to priests, as well as to Evangelical ministers, Jewish rabbis, or Muslim Imams, in the current application of Article 219 of the Penal Code. It is true though, that there have been no court cases in which clerics or ministers of other religions have been prosecuted for or convicted of authorizing or performing marriages while being aware of some cause for civil nullity. This is so in spite of the indisputable fact that the number of simulated marriages to achieve Spanish nationality has increased hugely.

11. *Offences against public peace in a place of worship or during a religious practice*

Specific penal punishment for words spoken or actions carried out that could subvert public order or by clergy or religious orders of the Catholic religion, usual in some 19th century penal codes, disappeared from the legal texts of the 20th century.

III. Offences committed in religious or cultural rituals

12. *Female genital mutilation*

The increase in immigration of Muslims of Sub-Saharan origin who practise female genital mutilation on very young girls has created a great deal of social alarm. With the aim of putting an end to such practices, in 2003,

[17] High Court Rulings of November 29, 1944 and September 24, 1954.

the Penal Code was reformed, adding a second paragraph to Article 149, which expressly contemplates punishment for female genital mutilation, considering it an offence involving grave physical harm. Furthermore, considering also what is established in Article 23.4 of Organic Law of July 1, 1985 of Judicial Power, prosecution for this offence is possible even when it is committed in another country, provided that the accused is on Spanish soil.

The material element is causing genital mutilation in any of its manifestations. Wilful misconduct is required or at least causal intent, which should reflect on the outcome. The punishment established for this offence is six to twelve years in prison. If the victim is a minor or disabled, punishment may include disqualification from the exercise of guardianship for a term of four to ten years, provided the judge rules that this is in the interests of the minor or the disabled victim.

IV. Religious motivation as aggravation or attenuation

13. *Offences aggravated by religious motivation*

Article 22.4 of the Penal Code contemplates a generic aggravating circumstance – which is applicable to the commission of any offence; namely: "commission of the offence because of motives which are... anti-Semitic... (or because of) the religion or beliefs of the victim", or other personal circumstances such as ethnic background, race, or nationality, sex, or sexual orientation, physical illness or disability. The application of this aggravating circumstance, aimed at reinforcing the protection of equality and the fight against discrimination, requires the criminal action carried out to be exclusively motivated by the religious beliefs – or ethnicity, gender, nationality, etc – of the victim.

14. *Offences attenuated by religious motivation*

The Penal Code does not contemplate the religious beliefs of persons as a generic or specific extenuating circumstance. Nevertheless, it is possible to attenuate responsibility in relation to incomplete defences – when all the necessary requisites do no concur for absolving responsibility – by way of acting in the fulfillment of a duty or in exercising a right (Article 20.7 of the Penal Code); in the case in question, an extenuating circumstance would be carrying out the right to ideological or religious freedom.

In any event, jurisprudence has traditionally considered that to act according to the dictates of rooted moral or religious convictions constitutes extenuating circumstances for penal responsibility.

In the Ruling of November 25, 1955, the High Court found a group of Catholics guilty of the offence of arson for breaking into a protestant temple and attempting to burn some bibles at the altar, even when the very qualified extenuating circumstance was applied of acting in accordance with moral convictions: "the defendants, holding deeply rooted Catholic beliefs, such as protesting against the intense and public propaganda of Protestant ideas being carried out by the Pastor and affiliates of a Protestant sect… which hampered their sense of reason". It seems evident that the Ruling is tinged with a certain justification of the action of the guilty party, typical of a Catholic State, which is manifested in the substantial reduction of the punishment. However, in later rulings, from the constitutional period, the High Court has taken into account the religious beliefs, and acts in accordance with those beliefs, to diminish penal responsibility, particularly with respect to the criminal behaviour of Jehovah's Witnesses.

The case contained in the Ruling of March 27, 1990 is truly dramatic. An unconscious woman was taken to an emergency ward after having been repeatedly stabbed by her husband. She was accompanied by someone claiming to be a friend, belonging to the Jehovah's Witnesses. The hospital doctors immediately carried out a blood transfusion, given the large quantity of blood that she had lost. The friend accompanying her subsequently warned the medical team that the woman was likewise a Jehovah's Witness, and that such a treatment was against her beliefs. As the friend was not a family member, he was separated from her, and taken to the waiting room. Nevertheless, taking advantage of a nurse's inattention, the man entered the woman's hospital room, and pulled out the tube which was giving the woman the blood transfusion, resulting in her death. The Court upheld the conviction of the Jehovah's Witness for intentional homicide since he was aware of the illegal nature and results of his action. Notwithstanding, the incomplete extenuating circumstance of a very qualified insanity was applied "because of the dogmatism and the rigidity of his ideas". In a similar way, in the Ruling of June 27, 1997, the Court found parents who were Jehovah's Witnesses guilty of homicide for refusing to allow their son to receive a blood transfusion when he was suffering from an advanced form of leukemia, subsequently dying from it. The extenuating circumstances of rage or obfuscation were applied because of the intensity and strength of the parents' religious convictions.

V. Criminal law and sects

15. *Offences linked to the sectarian milieu*

Apart from committing various offences – prostitution, fraud, corruption of a minor – under the guise of a religious aim, the behaviour most typically linked to sects is that of using aggressive means to kidnap and retain followers. The punishment of this behaviour forms part of one of the cases by which the group can be considered an illicit association. Indeed, Article 515.3 of the Penal Code, without expressly mentioning sects, penalizes an illicit association, even though it has a legitimate aim, which employs violent means or seeks alteration or control of personalities to achieve that aim. The courts, in applying Article 515, will also have to determine whether the association should be dissolved as well as the punishment, for their participation and responsibility, of its members: the founders, directors, and presidents, who may receive a prison term of two to four years and a fine of twelve to twenty four months; and for others complicit in the crime, prison from one to three years, and a fine of twelve to twenty four months.

Lars Friedner

RELIGION IN CRIMINAL LAW: SWEDEN

As will become apparent in the following, Sweden is to a great extent a secularized state. The separation of Church and State, at the turn of the millennium,[1] is another factor that has diminished the number of special regulations concerning religion and criminal law.

Blasphemy[2] was once an offence under Swedish criminal law, though this special offence was abolished in 1970.[3] The main reason for this decision was the opinion that the protection of religions and churches did not call for such restrictions on freedom of expression and freedom of the press. It was also argued that there were several other offences through which the law provided protection for religions in the same way as the protection provided by the offence of *blasphemy*. The offences of *agitation against a national or ethnic group*,[4] *disorderly conduct*,[5] *defamation*,[6] *disturbing a public meeting*,[7] and *disturbing a function*,[8] were referred to as being such offences.[9] This latter offence is basically aimed at the duties of officials (for instance police officers), as it is consequently no longer applicable to priests of the Church of Sweden, the former state church, as they are now not to be regarded as state officials. On the other hand the word 'duties' also includes weddings and funerals. This means that a wedding or a

[1] Church of Sweden Act (Sw. *Lagen om Svenska kyrkan*) 1998:1591, Act on Introduction of the Church of Sweden Act (Sw. *Lagen om införande av lagen om Svenska kyrkan*)1998:1592, Religious Communities Act (Sw. *Lagen om trossamfund*) 1998:1593; see i.e. *Friedner*, Church and State in Sweden 1999, European Journal for Church and State Research 2000, vol. 7, p. 225ff.

[2] Since 1948 the actual name of the offence has been *crime against the peace of creed*, see NJA II 1948 p. 359 f.

[3] Official Government Report – SFS 1970:225.

[4] Sw. *Hets mot folkgrupp*, BrB (Penal Code) 16:8.

[5] Sw. *Förargelseväckande beteende*, BrB 16:16.

[6] Sw. *Ärekränkning*, BrB 5:1-3.

[7] Sw *Störande av allmän sammankomst*, BrB 16:4.

[8] Sw *Störande av förrättning*, BrB 16:4.

[9] NJA II 1970 p. 553.

funeral, officiated by a priest or another religious leader is protected by this provision.[10]

Among the other offences mentioned, the offence of *agitation against a national or ethnic group* is specifically aimed at the matter of religion ("...anyone who...threatens or expresses disrespect for a group of people or another such group of persons alluding to race, skin colour, national or ethnic origin, profession of creed, or sexual orientation...."[11]). The crime of *disturbing a public meeting* enumerates "public divine service (and) other public worship" as examples of public meetings that are protected by the law.[12] The other offences mentioned merely include protection for religious activities and beliefs, without this being specifically mentioned. Except for a case from 2005,[13] there have been no prosecutions for these offences, with religious implications, reported in Sweden since the 1970 amendment.

The matter of *blasphemy* has also been debated in Sweden since 1970. Two members of parliament submitted a bill seeking to reintroduce the offence of *blasphemy* in Sweden.[14] However, the Riksdag (Swedish Parliament) rejected the bill.[15]

The offence of *agitation against a national or ethnic group*, mentioned above, does not seem to encompass agitation against members of non-religious philosophical associations. However, the question has not been tested in any reported case.

There is no special offence in Sweden regarding desecration of places of worship or sacred objects. But, of course, the general offences of *disorderly conduct* or *inflicting damage*[16] could apply to such situations.

The offence of *disturbing a public meeting* is aimed at, as mentioned, *public* worship. This would mean that a meeting in private is not protected by the law,[17] only meetings which anyone is free to enter. (On the other hand, a meeting in private is probably very often protected by the

[10] The Marriage Code (Sw *Äktenskapsbalken*) 4:3; Act of the Right for Officiating Marriages within Religious Communities other than the Church of Sweden (Sw. *Lag om rätt att förrätta vigsel inom andra trossamfund än Svenska kyrkan*) 1993:305. The Church of Sweden also, in some ways, still exercises state authority within the funeral system, Burial Act (Sw. *Begravningslagen*) 1990:1144, 1:1.

[11] BrB 16:8.

[12] BrB 16:4.

[13] NJA 2005 p. 805, see below.

[14] Mot 1999/2000:K286. The aim of the bill was actually that the Riksdag (Parliament) should encourage the Government to take measures for a new act on "violating religions".

[15] Bet. 2000/01:KU09, Prot. 2000/01:55.

[16] Sw *Skadegörelse*, BrB 12:1.

[17] Holmqvist&al, *Brottsbalken – en kommentar Kap.* 13-24, p. 16:16.

general offence of *breach of domiciliary peace.*[18]) As this offence covers most types of public meetings, it is likely that a meeting of a non-religious philosophical association is also protected. The punishment for *disturbing a public meeting* is a fine (the norm) or a maximum of six months' imprisonment.[19]

The punishment for the offence of *agitation against a national or ethnic group* is a maximum of two years' imprisonment, in minor cases just fines. Grave crimes are punished by imprisonment: minimum six months, maximum four years.[20]

In Sweden, a *crime against the peace of a tomb*[21] is punished by fines or a maximum of two years' imprisonment. The offence is defined as "moving, damaging, or outrageous treatment of a corpse or of the ashes of a deceased person, opening of a grave, or otherwise causing damage or mischief to a coffin, urn, grave, or other resting-place of the deceased or at a sepulchral monument, without authorization".[22] The offence applies regardless of the religion of the deceased.

Proselytizing or apostasy are not offences in Sweden, though this was not always so. Until 1860 it was forbidden for Swedish citizens to leave the Lutheran state church.[23] Private meetings for divine services and worship were also forbidden.[24] Apostasy from the "true evangelical creed" was punished by expatriation and disinheritance.[25]

As long as Sweden had a state church, until the year 2000, the offence of *pretence of public office*[26] also covered officials of the Church when exercising state authority. As Sweden has a system where the Church of Sweden and many other religious communities have the right to officiate at marriages, it is likely that the priests of the Church of Sweden are still covered by this rule when they, on behalf of the State, solemnise marriages (although this has not been examined since the new relationship between State and Church was established).[27] In that case, the same rule

[18] Sw. *Hemfridsbrott*, BrB 4:6.
[19] BrB 16:4.
[20] BrB 16:8.
[21] Sw. *Brott mot griftefrid*, BrB 16:10.
[22] BrB 16:10.
[23] *Göransson, Svensk kyrkorätt – en översikt* (Stockholm 1993), p. 39.
[24] Royal Ordinance 1726 ("*konventikelplakatet*"), here quoted after *Göransson*, p. 38.
[25] 1734 Statute Book, Act on Missdeed (Sw. *missgärningsbalken*) 1:3, here quoted after *Göransson*, ibid.
[26] Sw *Föregivande av allmän ställning*, BrB 17:15.
[27] The Marriage Code (Sw *Äktenskapsbalken*) 4:3. The Church of Sweden also, in some ways, still exercises state authority within the funeral system, Burial Act (Sw. *Begravningslagen*) 1990:1144, 1:1.

covers priests and other officials from other churches and religions, when they, in the same way, exercise state authority.[28]

Breach of professional confidentiality[29] applies to all state officials, as well as others who have an obligation through an Act of Parliament or an Ordinance to keep any information secret. Thus, until the year 2000, the offence also covered the priests of the Church of Sweden, as their obligation of secrecy was laid down by an Act of Parliament.[30] As this Act has now been repealed,[31] the offence no longer covers any church or religious community.

Female genital mutilation is forbidden in Sweden.[32] The punishment is imprisonment, maximum four years. Grave crimes are punished by imprisonment, minimum two years, maximum ten years.[33] The elements of the offence are "to perform an operation on the outer female genitals with the purpose of mutilating them or bringing other permanent changes to them".[34] It should be noted that this offence, as opposed to many other offences in Swedish law, explicitly applies regardless of any consent by the victim.[35] It should also be observed that, unlike many other offences, the perpetrator can be sentenced by a Swedish court although the deed was not an offence in the country where it was committed.[36] It is widely discussed in Sweden whether female genital mutilation is a religious custom or if it has its roots in ethnic or cultural factors.[37]

Formally, there are no offences in Sweden that are aggravated or extenuated by religious motivation. However, in practice there is one well-known case, concerning a pastor of the Pentecostal Movement. The pastor preached a sermon in his church, where he spoke disrespectfully of homosexual people. He was prosecuted for the offence of *agitation against a national or ethnic group*. The Supreme Court ultimately acquitted him on the ground that although he had obviously spoken

[28] Act of the Right for Officiating Marriages within Religious Communities other than the Church of Sweden (Sw. *Lag om rätt att förrätta vigsel inom andra trossamfund än Svenska kyrkan*) 1993:305.

[29] Sw *Brott mot tystnadsplikt*, BrB 20:3.

[30] Church Act (Sw. *Kyrkolagen*) 1992:300, 36:1.

[31] Act on the Introduction of the Church of Sweden Act (Sw. *Lag om införande av lagen om Svenska kyrkan*) 1998:1592, 2 §.

[32] Act on Ban on Female Genital Mutilation (Sw. *Lag om förbud mot könsstympning av kvinnor*) 1982:316, 1 §; NJA II 1982 p. 423, NJA II 1998 p. 378 f.

[33] ibid 2 §.

[34] ibid 1 §.

[35] Ibid.

[36] ibid 3 §.

[37] i.e. www.rb.se (website for Save the Children Sweden).

disrespectfully of homosexual people he did so in the course of a religious ceremony, where his freedom of religion was to be protected.[38]

There are no special regulations in Sweden concerning the conduct of religious sects.

One situation relevant to criminal law and religion that has been widely discussed in Sweden is the question of 'ritual slaughter'.[39] According to the Animal Protection Act,[40] a domestic animal shall at the slaughter be unconscious when the blood is drawn.[41] However, this method of slaughter seems to be against some Jewish and Muslim traditions. Thus, Jews and Muslims practising such traditions cannot legally have ritual slaughter carried out in Sweden. There have been no reports of religiously motivated crimes against the Animal Protection Act.

[38] NJA 2005 p. 805.

[39] SOU 1999:9

[40] Sw. *Djurskyddslagen* (1988:534); some exceptions are accepted regarding poultry and rabbits, see Animal Protection Act 14 §and Animal Protection Ordinance (Sw. *Djurskyddsförordningen*) 1988:539, 31 §

[41] Animal Protection Act (Sw. *Djurskyddslagen*) 1988:534, 14 §;

NORMAN DOE, RUSSELL SANDBERG AND FRANK CRANMER

The Centre for Law and Religion, Law School, Cardiff University

RELIGION AND CRIMINAL LAW IN THE UNITED KINGDOM

Criminal liability in the United Kingdom is based on proof of the definitional elements of the crime in question. Generally, this requires proof of the external element (*actus reus*), which may involve conduct, consequences, or circumstances (and sometimes omissions), including causation and voluntariness; proof of the internal or mental element (*mens rea*), which varies between crimes (and may include intention, belief, knowledge, recklessness and negligence); and the absence of a defence (justification or excuse), such as automatism, intoxication, duress, provocation, and self-defence. Criminal offences may also be ones of strict liability (where liability is imposed without the necessity of proving *mens rea* with respect to one or more elements of the crime) or, more rarely, absolute liability (no proof of a *mens rea* is required). Whilst there are many sociological studies on the relationship between religiosity and crime, there are few on religion and the criminal law in the UK.[1] Most criminal offences are defined in parliamentary legislation (statutes), though the courts still claim a residual authority to recognise crimes at common law.[2] The category "religious offences" is known in Parliament and to academics,[3] but not in statute.[4] The focus of the following is primarily the law in England and Wales.[5]

[1] See, however, N. Addison, *Religious Discrimination and Hatred Law* (Routledge-Cavendish, London, 2007) Ch. 7, and R. Sandberg and N. Doe, 'The changing criminal law on religion', *Law and Justice* (forthcoming).

[2] *R v Jones* [2006] UKHL 16, [2006] 2 WLR 772 *per* Lord Bingham.

[3] Eg House of Lords Select Committee on Religious Offences in England and Wales, Report 2003.

[4] It would have become a statutory category had the Religious Offences Bill 2002 become law.

[5] Occasional references are made to the law in Scotland (which shares much with that in England and Wales) as well as, where appropriate, to the position in Northern Ireland.

I. The protection of religion in the criminal law

1. *Blasphemy*

The ancient offences of blasphemy and blasphemous libel have recently been abolished by section 79 of the Criminal Justice and Immigration Act 2008: 'The offences of blasphemy and blasphemous libel under the common law of England and Wales are abolished'.[6] The abolition concludes a long-running debate. Although many had already pronounced the offence dead, or at least moribund, its abolition in such an understated way caught many by surprise.[7] For the courts blasphemy was 'not only an offence to God and to religion, but a crime against the laws, state and Government'; and undermining religion was 'to dissolve all those obligations whereby the civil societies are preserved'; since 'Christianity is parcel of the Laws of England', it followed that 'to reproach the Christian religion is to speak in subversion of the law'.[8] Blasphemy law rested mainly on court decisions in the seventeenth to nineteenth centuries,[9] and was often difficult to define.[10] But despite adaptability to social change,[11] it was possible to outline the essence of the offence.[12]

The *actus reus* of blasphemy was to publish 'blasphemous' material in any form;[13] it had to be in conflict with the tenets of the Church of England and couched in indecent or offensive terms likely to shock and outrage the feelings of the general body of Church of England believers. The extent to which the law protected Christian denominations other than the Church of England was an open question.[14] It was made

[6] For the process of abolition, see R. Sandberg and N. Doe, 'The strange death of blasphemy', *Modern Law Review* (forthcoming December 2008).

[7] Eg A. Denning, *Freedom Under the Law* (London: Stevens, 1949) 46; R. Ahdar and I. Leigh, *Religious Freedom in the Liberal State* (Oxford: Oxford University Press, 2005) 368.

[8] *Taylor's Case* (1676) 1 Vent 293. See HL Select Committee Report 2003, Vol. I, App. 3, para 2.

[9] Blasphemy was originally both a statutory and a common law offence. However, the Criminal Law Act 1967 repealed the Blasphemy Act 1697.

[10] See, eg, House of Lords Select Committee, n 3 above, Appendix 3, paragraph 1; A. Bradney, *Religions, Rights and the Law* (Leicester: Leicester University Press, 1993) 82; D. Feldman, *Civil Liberties and Human Rights in England and Wales* (Oxford: Oxford University Press, 2002) 913.

[11] C Munro, 'Prophets, Presbyters and Profanity' [1989] *Public Law* 369 at 371.

[12] P W Edge, *Legal Responses to Religious Difference* (The Hague: Kluwer Law, 2002) 207-211.

[13] Material could be published in a written or verbal form: *R v Gott* (1922) 16 CR App R 87.

[14] Eg *Gathercole's Case* (1838) 2 Lewin 237: 'any general attack on *Christianity* is the subject of criminal prosecution, because Christianity is the established religion of the

clear in *Williams*[15] that other Christian denominations and other religions were protected 'to the extent that their fundamental beliefs are those which are held in common with the established Church'.[16] This requirement did mean however, that the offence of blasphemy did 'not protect religious *beliefs* as such' but rather was 'concerned with attacks on those beliefs expressed in highly offensive *ways*':[17] thus, 'if the decencies of controversy are observed, even the fundamentals of religion may be attacked',[18] and 'reasonable men do not apprehend the dissolution or the downfall of society because religion is publicly assailed by methods not scandalous'.[19]

The *mens rea* of blasphemy was established (in the last successful prosecution) by the House of Lords in *R v Lemon, R v Gay News*,[20] which held that the defendant must have intended to publish the blasphemous material. There was no requirement that the defendant had an intention to blaspheme;[21] it was sufficient for the prosecution to prove that the publication had been intentional and that the matter was blasphemous. The *Gay News* case was the first successful prosecution for almost sixty years.[22] During that period, blasphemy was policed extra-legally; it was curtailed 'by the fears, anxieties and sensitivities of individuals' rather than by law.[23]

The *Gay News* case also showed that the law on blasphemy was compliant with the European Convention on Human Rights, which, of course, safeguards both freedom of religion (Article 9) and freedom of expression (Article 10). However, Strasbourg has held that although the freedom to manifest religion does not include a right to be exempt from all criticism,[24] freedom of expression contains 'a duty to

country'. See also *Stephen's Digest of the Criminal Law* which defined blasphemous matters as those 'relating to God, Jesus Christ or the Bible, or the formulation of the Church of England as by law established' (London: Sweet & Maxwell, 1950) article 2.14, quoted in *R v Lemon, R v Gay News* [1979] AC 617.

15 (1797) 26 St Tr 654.

16 See also *R v Chief Stipendiary Magistrate ex parte Choudhury* [1991] 1 QB 429; HL Select Committee, Vol. 1, App. 3, para 4.

17 Ahdar and Leigh (2005) 367.

18 *R v Ramsay and Foote* (1883) 15 Cox CC 231.

19 *Bowman v Secular Society Ltd* [1917] AC 406.

20 [1979] AC 617.

21 Edge (2002) 209-210.

22 Since *R v Gott* (1922) 16 CR App R 87.

23 R Webster, *A Brief History of Blasphemy* (Southwold: Orwell Press, 1990) chapter 1.

24 *İA v Turkey* (Application no. 42571/98) 13 September 2005, para 28: 'Those who choose to exercise the freedom to manifest their religion, irrespective of whether they do so as members of a religious majority or a minority, cannot reasonably expect to be exempt

avoid expressions that are gratuitously offensive to others and profane'.[25] It was therefore not surprising that a claim that the prosecution for blasphemy in *Gay News* was incompatible with ECHR was unsuccessful in Strasbourg.[26] The Commission held that blasphemous libel restricted freedom of expression but this was justified (to protect the religious feelings of citizens), legitimate and necessary in a democratic society provided the principle of proportionality is respected.[27] Strasbourg has since followed a similar approach in relation to other States.[28]

Following *Gay News*, blasphemy seemed to experience something of a revival. After the publication of Rushdie's *The Satanic Verses*, it was held that blasphemy law applied only to Christianity and there was no justification for a court to extend this, not least since this was likely to do more harm than good.[29] A subsequent Strasbourg application was declared inadmissible.[30] Blasphemy law was also enforced by public bodies (one such decision, *Wingrove*, was upheld in Strasbourg).[31]

Since 1979, numerous commentators and politicians called for the abolition of blasphemy.[32] In 2003, the House of Lords Select Committee on Religious Offences in England and Wales concluded that: (1) the future of the offence 'may not depend upon legislation but upon the

from all criticism. They must tolerate and accept the denial by others of their religious beliefs and even the propagation by others of doctrines hostile to their faith.'

[25] *İA v Turkey* (Application no. 42571/98) 13 September 2005, para 24.

[26] *Gay News Ltd v United Kingdom* (1983) 5 EHRR 123.

[27] The failure of the Article 10 claim was also fatal for the Article 9 claim since interference would be justified under Article 9 (2) on the same grounds as under Article 10 (2). An argument on grounds of Article 14 (discrimination in the enjoyment of a Convention right) was also dismissed since there was no evidence that the applicants were discriminated against on account of their homosexual views or of beliefs not shared by confessing Christians.

[28] See eg *Otto-Preminger Institute v Austria* (1995) 19 EHRR 34.

[29] *R v Chief Stipendiary Magistrate ex parte Choudhury* [1991] 1 QB 429.

[30] *Choudhury v United Kingdom* (1991) 12 HRLJ 172. The Applicant applied to European Commission of Human Rights on grounds of violation of Articles 9 and 14. The Commission dismissed the claim on the grounds that 'no State authority or any body under which the United Kingdom Government may be responsible under the Convention, directly interfered in the applicant's freedom to manifest his religion or belief'.

[31] *Wingrove v United Kingdom* (1997) 24 EHRR.

[32] David Blunkett, HC Deb Column 707 26 Nov 2001; Law Commission (1981): Offences against Religion and Public Worship (Working Paper No. 79).

[33] Ibid, para 139.

contemporary climate, both social and legal, which could lead to a decision to take no action at all';[33] the offence was a dead-letter: 'any prosecution for blasphemy today ... is likely to fail on grounds either of discrimination or denial of the right to freedom of expression';[34] (3) the *Wingrove* decision that blasphemy was in the UK's 'margin of appreciation' did not mean that it will continue to be Convention compatible;[35] (4) it was uncertain whether the offence applied to the Church of England or Christianity (and thus the law is not compatible with Article 7 ECHR); and its discrimination against non-Christian faiths and the disproportionality of the unlimited penalty may cause problems.[36]

However, in 2007 in *Green v The City of Westminster Magistrates Court*,[37] a private prosecution for blasphemous libel concerning *Jerry Springer: The Opera*, the High Court held that: the offence still existed; it could be accurately stated; it was ECHR-compliant (under Art. 10(2)); s. 2(4) of the Theatres Act 1968 prevented prosecution for blasphemy in respect of a play;[38] and there was no *prima facie* case to answer: the play as a whole was not and could not reasonably be regarded as aimed at Christianity or at what Christians held sacred. The High Court thus undermined many of the human-rights based reasons given by the Select Committee to justify abolition. Yet, in their place, it added two new dimensions to the debate: the significant curtailing of blasphemy law by the Theatres Act 1968, and the view that the offence of blasphemy was alive and could still be elucidated. Although *Green* revealed that the potential for a blasphemy prosecution was small, it served as a reminder that the offence lay dormant rather than dead (and could be revived in much the same way as it was in the *Gay News* case). Although the House of Lords refused to hear the case judicially,

[34] Ibid, Appendix, para 9.

[35] Ibid, Appendix 3, para 12: 'the Court's decision in *Wingrove* that there was not 'as yet...sufficient common accord' to mean that the English law of blasphemy was in breach of the European Convention does not mean that it will not rule otherwise in the future'.

[36] Ibid., Appendix 3, para 15.

[37] [2007] EWHC 2785 (Admin).

[38] Theatre Act 1968, s.2(4): 'No person shall be proceeded against in respect of a performance of a play or anything said or done in the course of such a performance ... for an offence at common law where it is of the essence of the offence that the performance or, as the case may be what was said or done was obscene, indecent, offensive, disgusting or injurious to morality'; see also the Broadcasting Act 1990, Sched. 15, para. 6 (applicable to the BBC).

it was not to be long before Parliament addressed the offence of blasphemy.

On 9 January 2008 in the House of Commons, Dr Evan Harris moved a new clause to the Criminal Justice and Immigration Bill to abolish what he called 'the ancient discriminatory, unnecessary, illiberal and non-human rights compliant offences of blasphemy and blasphemous libel'. As well as the usual criticisms about legal uncertainty, discrimination and alleged incompatibility with the ECHR (but there was no reference to *Green*), Harris further argued that: there were 'enough laws dealing with outraging public decency and public order offences [already exist] to ensure that the removal of these two offences will not lead to widespread outrageous behaviour in public'. Moreover, in spite of *Green*, Harris argued for abolition because (though not used for a long time) the law had 'a chilling effect', leading to self-censorship. Referencing the objections to abolishing blasphemy at the time of debating the Racial and Religious Hatred Bill, Dr Harris also argued that there was no longer 'an excuse for prevarication' since 'religious hatred was dealt with two years ago'.[39]

However, Harris withdrew his proposal in response to an undertaking by the Government to bring forward its own new clause in the House of Lords, subject to consultation with the Church of England. The Government felt that it was 'high time that Parliament reached a settled conclusion on the issue', and that the decision in *Green* concerning the Theatres Act reinforced the idea that the offences appeared to be moribund.[40] On 5 March 2008, an amendment abolishing blasphemy was moved by the Government in the Lords.[41] The Government's reasons were: first, since the law 'has fallen into disuse', this 'runs the risk of bringing the law as a whole into disrepute'; second, there is now 'new legislation to protect individuals on the grounds of religion and belief' (namely the Racial and Religious Hatred Act 2006).[42] The first reason seems questionable, given that *Green* surely showed the law was being used. The Government was on steadier ground in relation to its second reason: although *Green* showed that blasphemy still existed, it indicated that the offences had been severely curtailed. The amendment was passed by 148 votes to 87 by the House of Lords and then by 378 votes to 57 in the House of Commons.

[39] HC Hansard (9 Jan 2008) Columns 442-448.
[40] Ibid, Columns 453-454.
[41] HL Hansard (5 Mar 2008) Column 1118.
[42] Ibid, Column 1118.

2. *Stirring up Religious Hatred*

The Racial and Religious Hatred Act 2006, a controversial measure,[43] which had a turbulent legislative history,[44] had been promised in the Labour Party manifesto during the 2005 general election.[45] The Act amended the Public Order Act 1986 to create Part 3A, 'Hatred against persons on religious grounds'; it creates new offences of stirring up hatred against persons on religious grounds.[46] It also amends the Police and Criminal Evidence Act 1984 so that powers of citizens to arrest do not apply to the offences of stirring up religious hatred – only the police can arrest.[47] The new offences apply to the use of words or behaviour or display of written material,[48]

[43] See Addison, 139f: the proposals aroused suspicion from 'an unusual coalition of comedians, Evangelical Christians and atheists'; the comedian Rowan Atkinson considered that it would make it impossible to satirise religion; the National Secular Society that it would do the same for criticism of religion; there was also a fear that 'religious vilification' legislation in Victoria, Australia had been used by one religious group against another: *Islamic Council of Victoria v Catch the Fire Ministries Inc* [2004] VCAT 2510. The proposals were supported by the Muslim Council of Britain. And similar legislation already existed in Northern Ireland: Public Order (Northern Ireland) Order 1987.

[44] The Act took four attempts to get onto the statute books. Even then the Act took a different form than the Government had intended. The House of Lords had defeated the Government on many key points and the Government was unable to get the Bill back to original state in House of Commons since it lost by one vote when the then Prime Minister Tony Blair left early. The Bill thus passed into law with the Commons supporting some of the Lords' amendments. For a fuller account of the Act's extraordinary legislative history, see N. Addison, 139-141. The Act came into force on 16 Feb. 2006.

[45] That is, the manifesto for England and that for Wales (not Scotland): 'It remains our firm and clear intention to give people of all faiths the same protection against incitement to hatred on the basis of their religion. We will legislate to outlaw it and will continue the dialogue we have started with faith groups from all backgrounds about how best to balance protection, tolerance and free speech'.

[46] There are existing offences in Part 3 of the 1986 Act against stirring up racial hatred.

[47] Explanatory Notes to Racial and Religious Hatred Act 2006, prepared by the Home Office (3-3-2006): the notes do not form part of the Act; s. 2. amends s.24a of the Police and Criminal Evidence Act 1984.

[48] The new s.29B: 'Use of words or behaviour or display of written material (1) A person who uses threatening words or behaviour, or displays any written material which is threatening, is guilty of an offence if he intends thereby to stir up religious hatred. (2) An offence under this section may be committed in a public or a private place, except that no offence is committed where the words or behaviour are used, or the written material is displayed, by a person inside a dwelling and are not heard or seen except by other persons in that or another dwelling. (3) A constable may arrest without warrant anyone he reasonably suspects is committing an offence under this section. (4) In proceedings for an offence under this section it is a defence for the accused to prove that he was inside a dwelling and had no reason to believe that the words or behaviour used, or the written material displayed, would be heard or seen by a person outside that or any other dwelling. (5) This section does not apply to words or behaviour used, or written material displayed, solely for the purpose of being included in a programme service'.

publishing or distributing written material,[49] the public performance of a play,[50] distributing, showing or playing a recording,[51] broadcasting or including a programme in a programme service,[52] and the possession of written materials or recordings with a view to display, publication, distribution or inclusion in a programme service.[53] For each offence the words, behaviour,

[49] The new s.29C: 'Publishing or distributing written material (1) A person who publishes or distributes written material which is threatening is guilty of an offence if he intends thereby to stir up religious hatred. (2) References in this Part to the publication or distribution of written material are to its publication or distribution to the public or a section of the public.'

[50] The new s.29D: 'Public performance of play (1) If a public performance of a play is given which involves the use of threatening words or behaviour, any person who presents or directs the performance is guilty of an offence if he intends thereby to stir up religious hatred. (2) This section does not apply to a performance given solely or primarily for one or more of the following purposes— (a) rehearsal, (b) making a recording of the performance, or (c) enabling the performance to be included in a programme service; but if it is proved that the performance was attended by persons other than those directly connected with the giving of the performance or the doing in relation to it of the things mentioned in paragraph (b) or (c), the performance shall, unless the contrary is shown, be taken not to have been given solely or primarily for the purpose mentioned above. (3) For the purposes of this section— (a) a person shall not be treated as presenting a performance of a play by reason only of his taking part in it as a performer, (b) a person taking part as a performer in a performance directed by another shall be treated as a person who directed the performance if without reasonable excuse he performs otherwise than in accordance with that person's direction, and (c) a person shall be taken to have directed a performance of a play given under his direction notwithstanding that he was not present during the performance; and a person shall not be treated as aiding or abetting the commission of an offence under this section by reason only of his taking part in a performance as a performer. (4) In this section "play" and "public performance" have the same meaning as in the Theatres Act 1968. (5) The following provisions of the Theatres Act 1968 apply in relation to an offence under this section as they apply to an offence under section 2 of that Act— section 9 (script as evidence of what was performed), section 10 (power to make copies of script), section 15 (powers of entry and inspection).'

[51] The new s.29E: 'Distributing, showing or playing a recording (1) A person who distributes, or shows or plays, a recording of visual images or sounds which are threatening is guilty of an offence if he intends thereby to stir up religious hatred. (2) In this Part "recording" means any record from which visual images or sounds may, by any means, be reproduced; and references to the distribution, showing or playing of a recording are to its distribution, showing or playing to the public or a section of the public. (3) This section does not apply to the showing or playing of a recording solely for the purpose of enabling the recording to be included in a programme service.'

[52] The new s.29F: 'Broadcasting or including programme in programme service (1) If a programme involving threatening visual images or sounds is included in a programme service, each of the persons mentioned in subsection (2) is guilty of an offence if he intends thereby to stir up religious hatred. (2) The persons are – (a) the person providing the programme service, (b) any person by whom the programme is produced or directed, and (c) any person by whom offending words or behaviour are used.'

[53] The new s.29G: 'Possession of inflammatory material (1) A person who has in his possession written material which is threatening, or a recording of visual images or sounds which are threatening, with a view to— (a) in the case of written material, its being displayed, published, distributed, or included in a programme service whether by himself or

written material, recordings or programmes must be threatening and intended to stir up religious hatred.[54] Religious hatred means 'hatred against a group of persons defined by reference to religious belief or lack of religious belief'.[55] The meaning of 'religious belief or lack of religious belief' is deliberately broad.[56] The Act extends to England and Wales, and aims to ensure the criminal law protects all groups of persons defined by their religious beliefs or lack of religious belief from having religious hatred intentionally stirred up against them.[57]

The offences of stirring up religious hatred are not intended to limit or restrict discussion, criticism or expressions of antipathy, dislike, ridicule or insult or abuse of particular religions or belief systems or lack of religion or of the beliefs and practices of those who hold such beliefs; nor do they apply to proselytisation, evangelism or the seeking to convert people to a particular belief or to cease holding a belief.[58] Moreover, the

another, or (b) in the case of a recording, its being distributed, shown, played, or included in a programme service, whether by himself or another, is guilty of an offence if he intends religious hatred to be stirred up thereby. (2) For this purpose regard shall be had to such display, publication, distribution, showing, playing, or inclusion in a programme service as he has, or it may reasonably be inferred that he has, in view.' Namely, possession of threatening material with a view to using it in a way that is intended to stir up religious hatred: Explanatory Notes, para. 15.

[54] Explanatory Notes, para. 14: '[i]n the case of the offence at 29B, this does not apply where the words or behaviour are used or displayed inside a private dwelling and there is no reason to believe that they can be heard or seen by a person outside that or any other private dwelling'.

[55] S.29A; Explanatory Notes, para. 11: '[t]he definition is designed to cover hatred against a group of persons defined by their religious belief or lack of religious belief but does not seek to define what amounts to a religion or a religious belief. It will be for the courts to determine whether any particular belief is a religious belief for these purposes'.

[56] Explanatory Notes, para. 12: '[t]he reference to "religious belief or lack of religious belief" is a broad one, and is in line with the freedom of religion guaranteed by Article 9 of the ECHR. It includes, although this list is not definitive, those religions widely recognised in this country such as Christianity, Islam, Hinduism, Judaism, Buddhism, Sikhism, Rastafarianism, Baha'ism, Zoroastrianism and Jainism. Equally, branches or sects within a religion can be considered as religions or religious beliefs in their own right. The offences also cover hatred directed against a group of persons defined by reference to a lack of religious belief, such as Atheists and Humanists. The offences are designed to include hatred against a group where the hatred is not based on the religious beliefs of the group or even on a lack of any religious belief, but based on the fact that the group do not share the particular religious beliefs of the perpetrator'.

[57] Explanatory Notes, para. 9.

[58] S.29J: 'Protection of freedom of expression. Nothing in this Part shall be read or given effect in a way which prohibits or restricts discussion, criticism or expressions of antipathy, dislike, ridicule, insult or abuse of particular religions or the beliefs or practices of their adherents, or of any other belief system or the beliefs or practices of its adherents, or proselytising or urging adherents of a different religion or belief system to cease practising their religion or belief system'; Explanatory Notes, 16.

Act does not apply to fair and accurate reports of anything done in the United Kingdom and Scottish Parliaments, the National Assembly for Wales, or the fair and accurate contemporaneous reports of judicial proceedings.[59] No prosecution for the offences of stirring up religious hatred shall proceed without the consent of the Attorney General. The maximum penalty for a conviction of stirring up religious hatred is seven years in prison.[60] The Act also deals with offences committed by corporations,[61] and it contains an interpretation section defining relevant words.[62]

In short, the Act creates numerous criminal offences protecting groups of believers from being threatened in a way that is defined by reference to religious belief or lack of religious belief.[63] However, contrary to Government's original intentions, a prosecution can only be brought if the defendant intended to stir up religious hatred.[64] This, coupled with a freedom of speech clause included in the final Act, has decreased the likelihood of a successful prosecution under the Act.[65] The focus of the new law differs from that of the law on blasphemy.[66] Unlike the law of blasphemy, which sought to protect Christian religious beliefs as a source of public morality and social cohesion, the Racial and Religious Hatred Act 2006 simply seeks to outlaw antisocial behaviour committed against people on grounds of religion. The protection extends far beyond the sensibilities of the established church: indeed, the protection is not focused on 'religion' as such but rather upon deviant acts that happen to involve 'religion'. Some commentators have seen aspects of the Act as possible replacements for blasphemy law,[67] and this was the original

[59] S.29K; see also Explanatory Notes, para. 17; originally, proceedings in the National Assembly for Wales were not covered by this provision, but this was changed by the Criminal Justice and Immigration Act 2008, Sched. 16, s.15.

[60] S. 29L; see also Explanatory Notes, para. 18.

[61] S. 29M.

[62] S. 29N.

[63] For a full account, see I. Hare, 'Crosses, Crescents and Sacred Cows: Criminalising Incitement to Religious Hatred' [2006] PL 521; and K. Goodall, 'Incitement to Religious Hatred: All Talk and No Substance' (2007) 70(1) MLR 89.

[64] The Government had wanted the offence to be charged either when the defendant had the intention to stir up religious hatred or was being reckless as to whether religious hatred would be stirred up thereby. The Government had also wanted to include 'abusive or insulting' words or behaviour in addition to 'threatening'.

[65] See A. Jeremy 'Practical Implications of the Enactment of the Racial and Religious Hatred Act 2006' (2007) 9 *Ecclesiastical Law Journal* 187.

[66] See R. Sandberg, 'Religion and Morality: A Socio-Legal Approach' [2007] *DISKUS* (online).

[67] See N. Addison, 133.

intent of the Government.[68] Scotland has no legislation on religious hatred (though a report appeared on it in 2002).[69]

3. *Desecration of a Place of Worship or Sacred Objects*

There are no specific offences for such conduct. The matter would be dealt with under the Criminal Damage Act 1971.[70] However, see below for religiously aggravated criminal damage.

4. *Hindering or Disrupting a Religious Meeting (and Philosophical Meetings)*

See below in Part III for offences relating to disturbances at places of public worship.

5. *Menaces, Violence or Force against Freedom of Religion*

(1) Obstruction of Ministers of Religion

Under the Offences Against the Person Act 1861, it is an offence to obstruct, by threats or force, any clergyman or other minister in or from celebrating divine service or otherwise officiating in any church, chapel, meeting house or other place of divine worship. Similarly, it is an offence to strike or offer any violence to (or to arrest pursuant to any civil process) any clergyman or other minister who is engaged in (or is, in the knowledge of the offender, about to engage in) any of these rites or duties (or is in the offender's knowledge, going to or returning from their performance).[71] The offence extends to protect all theistic (and polytheistic) religions but does not protect 'non-theistic' ones.[72] One of

[68] See the comments of David Blunkett, cited above.

[69] Namely, the Report of Cross-Party Working Group on Religious Hatred, *Tackling Religious Hatred*: http://www.scotland.gov.uk/Publications/2002/12/15892/14536. There does not appear to have been any subsequent legislation. It is not clear that such legislation is necessary anyway: the matter would more than likely be covered by breach of the peace law. It should also be borne in mind that, in Scotland, 'religious hatred' usually means Protestant-Catholic sectarianism first and foremost.

[70] S.1: 'A person who without lawful excuse destroys or damages any property belonging to another intending to destroy or damage any such property or being reckless as to whether such property would be destroyed or damaged shall be guilty of an offence'.

[71] Offences Against the Person Act 1861, s. 36; Criminal Law Act 1967, s. 1.

[72] HL SC Religious Offences, 2003, para. 28.

[73] Canon F15(3); Opinions of the Legal Advisory Commission, 48.

the duties of churchwardens in the Church of England is to maintain order at the time of divine service but their power to apprehend or eject must be exercised 'without unnecessary violence [to] any person creating a disturbance'.[73]

(2) Religious Harassment

Although enacted to deal with stalking, the Protection from Harassment Act 1997 covers several forms of harassment. Under the Act only individuals can be harassed but a religious organisation can bring a claim to protect its members. First, a person must not pursue a "course of conduct" that "amounts to harassment of another" if they "know or ought to know" that it "amounts to harassment of the other".[74] A "course of conduct" is conduct on at least two occasions in relation to that person.[75] The Serious Organized Crime and Police Act 2005 extended the offence:[76] it is an offence to pursue a "course of conduct" that "amounts to harassment of two or more persons" if the defendant knows or ought to know that the conduct "involves harassment of those persons".[77] The mental element required is that the defendant 'ought to know that it amounts to or involves harassment of another if a reasonable person in possession of the same information would think the course of conduct amounted to or involved harassment of the other'. It is thus not necessary to prove an intention to cause fear of violence or a sense of harassment.[78] Second, a higher-level offence is committed where the defendant's behaviour is so threatening that the victims fear violence against them on at least two occasions provided that the defendant "knows or ought to know that his course of conduct will cause the other so to fear on each of those occasions". The *mens rea* is

[74] Ss.1 and 2.

[75] S.7(3).

[76] S. 125(2)(c).

[77] S. 1(1A) of the 1997 Act: this also requires the defendant to intend to persuade any person (not necessarily one of those mentioned above) either "not to do something that he is entitled or required to do" or "to do something that he is not under any obligation to do".

[78] S. 1(2). S. 1(3) states that neither section 1(1) or 1(1A) applies to a course of conduct if the defendant can show that course of conduct was "pursued for the purpose of preventing or detecting crime", "pursued under any enactment or rule of law or to comply with any condition or requirement imposed by any person under any enactment", or "that in the particular circumstances the pursuit of the course of conduct was reasonable".

[79] S.4; as to the *mens rea*, the defendant "ought to know that [his course of conduct] will cause another to fear that violence will be used against him on any occasion if a

the same as for the lower-level offence.[79] The Act provides defences to the offence.[80]

In *Church of Latter Day Saints v Price* it was held that the Mormon Church could obtain an anti-harassment injunction against an individual because of his continual harassment of Mormon missionaries and churches (4,000 cold calls, preached at them for 30 minutes on the tube and he chased them down the street).[81] In *Singh v Bhaker*, following a Sikh arranged marriage, a female Singh moved into the home of her mother-in-law. She was forced to do menial housework – eg cleaning toilets without a brush – and was kept a virtual prisoner in the house. Singh claimed that she was not allowed to visit the local Sikh temple and was forced to have her hair cut to shoulder length, against her religious beliefs. The court held against the mother-in-law.[82]

(3) Anti Social Behaviour Orders (ASBOS)

Courts can make a civil Anti-Social Behaviour Order (ASBO) on application of a local authority, chief office of police, chief constable of the British Traffic Police Force or social landlords.[83] Applications may be made in respect of anyone aged over 10 "if it appears to the authority" that the person has acted in an anti-social manner, that is to say, in "a manner that caused or was likely to cause harassment, alarm or distress to one or more persons not of the same household as himself"; and such an order is necessary to protect relevant persons from further anti-social acts by him.[84] The Crime and Disorder Act 1998 states that "the court shall disregard any act of the defendant which he shows was reasonable in the circumstances".[85]

reasonable person in possession of the same information would think the course of conduct would cause the other so to fear on that occasion" (s 4(2)).

[80] It is a defence to show that course of conduct was to prevent or detect crime or was "pursued under any enactment or rule of law or to comply with any condition or requirement imposed by any person under any enactment". However, the third defence differs: under section 3(c), it is a defence for the defendant to show that "the pursuit of his course of conduct was reasonable for the protection of himself or another or for the protection of his or another's property".

[81] [2004] EWHC Admin 325.

[82] [2006] Fam Law 1026.

[83] Under the Crime and Disorder Act 1998, Police Reform Act 2002 (sections 61-66) and the Anti Social Behaviour Act 2003 (sections 85-86). Around 98% of applications accepted (*Telegraph*, 18/12/05).

[84] No intention on the part of the defendant has to be proved.

[85] S.1(5).

The ASBO prohibits the defendant from doing anything described in the order, such as doing specified acts or entering a defined area.[86] The breach of an ASBO is a *criminal offence* unless the defendant has "reasonable excuse" for his actions. Punishment is up to five years in prison.[87] ASBOs involving religion have included: one against a publican on grounds that a sign in his car park named 'The Porking Yard' was regarded as offensive to local Muslims attending a nearby Mosque; and one against a street preacher stopping him from using a loudspeaker or other amplification as part of his street preaching.[88]

(4) Genocide, Offences against Humanity, and Religion

Under the International Criminal Court Act 2001 it is an offence against the law of England and Wales for a person to commit genocide which is defined to mean any acts committed 'with intent to destroy in whole or in part, a national, ethnical, racial or religious group'.[89] Moreover, crimes against humanity are also dealt with in the statute: a crime against humanity is any act committed as part of a widespread or systematic attack directed against any civilian population with knowledge of the attack, including persecution against any identifiable group or collectivity on religious (as well as political, racial, national, ethnic, cultural, or gender) grounds.[90]

6. *Discrimination on Religious Grounds*

This is treated by civil not criminal law.[91]

[86] The Police Reform Act 2002 removed the local basis of the ASBO so that an order can effectively travel with the person to whom it applies. The ASBO is in effect for a period specified in the order or until further notice.

[87] Over 1,000 people jailed by end of 2005 (*Telegraph*, 18/12/05). The Telegraph in 2005 stated that the number of ASBOs was increasing at such a rate that if it continued to increase by same amount "by some point in about March 2016 everyone in the UK will have one" (*Telegraph*, 18/12/05).

[88] Addison, 137-138.

[89] Schedule 8: killing members of the group; causing serious bodily or mental harm to members of the group; deliberately inflicting on the group conditions of life calculated to bring about its physical destruction in whole or in part; imposing measures intended to prevent births within the group; forcibly transferring children of the group to another group.

[90] International Criminal Court Act 2001, s.50(6), Schedule 8.

[91] See generally Addison, and R. Sandberg, 'Flags, beards and pilgrimages: a review of the early case law on religious discrimination', (2007) 9 *Ecclesiastical Law Journal*, 87-91.

7. *Disrupting a Funeral*

It is an offence to obstruct (or attempt to obstruct), by threats or force, any clergyman or other minister in the performance of a duty in the lawful burial of the dead in any churchyard or other burial place.[92]

8. *Abuse of a Corpse and Desecration of Graves*

It is an offence to dig up a corpse unlawfully;[93] if the corpse is buried in consecrated ground (of the Church of England), a faculty is required from the consistory court, and if reburial is to be in unconsecrated ground, a licence from the Home Office is also required.[94] Under the Local Authorities' Cemeteries Order 1977, s. 18 it is an offence wilfully to interfere with any grave, vault, tombstone or other memorial or any flowers or plants or any such matter or to play any game or sport therein.[95]

9. *Proselytising*

This is not a criminal offence.[96]

10. *Apostasy*

This is not a criminal offence.

11. *Misuse of religious garment or false state of office*

It is an offence if a person knowingly and wilfully solemnizes a marriage according to the rites of the Church of England or Church in Wales falsely pretending to be in Holy Orders. Such persons are liable to imprisonment for a term not exceeding fourteen years.[97] It is unlawful (but no longer a crime) under the Ecclesiastical Titles Act 1851 for a minister to assume the name, style or title of archbishop of any province, bishop of any diocese or dean of any deanery already settled as titles operative in the Church of England.[98]

[92] Offences Against the Person Act 1861, s. 36; Criminal Law Act 1967, s. 1.
[93] *R v Sharpe* (1857) Dears & B 160.
[94] Burial Act 1857, s.25.
[95] SI 1977 No. 204, Art. 18; Art. 19 penalties: on summary conviction £1000.
[96] However, see above for harassment.
[97] Marriage Act 1949, s.75(1)(d); also s.78: the Church of England includes the Church in Wales.
[98] The criminal offence was repealed by the Ecclesiastical Titles Act 1971.

II. Criminal offences committed by ministers of religion

Needless to say, ministers of religion are subject to the general criminal law.[99] Very few criminal laws explicitly treat the commission of offences by ministers of religion.

12. *Breach of Confidentiality*

Disclosure by clergy of information received in the exercise of ministry may be prevented by recourse to civil law, not generally by the criminal law.[100] It is uncertain whether priest-penitent communications are privileged, thereby entitling the cleric to refuse to answer questions relating to them.[101] In criminal proceedings, it is unlikely that a trial judge would require evidence of a confession made to a priest.[102]

13. *Marriage*

There are several offences, involving religion, relating to the *solemnization of marriage*. First, under the Marriage Act 1949, it is an offence if any person knowingly and wilfully: (a) solemnizes a marriage at any other time than between the hours of 8am and 6pm; this does not apply to a marriage by special licence, a marriage according to the usages of the Society of Friends (Quakers) or a marriage between two persons professing the Jewish religion according to the usages of the Jews; (b) solemnizes a marriage according to the rites of the Church of England or the Church in Wales without banns of matrimony having been duly published (not being a marriage solemnized on the authority of a special licence, a common licence or certificates of a superintendent registrar); (c) solemnizes a marriage according to the rites of the Church of England or the Church in Wales (not being a marriage by special licence) in any place other than a church or other building in which banns may be published; (d) solemnizes a marriage according to the rites of the Church of England or the Church in Wales falsely pretending to be in Holy Orders.

[99] See *Blake v DPP* (1993) Crim LR 586 (criminal damage by Church of England cleric).

[100] However, see J. Behrens, 'No secrets in the church: the implications of the Data Protection Act 1998', (2003) 7 *Ecclesiastical Law Journal*, 17.

[101] M. Hill, *Ecclesiastical Law* (3rd edn., Oxford UP, 2007) para. 5.62.

[102] Police and Criminal Evidence Act 1984, ss.76,78,82(3): there is a discretion to admit/exclude.

Such persons are liable to imprisonment for a term not exceeding fourteen years.[103]

Secondly, as to the *place of solemnization*, it is an offence if any person knowingly and wilfully solemnizes a marriage in any place other than a church or other building in which marriages may be solemnized according to the rites of the Church of England; the rule does not apply to a marriage by special licence, according to the usages of the Society of Friends or between two persons professing the Jewish religion according to the usages of the Jews. Such persons are liable to imprisonment not exceeding five years.[104] For both sets of offences, no prosecution shall be commenced after the expiration of three years from the commission of the offence.[105]

Thirdly, there are offences relating to *registration of marriages*. Any minister who refuses or without reasonable cause omits to register any marriage which he is required by law to register, and any minister having the custody of a marriage register book or a certified copy of a marriage register book or part thereof who carelessly loses or injures the book or copy or carelessly allows the book or copy to be injured while in his keeping, is liable on summary conviction to a fine.[106] Moreover, a minister who knowingly and wilfully registers any marriage which is void by virtue of any of the provisions of the Marriage Act (Part III) shall be liable to imprisonment for a term not exceeding five years;[107] no prosecution shall be commenced after the expiration of three years from the commission of the offence.[108]

Fourthly, under the Gender Recognition Act 2004, a Church of England minister is not obliged to solemnise the marriage of a person if the minister reasonably believes that the gender of the person is an acquired

[103] Marriage Act 1949, s.75(1)(a)-(d); also s.78: the Church of England includes the Church in Wales. The current law on marriage in Scotland is set out in the Marriage (Scotland) Act 1977, as amended. That Act, *inter alia*, abolished the requirement for banns and substituted the Marriage Notice Form from the District Registrar. Following the ceremony, the officiant and the parties complete a Marriage Schedule and return it to the Registrar. The Kirk responded by passing Act III of 1978, repealing the Act anent Proclamation of Banns, but at the same time making provision for 'any person usually resident in Scotland and requiring proclamation of banns in order to be married furth of Scotland to have banns proclaimed in any parish church within the registration district within which he or she normally resides'.

[104] Marriage Act 1949, s.75(2).

[105] Marriage Act 1949, s.75(4).

[106] Marriage Act 1949, s.76(1).

[107] Marriage Act 1949, s.76(3).

[108] Marriage Act 1949, s.76(6).

gender under the Act; an unauthorised disclosure of information relating the 'gender history' of the person is an offence.[109] The rule applies only to those who have gained information in an official capacity but this may include receipt of information in connection with a voluntary organisation. There are exceptions for religious purposes (as well as legal, medical and financial purposes); as to religious purposes, disclosure is permitted to enable any person to make a decision whether to officiate at or permit the solemnisation of the marriage.[110] The position is broadly the same in Scotland.[111]

14. *Civil Partnerships and Religious Premises and Services*

A civil partnership may not be entered on religious premises and no religious service may be used while the registrar is officiating at the signing of a civil partnership document. It is an offence for a civil partnership registrar to officiate at the signing of a civil partnership schedule by the proposed civil partners at a place other than the place specified in the notices of the proposed civil partnership and the civil partnership schedule.[112] Other offences relating to public worship are dealt with in the next section.

III. Criminal offences related to worship and ritual

There are several nineteenth-century offences which deal with disorder in places of public religious worship and cemeteries. These are widely regarded as obsolete, but nevertheless attract occasional prosecutions.

[109] Gender Recognition Act 2004, s.22: the unauthorised disclosure is punishable by a fine of up to £5,000.

[110] Gender Recognition (Disclosure of Information) (England, Wales and Northern Ireland) (no 2) Order 2005, SI 2005/916: disclosure is also permitted in relation to appointment of a person as a minister, office-holder or to any employment for the purposes of the religion, whether to admit them to any religious order, or to determine 'whether the subject is eligible to receive or take part in any religious sacrament, ordinance or rite, or take part in any act of worship or prayer, according to the practices of an organised religion' (Art. 4). If a decision other than one relating to marriage is involved, the person disclosing must reasonably consider that that person may need the information in order to make a decision which complies with the doctrines of the religion in question or avoids conflicting with the strongly held religious convictions of a significant number of the followers of that religion.

[111] The Gender Recognition (Disclosure of Information) (Scotland) Order (SSI/2005/No 125 2005) makes broadly similar provision for Scotland to that in England, Wales and Northern Ireland: see http://www.opsi.gov.uk/legislation/scotland/ssi2005/20050125.htm

[112] Civil Partnership Act 2004, ss.2(5) (premises), 6(1)(b) (religious services), 31(2) (offences).

14A. *Funerals Burials and Cemeteries*

First, under the Cemeteries Clauses Act 1847, it is an offence to 'play at any game or sport, or discharge firearms, save at a military funeral' in any cemetery or to 'wilfully and unlawfully disturb any persons assembled in the cemetery for the purposes of burying a body' or to 'commit any nuisance within' a cemetery.[113] This now applies only to private cemeteries. Cemeteries administered by local authorities are regulated by the Local Authorities' Cemeteries Order 1977: it is an offence wilfully to create any disturbance or nuisance in such a cemetery or wilfully to interfere with any burial taking place or with any grave, vault, tombstone or other memorial or any flowers or plants or any such matter or to play any game or sport therein.[114]

Secondly, the Burial Laws Amendment Act 1880 applies to burials 'with or without a religious service'. It is an offence to engage in 'riotous, violent, or indecent behaviour' at any burial under the Act, or to obstruct a burial. It is also an offence to 'bring into contempt or obloquy the Christian religion, or the belief or worship of any church or denomination of Christians, or the members or any minister of any church or denomination, or any other person'.[115] As with blasphemy law pre-abolition, this protects only the Christian religion and not other faiths. The offence is triable only in the Crown Court and is punishable with a maximum of two years' imprisonment.

14B. *Disturbances in Places of Worship*

With regard to protection against disturbance of public worship, under the Ecclesiastical Courts Jurisdiction Act 1860 it is a criminal offence to commit 'riotous, violent or indecent behaviour' in the course of lawful liturgical action.[116] The offence may be committed in any cathedral, church or chapel of the Church of England or in any chapel of any religious denom-

[113] S.59.

[114] SI 1977 No. 204, Art. 18; Art. 19 penalties: on summary conviction £1000.

[115] S.7: there is no definition of 'any other person'; for objections to s. 7, see HL SC, Religious Offences, 2003, para. 29.

[116] s. 2; for 'indecency' see *Worth v Terrington* (1845) 13 M&W 761 at 795; indecency need not simply signify that which tends to deprave or corrupt nor does it have to have sexual connotation – it simply means creating a disturbance: *Abrahams v Cavey* [1968] 1 QB 479 ('Oh you hypocrites, how can you use the word of God to justify your policies', shouted after the Foreign Secretary had read a passage from Micah 4 at a service arranged and televised for a Labour Party conference in a Methodist church was an offence); in *Jones v Catterall* (1902) 18 TLR 367 'idolatory' called out during the service was held to be 'indecent'.

ination or in any certified place of religious worship.[117] This applies not only when those acts are committed during the celebration of 'divine service' but at any time, including in any churchyard or burial ground.[118] Moreover, it is a criminal offence to molest, disturb, vex or trouble (or by any other unlawful means to disquiet or misuse) any preacher duly authorised to preach or any clergyman in holy orders ministering or celebrating any sacrament or any divine service, rite or office.[119] The offence may be committed by a clergyman acting in an indecent or violent way in his own church or churchyard.[120] A person may be removed for disturbing the congregation at the time of divine service even though no part of that service is actually proceeding at the time.[121] In the period 1997-2002 there were 60 prosecutions under this Act and 21 convictions.[122] According to "National Churchwatch" there were 6,829 crimes against places of worship in 12 (of 42) police areas in the year ending April 2002.[123] It has been considered that the penalties in the Act are of little deterrence value, that the Act is archaic, but that it is not obsolete and still sends an important message.[124] In Scotland, disturbance of public worship is punishable under the common law as a breach of the peace.[125]

15. *Female Genital Mutilation*

This is an offence under the Female Genital Mutilation Act 2003.[126] No offence is committed by an approved person (such as a registered medical

[117] Places of Worship Registration Act 1855.

[118] See also Burial Laws Amendment Act 1880, ss. 7,8.

[119] Ecclesiastical Courts Jurisdiction Act 1860, s. 2; *Cope v Barber* (1872) LR 7 CP 393; for a wide understanding of 'sacrament' and 'divine service', see *Matthews v King* [1934] 1 KB 505; 'clergyman in holy orders' normally excludes a minister not episcopally ordained: *Glasgow College v AG* (1848) 1 HL Cas 800 at 819,823. For the possiblility of proceedings under the 1860 statute in the diocese of Blackburn with respect to intrusion during a baptism service, see *Times* 18/11/94.

[120] *Vallancey v Fletcher* [1897] 1 QB 265.

[121] *Williams v Glenister* (1824) 2 B&C 699.

[122] HL Select Committee, Religious Offences in England and Wales, First Report 2003, para. 58.

[123] Ibid., para. 26: of these, 186 were violent crimes (including two murders) and 2,866 incidents of criminal damage.

[124] HL SC, Religious Offences, 2003, para. 134; see para. 132: the UK is 'not a secular state'.

[125] *Dougall v Dykes* 1861 4 Irvine 101. Breach of the peace is a much more general offence in Scotland than in England and Wales.

[126] S. 1(1): a person is guilty of an offence if he excises, infibulates or otherwise mutilates the whole or any part of a girl's labia majora, labia minora or clitoris; s.6: girl includes woman.

practitioner) who performs (eg) a surgical operation which is necessary for physical or mental health.[127] A person guilty of an offence under this Act is liable (a) on conviction on indictment, to imprisonment for a term not exceeding 14 years or a fine (or both), and on summary conviction, to imprisonment for a term not exceeding six months or a fine not exceeding the statutory maximum (or both).[128] In Scotland, it is an offence under the Female Genital Mutilation (Scotland) Act 2005.[129]

IV. Religious motivation, aggravation and attenuation

16. *Religiously Aggravated Offences*

An increase of racial violence and harassment resulted in a new category of racially-aggravated crimes under the Crime and Disorder Act 1998 and, following 9/11, the Anti-Terrorism Crime and Security Act 2001 extended these to deal with religiously-aggravated offences.[130] Section 28(1) of the Crime and Disorder Act 1998 provides two types of religious aggravation: one based on the demonstration towards the victim of religious hostility; the other based on religiously hostile motivation towards a religious group.[131] The Crown Prosecution Service has guidance on prosecutions in cases of religious crime.[132]

First: 'An offence is religiously aggravated…if at the time of committing the offence, or immediately before or after doing so, the offender demonstrates towards the victim of the offence hostility based on the victim's membership of (or presumed membership of) a…religious group'.[133] This does *not* require proof that the defendant was motivated by religious hostility;[134] the test is that the defendant formed the view that the victim was a member of a religious group and that the defendant

[127] S.1(2):

[128] S.5.

[129] It was already an offence for the whole of the UK under the previous legislation.

[130] See generally M. Idriss, 'Religion and the Anti-Terrorism Crime and Security Act 2001' (2002) *Criminal Law Review* 890.

[131] R. Card, *Card, Cross and Jones Criminal Law* (18th edn., Oxford University Press, Oxford, 2008) 7.102: 'The first type is "concerned" with the outward manifestation of… religious hostility, the other with the inner motivation of the offender': commenting on *Rogers* [2007] 2 AC 62 *per* Baroness Hale.

[132] www.cps.gov.uk/publications/docs/rrpbcrpol.pd

[133] Crime and Disorder Act 1998, s.28(1)(a). As the demonstration of hostility must be "immediately" before or after the act, a demonstration twenty minutes after the act will not suffice; however, the victim need not be present at the demonstration: *Perry v DPP* [2004] EWHC 3112 (Admin).

[134] Card (2008) 7.103; *DPP v Green* [2004] EWHC 1125 (Admin).

demonstrated hostility based on that membership.[135] "Membership" of a religious group includes 'association with members of that group';[136] and 'presumed membership' means presumed by the offender.[137]

Second, an offence is religiously aggravated if the offence is motivated (wholly or partly) by hostility towards members of a religious group based on their membership of that group.[138] This requires proof that the defendant was motivated by religious hostility.[139] Religious aggravation may exist regardless of whether the defendant is of the same religious group as the object of the offence.[140]

For both types, it is immaterial whether or not the religious hostility of the offender is also based, to any extent, on any other factor.[141] "Religious group" means 'a group of persons defined by reference to religious belief or lack of religious belief'.[142] "Religious belief" is not defined.[143] The reference to 'lack of religious belief' is important.[144] It has been suggested that: given 'the broad interpretation in Article 9

[135] Card (2008) 7.105: words used need not expressly identify the religious group: *AG's Reference (No 4 of 2004)* [2005] 1 WLR 2810 (CA) – on racial aggravation.

[136] "Membership" is not here defined. However, see Card (2008) 7.102: 'Clearly, a religious group includes converts and excludes apostates….the importance of the precise meaning of "membership" in s.28(1)(a) is lessened by s.28(2)…a person who has not converted but is the spouse or an adopted child of a member and thereby in association with that member and members of his family etc who are members of the group'.

[137] Crime and Disorder Act 1998, s.28(2).

[138] Crime and Disorder Act 1998, s.28(1)(b). Whereas proof of demonstration under s. 28 (1)(a) requires proof of what D did at the time of the offence, proof of motivation under s.28(1)(b) may be established by what D may have done or said on other occasions: *G v DPP; T v DPP* [2004] EWHC 183 (Admin): Card (2008) 7.113.

[139] Card (2008) 7.103; making "motive" relevant to criminal liability is exceptional in the criminal law: ibid., 7.110; see also 7.112: 'A person who, motivated by hostility towards members of the Jewish religious community, attacked a bricklayer whom he knew was not Jewish who was working on the building of a synagogue would fall foul of s 28(1)(b), for example. It was for this reason that it was not necessary to extend to s 28(1)(b) the provision that membership of a racial or religious group includes association with it'.

[140] This has been applied to racial aggravation: White [2001] 1 WLR 1352 (CA).

[141] Crime and Disorder Act 1998, s.28(3).

[142] Crime and Disorder Act 1998, s.28(5); under s.28(4) "racial group" means a group of persons defined by reference to race, colour, nationality (including citizenship) or ethnic or national origins; the term "ethnic" under the Race Relations Act 1976 has been construed widely to include 'a common religion different from that of neighbouring groups or from the general community surrounding it': per Lord Fraser in *Mandla v Dowell Lee* [1983] 2 AC 548 (HL).

[143] However, Sikhs, Muslims and Rastafarians are religious groups though the last two are not racial groups: *JH Walker Limited v Hussain and Others* [1996] ICR 291; *Crown Suppliers (PSA) Limited v Dawkins* [1983] ICR 517.

[144] It means that there may be an offence when D acts because the victim is not of a specific religion (eg): N. Addison *Religious Discrimination and Hatred Law* (2007) 126-127.

of the ECHR, it would seem likely that the domestic courts will interpret the offence as affording protection to a religion as widely understood.

The religiously aggravated crimes in the Crime and Disorder Act 1998 are based on pre-existing offences as aggravated versions of them carrying a higher maximum punishment.[145] The basic crime is aggravated by the demonstration or motivation of religious hostility. First, a new religiously aggravated offence is grafted onto crimes of assault (including two crimes under the Offences Against the Persons Act 1861). Under the Crime and Disorder Act 1998, s. 29(1): a person is guilty of an offence of religiously (and racially) aggravated assault if he commits an offence of malicious wounding or grievous bodily harm,[146] an offence of actual bodily harm,[147] or common assault, which is religiously aggravated.[148] A religiously aggravated offence of malicious wounding or grievous bodily harm and actual bodily harm (under the Offences Against the Person Act 1861), is triable either way, and the maximum imprisonment on conviction on indictment is seven years (as opposed to five years for the basic offence under the 1861 Act).[149] For common assault (committed by an assault or a battery), the religiously aggravated version is triable either way and punishable on conviction on indictment with maximum imprisonment of two years.[150]

Secondly, s.30 of the Crime and Disorder Act 1998 (as amended) provides: 'A person is guilty of an offence under this section if he commits an offence under section 1(1) of the Criminal Damage Act 1971 (destroying or damaging property belonging to another) which is racially or religiously aggravated for the purposes of this section'.[151] The offence is punishable on summary conviction by imprisonment for six months or

[145] N. Addison, *Religious Discrimination and Hatred Law* (2007) 127: 'It is important to note that [the Acts] did not actually create any new offence or make anything illegal that had been legal before. What they did was to increase the possible sentence for certain existing criminal offences if they were committed in a religiously (or racially) aggravated way'.

[146] Under the Offences Against the Person Act 1861, s.20.

[147] Under the Offences Against the Person Act 1861, s.47.

[148] Crime and Disorder Act 1998, s.29(1).

[149] Crime and Disorder Act 1998, s.29(2).

[150] Crime and Disorder Act 1998, s.29(3).

[151] Amended by the Anti-Terrorism, Crime and Security Act 2001, s.39(5)(b) and (6)(b). The *mens rea* for an offence under the Criminal Damage Act 1971, s.1(1) is intention or recklessness: however, if criminal damage is caused "recklessly" it is unlikely tat it has been 'motivated by hostility'.

a fine not exceeding the statutory maximum or both; and, on conviction on indictment, by imprisonment for fourteen years (ten years for the non-aggravated form) or a fine or both.[152]

Thirdly, s.31(1) of the Crime and Disorder Act 1998 (as amended) provides that a person is guilty of an offence if he commits – (a) an offence under section 4 of the Public Order Act 1986 (fear or provocation of violence);[153] (b) an offence under section 4A of that Act (intentional harassment, alarm or distress);[154] or (c) an offence under section 5 of that Act (harassment, alarm or distress),[155] which is religiously (or racially) aggravated for the purposes of this section. The offences of fear or provocation of violence (s.4) and intentional harassment, alarm or distress (s.4A) when aggravated religiously are punishable on summary conviction by six months, or a fine not exceeding the statutory maximum, or both; and on indictment by two years, or a fine or both. A religiously aggravated harassment, alarm or distress offence is triable only

[152] D. Ormerod, *Smith and Hogan Criminal Law* (11th edn., Oxford University Press, Oxford, 2005) 918: 'The offences are extremely broad and elevate what is sometimes a trivial amount of damage (for example, a broken window caused in the course of a dispute with no racial [or religious] background) into a racially [or religiously] aggravated offence because the offender uses a racial or religious insult at the time of the offence'.

[153] Public Order Act 1986, s.4(1): 'A person is guilty of an offence if he – (a) uses towards another person threatening, abusive or insulting words or behaviour, or (b) distributes or displays to another person any writing, sign or other visible representation which is threatening, abusive or insulting, with intention to cause that person to believe that immediate unlawful violence will be used against him or another by any person, or to provoke the immediate use of violence by that person or another, or whereby that person is likely to believe that such violence will be used or it is likely that such violence will be provoked'. In *Horseferry Road Stipendiary Magistrate ex parte Siadatan* [1991] 1 QB 260 it was held that publication of *The Satanic Verses* was not an offence under s.4 because it did not provoke "immediate unlawful violence".

[154] Public Order Act 19986, s. 4A(1): 'A person is guilty of an offence if, with intent to cause a person harassment, alarm or distress, he – (a) uses threatening, abusive or insulting words or behaviour, or disorderly behaviour, or (b) displays any writing, sign or other visible representation which is threatening, abusive or insulting', thereby causing that or another person harassment, alarm or distress. In *Percy v DPP* [2001] EWHC Admin 1125 the High Court accepted that 'there is a pressing social need in a multi-cultural society to prevent the denigration of objects of veneration and symbolic importance for one cultural group'.

[155] Public Order Act s.5(1): 'A person is guilty of an offence if he – (a) uses threatening, abusive or insulting words or behaviour, or disorderly behaviour, or (b) displays any writing, sign or other visible representation which is threatening, abusive or insulting, within the hearing or sight of a person likely to be caused harassment, alarm or distress thereby' (ie there is no need to prove intention to case harassment etc or that anyone has actually been harassed).

summarily and punishable by a fine.[156] There have been several cases involving religiously aggravated offences.[157]

Fourthly, s.32 of the 1998 Act (as amended) provides religiously (and racially) aggravated offences of harassment and putting people in fear of violence: a person is guilty of an offence under this section if he commits – (a) an offence under s.2 of the Protection from Harassment Act 1997 (offence of harassment) or (b) an offence under s. 4 of that Act (putting people in fear of violence) which is religiously (or racially) aggravated. An aggravated offence of harassment is triable either way and punishable on indictment with a maximum sentence of two years' imprisonment. An aggravated offence putting people in fear of violence is on conviction on indictment punishable by a maximum of seven years' imprisonment.[158]

When a court is considering the seriousness of an offence (other than the religiously aggravated offences under ss.29-32), if the offence was religiously aggravated, the court must treat that fact as an aggravating factor, and must state in open court that the offence was so aggravated; and this should attract a heavier sentence.[159] In other words, this means that other offences religiously aggravated might be punished more severely than the aggravated form of the offence.[160]

[156] Ormerod (2005) 986: the fine must not exceed level 4 on the standard scale; it is Crown Prosecution Service policy 'not to accept pleas to lesser offences, or omit or minimize admissible evidence of racial or religious aggravation for the sake of expediency'.

[157] S.5 is the most commonly used offence. In *Norwood v DPP* [2003] EWHC 1564 Admin, it was held that displaying a poster in a window showing the events of 9/11 and the words "Islam out of Britain" was a religiously aggravated offence under s.5, even though no Muslims had complained about the poster and the only evidence came from a non-Muslim police officer who had seen the poster. In *Hammond v DPP* [2004] EWHC 69 Admin: it was held that an elderly, autistics evangelic protester who preached in Bournemouth on a Sunday afternoon while holding a large sign with the words 'Stop Immorality. Stop Homosexuality. Stop Lesbianism. Jesus is Lord' was guilty under section 5. His actions caused a hostile crowd which was in part violent but the police decided to arrest him and not the opponents. In *Dehal v CPS* [2005] EWHC Admin 2154 it was held that a notice denouncing a president of a Gurdwara and as a hypocrite, a liar and a 'mad dog' was not an offence under either section 4A or 5 since there was no real fear of public disorder. Under sections 4, 4A and 5, it is a defence if the defendant was in a dwelling and that either the other person is was also inside that or another dwelling or the defendant had no reason to believe that there was any person within hearing or sight who was likely to be caused harassment, alarm or distress. Under sections 4A and 5, it is a defence if the defendant's conduct was reasonable.

[158] Ormerod (2005) 1003.

[159] Criminal Justice Act 2003, s.145(1) and (2); s.145(3): s.28 of the Crime and Disorder Act 1998 (the meaning of 'religiously aggravated') applies for the purposes of this section as it applies to the purposes of s.29 of that Act.

[160] See Addision, 128.

In Scotland, "offences aggravated by religious prejudice", religiously-aggravated offences, are governed by the Criminal Justice (Scotland) Act 2003.[161] An offence is aggravated by religious prejudice if: (a) at the time of committing the offence or immediately before or after doing so, the offender evinces towards the victim (if any) of the offence malice and ill-will based on the victim's membership (or presumed membership) of a religious group, or of a social or cultural group with a perceived religious affiliation; or (b) the offence is motivated (wholly or partly) by malice and ill-will towards members of a religious group, or of a social or cultural group with a perceived religious affiliation, based on their membership of that group.[162] The court must take the aggravation into account in determining the appropriate sentence. Where the sentence in respect of the offence is different from that which the court would have imposed had the offence not been aggravated by religious prejudice, the court must state the extent of and the reasons for that difference.[163] Evidence from a single source is sufficient to prove that an offence is aggravated by religious prejudice.[164] "Membership" in relation to a group includes association with members of that group; and "presumed" means presumed by the offender.[165] "Religious group" means a group of persons defined by reference to their: (a) religious belief or lack of religious belief; (b) membership of or adherence to a church or religious organisation; (c) support for the culture and traditions of a church or religious organisation; or (d) participation in activities associated with such a culture or such traditions.[166]

17. *Religious Motivation, Acts and Defences (Attenuation)*

Explicit defences based on religion are not common.[167] However, first, it is an offence to have in a public place 'any article which has a blade or is sharply pointed'; it is a defence if the person had 'good reason or lawful authority' for having the article or is able 'to prove that he had the article...for religious reasons'.[168] Secondly, it is not a criminal offence

[161] 2003 asp 7, s. 74(1): this section applies where it is—(a) libelled in an indictment; or (b) specified in a complaint, and, in either case, proved that an offence has been aggravated by religious prejudice.
[162] S. 74(2).
[163] S. 74(3) and (4).
[164] S.74(5).
[165] S.74(6).
[166] S.74(7).
[167] See S. Poulter, *Ethnicity, Law and Human Rights* (Oxford, 1998) ch. 8.
[168] Criminal Justice Act 1988, s.139.

for a Sikh to wear on a motor-cycle a turban in place of a crash helmet for the purposes of road traffic law.[169]

Thirdly, the Offences Against the Person Act 1861 deals with non-fatal offences against the person. The general rule is that consent by the victim cannot validly be given to actual bodily harm. However, there are exceptions to this.[170] It has been recognised judicially that a valid consent could be given to religious mortification, the infliction of pain on a penitent with his consent as part of his religious repentance.[171]

V. Criminal law and sects

18. *Sects*

There are no criminal offences explicitly dealing with sects.[172]

Conclusion

The criminal offences relating to religion outlined here may be classified in a number of different ways. First, there are several criminal offences of considerable antiquity. These are still on the statute books, but recent parliamentary discussion suggests that they may soon be reformed; this is most evident with regard to crimes involving disturbance at religious worship and the administration of rites. Second, whilst blasphemy has been abolished, the introduction of several religion-related crimes (particularly stirring up religious hatred, religion and civil partnerships, and the religiously aggravated offences) are actually symptomatic of wider changes in religion law in England and Wales. Discussion within parliament suggests that these are understood to accommodate the increase in religious pluralism in recent years. Thirdly, whilst generally both the *actus reus* and *mens rea* of offences are defined with reasonable clarity, in relation to some offences this is not the case: the absence of a clear *mens rea* in relation to offences concerning disturbance at religious

[169] Road Traffic Act 1988, s.16: originally the Motor-Cycle Helmets (Religious Exemption) Act 1976.

[170] For example: properly conducted games or sports; reasonable surgical interference; tattooing.

[171] *Brown* [1994] 1 AC 212 at 267 *per* Lord Mustill.

[172] This is because there is no legal concept of a 'sect' in English or Welsh (nor it seems Scots) law, and may also be related to the absence of a system in the UK of registration of religious groups.

worship is typical. Fourthly, the complexities of the definitional elements of offences may mean that there could be difficulties in pursuing successful prosecutions; this may prove the case particularly with stirring up religious hatred. Moreover, the impact of the ECHR in the criminal sphere is far from clear in relation to, for example, disclosure of information obtained in the confessional. Finally, reliance on religion does not generally function as a defence to criminal liability, though it may be relevant in the exercise of prosecutorial discretion and for mitigation at the point of sentencing.